Commerce and Character

AMERICAN POLITICAL THOUGHT

Jeremy D. Bailey and Susan McWilliams Barndt
Series Editors

Wilson Carey McWilliams and Lance Banning
Founding Editors

Commerce and Character

THE POLITICAL ECONOMY OF
THE ENLIGHTMENT AND
THE AMERICAN FOUNDING

Edited by Steven Frankel and John Ray

University Press of Kansas

© 2025 by the University Press of Kansas
All rights reserved

Published by the University Press of Kansas (Lawrence, Kansas 66045), which was organized by the Kansas Board of Regents and is operated and funded by Emporia State University, Fort Hays State University, Kansas State University, Pittsburg State University, the University of Kansas, and Wichita State University.

Library of Congress Cataloging-in-Publication Data is available.

Names: Frankel, Steven, 1968– editor. | Ray, John A., 1957– editor.
Title: Commerce and character : studies in the political economy of the Enlightenment and the American founding / edited by Steven Frankel, John Ray.
Description: Lawrence, Kansas : University Press of Kansas, 2025 | Series: American political thought | Includes bibliographical references and index.
Identifiers: LCCN 2024028941 (print) | LCCN 2024028942 (ebook)
  ISBN 9780700638307 (cloth)
  ISBN 9780700638314 (paperback)
  ISBN 9780700638321 (ebook)
Subjects: LCSH: Political science—United States—History. | Political science—Philosophy—History. | Lerner, Ralph. | Enlightenment—United States. | Capitalism—Political aspects—United States History. | United States—Politics and government—1789–1815. | BISAC: POLITICAL SCIENCE / Political Economy | PHILOSOPHY / Political
Classification: LCC JA84.U5 .C61986 2025 (print) | LCC JA84.U5 (ebook) | DDC 320.50973–dc23/eng/20241023
LC record available at https://lccn.loc.gov/2024028941.
LC ebook record available at https://lccn.loc.gov/2024028942.

British Library Cataloguing-in-Publication Data is available.
Authorised Representative Details: Easy Access System Europe
Mustamäe tee 50, 10621 Tallinn, Estonia | gpsr.requests@easproject.com

To Ralph Lerner with deepest gratitude

Contents

Acknowledgments, ix

Introduction, 1
  Steven Frankel and John Ray

Prologue: Commerce and Character: The Anglo-American as
  New-Model Man, 12
  Ralph Lerner

1 Locke, Hume, and Property: On the Philosophical
   Foundations of Capitalism, 39
   Michael Zuckert

2 Montesquieu: Commerce and Character, 54
   Paul A. Rahe

3 The Commercial Republic and Adam Smith's
   The Theory of Moral Sentiments, 82
   Ann Charney Colmo

4 Adam Smith, Alexis de Tocqueville, and American
   Greatness, 103
   Ryan Patrick Hanley

5 "The Masterpiece of Policy of Our Century":
   Rousseau's Response to the Enlightenment, 122
   Clifford Orwin

6 Thomas Jefferson: Commercial Republican,
   Creole Nationalist, 136
   Peter S. Onuf

7 The Good Republican: Madison's Model Citizen, *162*
   Colleen A. Sheehan

8 On the Significance of *Federalist* 6, *183*
   Peter McNamara

9 Tocqueville on Democracy and the Commercial Republic, *191*
   John C. Koritansky

Epilogue: Commerce and Character Revisited, *208*
   Ralph Lerner

Selected Bibliography, 243

List of Contributors, 253

Index, 257

Acknowledgments

A few years ago, we were approached by a generous Xavier University alum, Stephen Smith, to start a center devoted to the study of political economy. We immediately thought of Ralph Lerner's beautiful book on the founding, *The Thinking Revolutionary*, and specifically his essay titled "Commerce and Character." Borrowing heavily from the issues and thinkers examined in that essay, we formulated an honors program that has enjoyed great success among both students and faculty. This volume represents a sort of manifesto for that program.

We thank Ralph Lerner for his intellectual guidance and the contributors who helped us expand and deepen the theme. We also thank Timothy W. Burns, Andrea E. Ray, and Linda Lotz for their invaluable assistance in preparing the manuscript and the Institute for Humane Studies for its generous support.

Introduction

Why did the founders prefer commercial republics? In reflecting on this question, this volume takes inspiration from Ralph Lerner's important essay "Commerce and Character: The Anglo-American as New-Model Man," which first appeared in the *William and Mary Quarterly* in 1979.[1] It immediately received widespread attention and admiration, including the Lester J. Cappon Award. "Commerce and Character" was later republished as the final chapter in a collection of Lerner's essays on the American founding titled *The Thinking Revolutionary: Principle and Practice in the New Republic*.[2] That volume was also feted, receiving the Benchmark Book Award in 1987.

The Thinking Revolutionary argues that the founders were not simply products of their age whose thought was determined by causes beyond their ken; rather, they were individuals who "thought for themselves and then deployed the results of that thinking coolly to reason with the reasonable, to persuade the persuadable, and to impress the impressionable" (*TR*, x). As Lerner documents in his prologue, contemporary historians tend to explain "high human actions by recurring to the acts and beliefs of the many (for the thoughtful, as distinguished from the influential, are always few)." In sharp contrast, Lerner shows that the founders' "highest and deepest motives derived from their reasoned understanding" (x). They were, in short, thinking revolutionaries.

"Commerce and Character" is consistent with the themes of *The Thinking Revolutionary* but dramatically broader. Rather than focusing exclusively on the American founding, "Commerce and Character" attempts to give "a coherent account of the revolutionary design" not just as it emerges in the American founding but also as "a singular movement within modern enlightened thought" (*TR*, xiv). Consequently, the scope of the essay includes not only Americans such as John Adams and Benjamin Rush but also Europeans such as Adam Smith and David Hume. Its intellectual reach is also broader, ranging from political rhetoric to political philosophy. In this way, the essay invites us to ponder not only modern foundings and revolutions but also the relationship between politics and philosophy.

One of the issues raised by *The Thinking Revolutionary* is the effort by contemporary historians to historicize the founding. Lerner shows how these historians tend to impose an ideological framework of interpretation on their analysis of the founders. Such an approach proves to be an obstacle to assessing the founders' writings on their merits. "Commerce and Character" invites us to consider, weigh, and *wonder at* the arguments themselves, which proves to be no easy task. The success enjoyed by the commercial republic obscures its novelty as well as the attractiveness of other regimes: "We no longer startle at the strange blend of limitless aspiration, quasi-heroic effort, and sensible calculation that characterizes their model man of the future. And, of course, we rarely wonder at how much domestic tranquility owes to the influence of commerce upon men's tastes, thoughts, and manners" ("CC," 3). With great precision, Lerner shows how the intellectual horizon of the Enlightenment shaped the thinking of the American revolutionaries. This horizon undergirds much (but not all) of our own thinking on human nature and property, including contemporary criticism of the Constitution of 1787. To analyze the founders properly, we need to recover the novelty of their arguments and consider the alternatives, both ancient and modern. Such a consideration begins with curiosity and wonder at their achievement.

What makes Lerner's introduction to philosophy through the lens of politics all the more remarkable is the seemingly unfertile ground on which he plans his project—namely, the creation of a commercial republic. Such a regime, where moneymaking is the daily activity of citizens, hardly seems like the stuff of wonder and marvel. But this too turns out to be a deliberate choice. The focus on economics is, as Lerner points out, intended to supplant more pious or nobler ends: "As men looked more to their economic interest, that interest would loom larger in their eyes and thoughts. Other concerns would matter less—sometimes because the accumulation of wealth was seen as the key to satisfying all desires, sometimes because a conflicting noneconomic interest (family feeling, attachment to a landed estate) was seen as only sentimental, illusory" ("CC," 9). Trade and commerce require partners, not enemies. Politics produces divisions and conflicts that make commerce impossible. The project that men like Montesquieu had in mind forces them to "learn how to subordinate disruptive political interests to those of commerce" (14, cf. 16). The success of the commercial republic means that one of the fundamental questions of political philosophy—the relation of politics and economics—is settled in favor of economics. Lerner teaches us to reopen this question.

Why did the founders prefer commercial republics? Certainly not because they were "money-grubbers [or] philistines [or] indifferent citizens . . . Rousseau's statement [that finance "is slave language; it has no place in the city's lexicon"] could not be farther from their conclusion" ("CC," 21). To the contrary, they grasped the defects and the problems introduced by commercial republicanism and, by and large, shared an appreciation of its virtues. They were, in this respect, "a band of brethren in arms" who advanced the case for "a new ordering of political, economic, and social life" (3).

What was their common project? Lerner's preliminary answer is as follows:

> It was their shared commitment to ordered liberty and their desire to promote it by emancipating men from many of the modes of thought of the past that led these thinkers to commend the commercial republic in the first place. What was a republic might, in this sense, be ascertained better by regarding the sphere of liberty rather than the formal organization of a state. Thus, for Montesquieu, England was a republic masquerading as a monarchy; for Smith, the trading world as a whole was a mercantile republic. ("CC," fn. 1)

It is strange that Lerner puts this seemingly critical summary in a footnote and instead turns to the question of how to read the founders' texts.

This sudden shift reminds the reader that additional effort is necessary to recover the founders' wisdom because their teachings are not as readily accessible as they seem at first glance.[3] The general elements of the revolution are clear: it will be a popular movement that aims to liberate men rather than elevate a few; commerce will be the engine for this liberation. However, the considerations that prompted such a formula remain obscure, as do the trade-offs they involve. Lerner invites us to pay attention to such calculations.

Further complicating our search for the origins of this revolution is that the proffered arguments are not necessarily the deepest or truest ones. According to Lerner, the founders of modernity were forced to employ rhetoric partly to avoid persecution by the ruling powers and partly to persuade their broader audience. Therefore, before we can appreciate the argument, we must read it critically, with an eye toward deliberate distortions and blind spots. Lerner focuses on those aspects that distort or exaggerate the defects of noncommercial regimes or paint an overly rosy picture of a commercial republic and its prospects. The critique amounts to this: regimes devoted to glory, honor, or piety were indifferent to the welfare of the community. Their leaders preferred to shower society's benefits on a few—namely, themselves—at the expense of everyone else. Because kings, aristocrats, and clergy were so effective at promoting these illusory and meretricious ends as the greatest good, the founders had to employ rhetoric, not to say exaggeration, to challenge and expose them. They had to discount honor and piety, for example, as mostly hypocritical pretensions. Adam Smith set out to mock the piety of the Spanish conquistadors and their mission to convert the native peoples of the New World: "A plundering horde of mendicant friars 'most carefully' taught the poor 'that it is a duty to give, and a very great sin to refuse them their charity'; this licensed, consecrated beggary 'is a most grievous tax upon the poor people'" ("CC," 7). Lerner teaches us to see that Smith's heated rhetoric hides a theological-political critique of revelation. Once such a critique is taken for granted, we can no longer perceive the heart of Smith's analysis. We no longer wonder at and hence challenge Smith's subtle ruse of substituting an aristocratic sense of greatness with the sober and universal "impartial spectator," which Lerner slyly describes as the "uncommon vantage of common humanity" (6).

This attack on piety is complemented by an equally ferocious attack on virtue, which Hume describes as "a mere philosophical whim or fiction" ("CC," 5–6). Instead of imagining republics that likely never existed, these modern revolutionaries began with men as they found them, pursuing passions such as the desire for survival and for comfort (5–6, cf. 12). The ancient demand for self-denial, even self-sacrifice, in favor of the public good is unrealistic. As Hume observes: "These principles [of ancient citizenship] are too disinterested, and too difficult to support, it is requisite to govern men by other passions, and animate them with a spirit of avarice and industry, art and luxury" (13). Most men are driven by their passions, not by some imaginary notion of excellence or virtue. To be fair, the "ancient policy of infusing each citizen-soldier with a passion for the public good might not be *utterly* futile, for it is at least conceivable that a community might be converted temporarily into a camp of lean and dedicated citizens" (13). But such models are as rare as they are useful for a founder who intends to build a stable and secure republic.

Lerner points out that, as they make their case for establishing a republic based on self-regarding passions rather than on virtue or piety, the founders also claim that political life will be more *rational* than the ancient alternatives. It is tempting to think that modern republics are more rational—that is, their citizens achieve theoretical excellence more frequently—than other regimes. Or, if that is too much to ask, at least we can imagine that such regimes are more rational because they reflect practical calculations and prudential considerations such as the security and comfort of their citizens. Lerner shows us that the latter account is closer to the mark, as the founders proudly employed the passions, even going so far as Hobbes in instrumentalizing reason as a mere tool of the passions. Seen in this light, it is reasonable that the founders lowered the goals of political life to fulfill the modest desires and needs of citizens. It is reasonable, in other words, to abandon theoretical virtue as a goal of politics.

But that may be selling the commercial republic short. Does such a regime not make men more rational by disabusing them of superstition and thereby preparing them for sober reflection? The critique of piety has the effect of encouraging citizens to abandon many of the more fanatical, not to say religious, passions (cf. "CC" 7, 11, 21). The modern regime effectively directs these passions more productively toward practical ends: the modern citizen seeks to find bargains on the weekends rather than glory or salvation. For those seeking wisdom, however, the question of the good can be pursued directly, without the distraction of superstition. The commercial republic, in short, offers "a surer guide to sane behavior" for the few and the many (8).

In addition to checking fanaticism and irrationality, such a regime may be more rational in teaching the virtue of moderation:

> That alternative was what we today would call the market model, what Smith called "the natural system of perfect liberty and justice." This way of getting rid of a kind of unreason did not presuppose that men at large would use their reason more. Far from seconding the proud aspirations of Reason to grasp the whole of society and to direct its complex workings in detail, the commercial republicans counseled humility. ("CC," 8)

The thinking revolutionaries secured the good of the regime as best they could. They also help us see that the good of their regime, and the happiness it affords them, is not the same as the true good. This sets careful readers on a course toward philosophy while at the same time moderating their hopes for politics. Lerner notes in the preface to *The Thinking Revolutionary*:

> The thinking revolutionary blazed a narrow path between mindless self-absorbtion and quixotic futility. His ideals, he hoped, might raise his followers' field of vision beyond the calculus of interest and appetite. At the same time, he accorded a new dignity to a broad range of ways in which individuals might

pursue happiness. In so doing, he hoped to arm ordinary citizens against the pretensions of would be tyrants. The highest claim to rule—wisdom or holiness or virtue—would no longer be the preserve of a monopolizing few or serve so readily to cloak the designs of the overbearing. In striking out on his new course, the thinking revolutionary was content to guard against the worst and to make room for the best. More than that he dared not claim. (*TR*, xiv)

What if, however, the most ambitious men are not satisfied by the hedging of the regime's goals? Alexander Hamilton voiced the hope that "the love of wealth [which is] as domineering and enterprising a passion as that of power or glory" would check other ambitions, but it was no sure solution ("CC," 17). What "is to be done about men whose aspirations fell only sometimes within the ordinary system of rewards held out by a republic—men of 'irregular ambition,' intent on seizing or even creating chances for self-promotion?" (18). The strategy of relying on passions invites other passions, such as ambition and the desire for power and glory, which might ultimately threaten the stability of the state. Here, the limit of the modern project, and perhaps of political life more generally, begins to emerge.

The final section of "Commerce and Character" considers these and other potential defects related to relying on the passions. The desire for comfort and security might lead to a disregard of nobility, piety, and honor altogether. Smith and Montesquieu worried that the pursuit of comfort might eventually narrow and corrupt men's souls so that "all the nobler parts of the human character" would be extinguished ("CC," 22). John Adams too worried that "an unrestrained indulgence in the passion for wealth would lead only to 'cowardice, and a selfish, unsocial meanness,' 'a sordid scramble for money'" (23). And Benjamin Rush feared that "the feast of reason and the flow of soul" would fall victim to a nation of businessmen (23).

Lerner refers to Tocqueville, but Tocqueville does not fully assuage these concerns. To the contrary, he concedes that "commerce may also predispose men to acquiesce in a new type of oppression." Tocqueville does, however, invite us to resist this oppression by pursuing "that form of greatness and of happiness which is proper to ourselves" ("CC," 26). Lerner too concludes by inviting us to consider the meaning of virtue and its place in political life. In this respect, he follows Tocqueville as his teacher. Indeed, Lerner not only gives Tocqueville the last word in the essay (and the book); in the preface of *The Thinking Revolutionary*, he gives him the first word as well:

It remained for Tocqueville—with a commercial, if barely industrialized, Jacksonian America before him—to make the full depiction. Wherever he turned, he saw men calculating and weighing and computing. Everything had more or less utility and hence could be hefted and judged with a trader's savvy. Because knowledge was seen to be a source of power, because knowledge paid, men sought it. The market mentality shrugged off that "inconsiderate contempt for practice" typical of aristocratic ages; the *use* to which the discoveries of the mind could be put became the leading question. Tocqueville traced the modern predilection for generalizations to a "lively yet indolent" democratic ambition: generalizations yielded large returns for very small investments of thought. Among commercial republicans even religion was brought down to earth: "in the very midst of their zeal one generally sees something so quiet, so methodical, so calculated that it would seem that the head rather than the heart leads them to the foot of the altar." Where the central concern was with utility, there could be little room for the play of the imagination, for poetry; men not only spoke prose but thought prose, all the days of their lives. (quoting "CC," 10)

Just as the thinking revolutionaries saw the potential of commerce to transform the republic into a wealthy and tolerant model of cosmopolitanism, they did not forget that such a regime poses a threat to the higher and more fragile human impulses.

Lerner's essay shows what can be accomplished by taking both philosophical books and the political rhetoric of statesmen seriously. The purpose of this volume, inspired by Lerner's scholarship, is to promote serious reflection, in the spirit of liberal education, about the relation between politics and economics in a modern commercial democracy, and especially in the origins of our own. We asked nine distinguished scholars to comment on "Commerce and Character" in light of their own scholarship.

Arguably the most profound Enlightenment thinkers on the key questions raised under the banner of "commerce and character" are John Locke, David Hume, Adam Smith, Montesquieu, and Jean-Jacques Rousseau. We offer chapters on each of these philosophical titans. Michael Zuckert takes us first to the philosophical underpinnings of the early Enlightenment's view of property. John Locke and David Hume were both defenders of the emerging protocapitalist order, an issue they approached through an examination of the status, nature, and justification of property. Yet as Zuckert shows, Locke and Hume developed radically different theories of property, and he assesses the merits of these two theories.

Paul Rahe observes that Montesquieu made the commercial revolution's impact on civilization thematic. He was the first to systematically trace the growth and extension of commerce through the ages and to chart how its increasing dominance altered social relations and the political options open to humankind. Montesquieu's *Spirit of the Laws* inspired the deepest ruminations on this subject by David Hume, Adam Smith, and Adam Ferguson. Rahe examines how, in Montesquieu's opinion, commerce reshapes mores and manners and alters the political playing field.

Ann Charney Colmo observes that Alexis de Tocqueville described the morality of the commercial republic as "self-interest properly understood." But for Adam Smith, writing prior to Tocqueville, a morality based on self-interest (or self-love, as he called it) was confused and circular: it was the self judging itself and unable to get out of itself. In *The Theory of Moral Sentiments* (1759), Smith stated that certain human sentiments would be a better basis for morality. Those sentiments were "principles in [man's] nature, which interest him in the fortune of others, and render their happiness necessary to him." He proposed a morality based on, and judged by, the "Impartial Spectator," which brought what Smith believed to be an indispensable element into his system: the social. He considered the social so important that he noted that although self-preservation is fundamental, violent death is not something we can experience ourselves. We have to experience it by seeing *someone else* die a violent death: even self-preservation has a social element. If the passions or sentiments could sometimes "seduce us from our duty," Smith harnessed both selfish and social passions through the capitalism of *The Wealth of Nations* and through the Impartial Spectator of *The Theory of Moral Sentiments*, each acting as an invisible hand.

Ryan Patrick Hanley observes that Adam Smith and Alexis de Tocqueville were both keen students of human greatness, and each were sensitive to the ways the idea of greatness was transformed by the advent of the democratic age. In particular, they understood that the traditional love of greatness characteristic of ancient and aristocratic orders was too strong to be extinguished by even the new and powerful forces of commercialization and democratization. Far from extirpating the love of greatness from modern hearts, commercialization and democratization redefined it in ways that prompted aspirants to greatness to seek new expressions of it and new paths to its realization. In particular, Smith and Tocqueville invite us to consider how the old love of greatness received new expressions in the wholly new world of America, such that we might better determine whether our reverence for both equality and greatness is likely to lead "to servitude or freedom, to enlightenment or barbarism, to prosperity or misery."[4]

Clifford Orwin admits that Lerner's "Commerce and Character" says very little about Rousseau; indeed, there is just one brief mention of him. This is not entirely surprising, given that the primary goal of Lerner's essay was to expound those thinkers who commended the influence of commerce on character. Rousseau, by contrast, enjoyed pride of place among critics of this view—certainly among those critics who were as thoroughly modern in their outlook as the proponents. Strikingly, Lerner's essay also indicates that these very proponents of commerce anticipated (or, in the case of Rousseau's contemporaries Smith and Hume, echoed) much of Rousseau's critique of it. They thought the pros of the new commercial world would outweigh its cons, whereas Rousseau tended to harp on the latter in dogged indifference to the former. Yet Rousseau's mature thought from the *First Discourse* onward seems to have sprung full grown from the brow of Montesquieu, the godfather of the burgeoning chamber of commerce. Orwin's chapter explores this paradox.

The next three chapters cover the three most influential American political thinkers of the revolutionary period: Thomas Jefferson, James Madison, and Alexander Hamilton. Thanks to Lerner's "Commerce and Character," Peter Onuf believes that students of political thought can gain fresh and illuminating perspectives on the author of the Declaration of Independence. Reviewing familiar primary sources and recent scholarship on Jefferson, Onuf provides a Lernerian interpretation of "thinking revolutionary" at the critical moment of political and military mobilization when "Americans" first imagined themselves as a people. If their collective identity drew on civic humanism and enlightened moral philosophy, it also reflected the experiences and aspirations of enterprising provincials in a prosperous Anglo-American commercial world. Jefferson was well prepared and well situated to articulate the principles that suddenly seemed so "self-evident" to Creole patriots who sought to vindicate their rights by reforming, not destroying, Britain's great and expansive "empire of liberty."

Up to this point in the volume, our distinguished scholars have largely been in agreement with Lerner's view of the Anglo-American "new-model man." We therefore welcome the sharply conflicting characterization by Colleen Sheehan in her chapter on Madison. Her contribution juxtaposes Lerner's portrait of the new American man with the picture Madison draws in a series of essays devoted to the character of the republican citizen in the modern world of commerce. In one of these essays, Madison takes on Montesquieu's idea of self-interest as a stabilizing force in society and government; in another, he explicitly addresses the character of the republican citizen in the new world. Madison's model republican citizen stands in contrast to both the noncivic, modern commercial individual envisioned by Montesquieu and the slaveholding, aristocratic professional citizen of book VII of Aristotle's *Politics*. With scientific and technological advances from the ancient to the modern world affecting citizens' ability to communicate effectively over a large territory, Madison crafted a republican design in which free, equal, self-sufficient, and educated citizens formed the basis of a new republican model. This new republican model, however, was designed to achieve age-old political ends such as the health, competence, intelligence, and virtue of its citizens. In essence, Madison views the health of the body, economic competence, and the intellectual and moral virtue of individual citizens as objects toward which good legislators direct their efforts and activities. In Madison's view, this new and more noble political course is grounded in the reason of the public, which in turn elevates and educates the interests of the people, which informs and refines public opinion. As such, Madison's "empire of reason" is not based on Hobbesian self-interest; nor is it reducible to the idea of self-interest rightly understood. Madison's vision for America and its citizens was anything but low or vulgar. His aspirations were nothing short of a republic in which citizens genuinely learned how to govern themselves. Implicit in the American social compact, he believed, is a civic promise—a promise to treat one another with the respect that is due to human beings qua human beings. This is the basis for civic trust, civic friendship, and the "benevolence and brotherly affection" that constitute the core of Madison's republic.

Peter McNamara explores Hamilton's rejection of the *doux commerce* thesis in *The Federalist*—a rejection noteworthy due to Hamilton's heavy reliance on Hume and Montesquieu, both of whom believed commerce to be a means to peace. McNamara outlines the argument of Federalist No. 6 and places it in the context of the *Federalist Papers* as a whole. Given that this great hope of the eighteenth century is shared by many people today, Hamilton's rejection leads to important and timely reflections on the relationship of politics to economics and the connection between political theory and political experience.

John C. Koritansky responds to the theory and practice of the classic Enlightenment with a chapter on Tocqueville's *Democracy in America*. As Koritansky observes, Tocqueville applauds the vitality Americans exhibit toward their commercial democratic republic. Tocqueville famously asserts that democratic Americans combat "individualism" and therefore resist the danger of soft egalitarian despotism in connection with their pursuit of self-interest under a "doctrine" of "self-interest rightly understood." Understanding just how this psychology operates requires an understanding of the curious irony of it—an irony that is especially obvious in terms of how Americans extend this "doctrine" to matters of religion and faith. The importance attached to this public doctrine points to the needful prerogative of a "legislator"—that is, someone who exercises a ruling science from the highest perspective.

The volume concludes with a chapter by Ralph Lerner responding to the issues raised by each contributor. Lerner's keen insight as a scholar is rivaled only by his spirit of generosity and disinterested devotion to the pursuit of truth.

NOTES

1. Ralph Lerner, "Commerce and Character: The Anglo-American as New-Model Man," *William and Mary Quarterly* 36, 1 (January 1979): 3–26; hereafter cited in text as "CC." This essay is reproduced in chapter 1 of this volume.

2. Ralph Lerner, *The Thinking Revolutionary: Principle and Practice in the New Republic* (Ithaca, NY: Cornell University Press, 1987); hereafter cited in text as *TR*.

3. Thus, Lerner suggests that even when we separate the rhetoric from the argument, we may not have arrived at the philosophical heart of the argument: "My intention here is not to trace the philosophic reasoning that led these men to reject the foundations of the older orders. That would lead us back to Locke and Spinoza, to Hobbes and Descartes, to Bacon and Machiavelli. Consider, rather, the public speech by which eighteenth-century thinkers—European and American—sought to persuade their contemporaries to adopt maxims. conclusions, and rules of action so much at odds with the certitudes of the day before yesterday" ("CC," 4).

4. Alexis de Tocqueville, *Democracy in America*, ed. and trans. Harvey C. Mansfield and Delba Winthrop (Chicago: University of Chicago Press, 2000), 676.

PROLOGUE

Commerce and Character:
The Anglo-American as New-Model Man

Ralph Lerner

> The hope of glory, and the ambition of princes, are not subject to arithmetical calculation.
> —*Franklin*

> In democracies nothing has brighter luster than commerce.
> —*Tocqueville*

Between them, Adam Smith and Alexis de Tocqueville have provided us with a detailed, fully realized portrait of the new man of commerce. Their psychological analysis—both of the universal type and of its American democratic exemplar—is by now familiar and persuasive. We no longer startle at the strange blend of limitless aspiration, quasi-heroic effort, and sensible calculation that characterizes their model man of the future. And, of course, we rarely wonder at how much domestic tranquility owes to the influence of commerce upon men's tastes, thoughts, and manners. In the eighteenth century, however, when this model of civil behavior was being formulated, all this stood in need of explication and argument. A case had to be made, and then won. The advocates—men as diverse as Montesquieu and John Adams, Adam Smith and Benjamin Franklin, David Hume and Benjamin Rush—were united at least in this: they saw in commercial republicanism a more sensible and realizable alternative to earlier notions of civic virtue and a more just alternative to the theological-political regime that had so long ruled Europe and its colonial periphery. However much these advocates differed—in their philosophic insight, in their perception of the implications of their proposal for the organization of economic life, even in the degree of their acceptance of the very commercial republic they were promoting—for all this, they may be considered a band of brethren in arms.[1]

The language of campaign and contention is no empty figure, for in many respects the commercial republic is defined best by what it rejects:[2] constraints and preoccupations based on visions of perfection beyond the reach of all or most; disdain for the common, useful, and mundane; judgments founded on a man's inherited status rather than on his acts. These were characteristics of an order or orders that the advocates of the commercial republic might still (in a limited way) admire but could not recommend. They saw fit, rather, to promote a new ordering of political, economic, and social life. Further, they perceived in the Anglo-American people and setting both the matter and the fitting occasion for their great project's success.

My intention here is not to trace the philosophic reasoning that led these men to reject the foundations of the older orders. That would lead us back to Locke and Spinoza, to Hobbes and Descartes, to Bacon and Machiavelli. Consider, rather, the public speech by which eighteenth-century thinkers—European and American—sought to persuade their contemporaries to adopt maxims, conclusions, and rules of action so much at odds with the certitudes of the day before yesterday. They had first to show their audience that the old preoccupations entailed unacceptable costs and consequences. Then—a much larger task—they had to propose a new model of political and social life, sketch its leading features in some detail, develop a case for preferring it, and defend it as sufficient to cope with the shortcomings of the existing order. In all these undertakings the advocates of the commercial republic show themselves to have been uncommon men, exceptionally clear- and sharp-sighted moderns who knew what they were rejecting and why.

PRIDEFUL PRETENSIONS DETECTED

The old order was preoccupied with intangible goods to an extent we now hardly ever see. The king had his glory, the nobles their honor, the Christians their salvation, the citizens of pagan antiquity their ambition to outdo others in serving the public good. However much men vied for a fine field, a good herd, a large purse, it was not by these alone that they would make their mark. So at least they said. A latter-day man might be inclined to discount these pretensions but could not dismiss them out of hand. Like Tocqueville, he might doubt "whether men were better in times of aristocracy than at other times," and he might ponder why those earlier men "talked continually about the beauties of virtue" while studying its utility "only in secret."[3] The sense of shame or pride that kept that study secret was itself a revealing social fact. To thinkers like Montesquieu, Hume, and Smith, those earlier pretensions evinced a state of mind in some respects admirable, in other respects astonishing, in most respects consequential, but at bottom absurd. A good part of the political program of these commercial republicans was getting other men to judge likewise.

Eighteenth-century men had to be brought to see how fanciful those noncommercial notions were. To the commercial republicans, aristocratic imagination and pretension were not totally devoid of social value. Honor could be specious and yet politically useful; pride could engender politesse and delicacy of taste, graces that make life easy. The weightier truth, however, was that concern with these fancies skewed public policy and public budgets, sacrificing the real needs of the people to the petty desires of their governors. As Montesquieu put it, these "imaginary needs are what the passions and foibles of those who govern ask for: the charm of an extraordinary project, the sick desire for a vain glory, and a certain impotence of mind against fantasies."[4]

It was not only the few who labored under such delusions. An entire populace might be so taken up with its peculiar vision of what was most important as almost to cease being recognizably human. As little as Rousseau could imagine a nation of true Christians, could Hume imagine a nation of latter-day Spartans consumed with a passion for the public good. Though the "positive and circumstantial" testimony of history kept Hume from dismissing the original Spartan regime as "a mere philosophical whim or fiction," it did not compel him to say much, if anything, good about "a people addicted to arms, who fight for honour and revenge more than pay, and are unacquainted with gain and industry, as well as pleasure."[5] If men would only recognize what is genuinely human, they would see these distorting preoccupations for the grotesques they truly were.

Disabusing the many was no small task. Those whom Smith pleased to call "the great mob of mankind" were the awe-struck admirers of wealth and greatness, of success, however well or ill deserved. Such popular presumption in favor of the powerful had its good side, too, making more bearable the obedience that the weak dared not withhold. But that was hardly the whole story, according to Smith, for men came to perceive heroic magnanimity where there was only "extravagant rashness and folly"; "the splendour of prosperity" kept them from seeing "the blackness of . . . avidity and injustice" in the acts of those in high places. Smith pointed to an escape from these conventional delusions. We have within us, he maintained, a means of distinguishing the admirable from the meretricious, the genuine from the fanciful—a means of more truly assessing both our own worth and "the real merit" of others. How, he asked, would a particular act appear to an "impartial spectator," the vicarious conscience of mankind within everyone's breast? From this uncommon vantage of common humanity, we could see what "the most successful warriors, the greatest statesmen and legislators, the eloquent founders and leaders of the most numerous and most successful sects and parties" rarely were able to see: how much of their success and splendor was owing to their excessive presumption and self-admiration. If such excess was useful and necessary—for the instigators to undertake what "a more sober mind would never have thought of," and for the rest of mankind to acquiesce and follow them—it was, nonetheless, excess bordering on insane vanity. Hardly anything Smith taught was more subversive of the older order than his cool deflation of the proud man's "self-sufficiency and absurd conceit of his own superiority."[6] He did not seek to have his readers deny or sneer at the real differences between men but rather to discount the claims of all who presumed on those differences, real or imagined.

These presumptuous men imposed terrible costs on the whole of society—political costs that were insupportable, economic costs that were irrational. Hume believed that to some extent ambitious pretensions were self-correcting: enormous monarchies overextend themselves, condemned to repeat the chain of causes and effects that led to the ruin of Rome. In this way "human nature checks itself in its airy elevation." But another kind of preoccupation with intangible goods was less surely or easily deflected. Though Hume found no counterpart in modern times to the factional rage of ancient oligarchs and democrats, another type unknown to the pagans still persisted. It was the effect of what Hume called "parties from principle, especially abstract speculative principle." That men should divide over distinct interests was intelligible, over affection for persons and families only somewhat less so. But that they should divide, with mad and fatal consequence, in "controversy about an article of faith, which is utterly absurd and unintelligible, is not a difference in sentiment, but in a few phrases and expressions, which one party accepts of without understanding them, and the other refuses in the same manner"—that they should so divide was even more absurd than the behavior of those Moroccans who waged civil war "merely on account of their complexion." For a variety of reasons Christianity had fostered a persecuting spirit "more furious and enraged than the most cruel factions that ever arose from interest and ambition."[7] On this point Hume and the commercial republicans generally could agree with the ancients: fanaticism prompted by principle was incompatible with civility, reason, and government.

The economic costs of pursuing imaginary preoccupations might be less bloody than the political costs, but they were no less real; for proof consider the colonies in the New World. The frugal, simple, yet decent civil and ecclesiastical establishments of the English colonies were, for Smith, "an ever-memorable example at how small an expence three millions of people may not only be governed, but well governed." They also were an indictment of contrasting pretensions and practices, most notably in the Spanish and Portuguese colonies where both rich and poor suffered the oppressive consequences. A plundering horde of mendicant friars "most carefully" taught the poor "that it is a duty to give, and a very great sin to refuse them their charity"; this licensed, consecrated beggary "is a most grievous tax upon the poor people.... The rich, too, were ill instructed: the elaborate ceremonials in those colonies habituated the rich to vanity and expense, thereby perpetuating "the ruinous taxes of private luxury and extravagance."[8] Though vanity (as with the French) might be productive of refinement, tastefulness and luxury, as well as industry, pride (as with the Spanish) generally produced nothing but laziness, poverty, and ruin.[9] Aristocratic pride, in particular, was singled out by the commercial republicans for censure. Whatever slight sense feudal institutions might once have made, they had become atavisms, sustained by bizarre notions of honor and shame. Family pride, absorption with honor and glory, habitual indulgence of one's fancy for ornament and elegance: all these unfitted a man to perceive, let alone tend to, his "real interest." "Nothing," Smith asserted, "could be more completely absurd" than adhering to a system of entails and, by extension, to the system of thought that made entails seem sensible. Clearly, no mode of thought was less likely to render a man inclined and able to pay "an exact attention to small savings and small gains."[10] In recommending an alternative mode, the commercial republicans thought they were returning to simple reason.

UTILITY RESPLENDENT

That alternative was what we today would call the market model, what Smith called "the natural system of perfect liberty and justice." This way of getting rid of a kind of unreason did not presuppose that men at large would use their reason more. Far from seconding the proud aspirations of Reason to grasp the whole of society and to direct its complex workings in detail, the commercial republicans counseled humility. They thought human behavior was adequately accounted for by dwelling upon the wants by which men are driven—wants that are largely, though not exclusively, physical; wants that are part and parcel of the self-regarding passions; wants that cannot in most cases be satisfied. Butchers and bakers, prelates and professors—all could be understood in more or less the same way. Once the similitude of our passions was recognized (however much the objects of those passions varied from man to man), our common neediness and vulnerability became apparent. This Hobbesian truth was axiomatic for the commercial republicans. Their reason told them that a surer guide to sane behavior could be found in the operations of a nonrational mechanism, the aggregate of small, anonymous calculations of things immediately known and felt by all. It was more reasonable to rely on the impersonal concourse of buyers and sellers than on the older standard of reasoned governance for proper hints and directions precisely because the market could better reckon with the ordinary passions of ordinary men. Indeed, where the ancient polity, Christianity, and the feudal aristocracy, each in its own fashion, sought to conceal, deny, or thwart most of the common passions for private gratification and physical comfort, the commercial republic built on those passions. Seen in this light, the market, and the state that secured its preconditions, were impersonal arenas where men could sort out their wants and tend to them.[11] The openness of these institutions to attempts at satisfying all kinds of wants would especially commend them to all kinds of men.

In seeking satisfaction under the new dispensation a man needed to be at once warm and cool, impassioned and calculating, driven yet sober. Eschewing brilliance and grandeur, the new-model man of prudence followed a way of life designed to secure for himself a small but continual profit. As Smith noted, he avoided whatever "might too often interfere with the regularity of his temperance, might interrupt the steadiness of his industry, or break in upon the strictness of his frugality." He deferred present ease for greater enjoyment later; he did his duty, but beyond that minded his own business. He was, in short, a private man whose behavior "commands a certain cold esteem but seems not entitled to any very ardent love or admiration."[12] Notwithstanding these reservations, preoccupation with incremental gains made sense to Smith the political economist. The energies set in motion would bring forth an array of small comforts and conveniences beyond the reach or imagining of serf or savage, relieving miseries once thought fated. As men looked more to their economic interest, that interest would loom larger in their eyes and thoughts. Other concerns would matter less—sometimes because the accumulation of wealth was seen as the key to satisfying all desires, sometimes because a conflicting noneconomic interest (family feeling, attachment to a landed estate) was seen as only sentimental, illusory. It was but a short step from this awakening to the adoption of what Tocqueville called "standards of prudent and conscious mediocrity," the adjustment of production and of products to satisfy ordinary men's demands for the gratification of their wants. In the end "there is no sovereign will or national prejudice that can fight for long against cheapness."[13]

The implications of all this for how and what men think were not lost upon Montesquieu and Smith. But it remained for Tocqueville—with a commercial, if barely industrialized, Jacksonian America before him—to make the full depiction. Wherever he turned, he saw men calculating and weighing and computing. Everything had more or less utility and hence could be hefted and judged with a trader's savvy. Because knowledge was seen to be a source of power, because knowledge paid, men sought it. The market mentality shrugged off that "inconsiderate contempt for practice" typical of aristocratic ages; the use to which the discoveries of the mind could be put became the leading question. Tocqueville traced the modern predilection for generalizations to a "lively yet indolent" democratic ambition: generalizations yielded large returns for very small investments of thought. Among commercial republicans even religion was brought down to earth: "in the very midst of their zeal one generally sees something so quiet, so methodical, so calculated that it would seem that the head rather than the heart leads them to the foot of the altar."[14] Where the central concern was with utility, there could be little room for the play of the imagination, for poetry; men not only spoke prose but thought prose, all the days of their lives.[15]

Quiet and prosaic though such men might be, they could be passionate, energetic, and willing to run risks. Just as Montesquieu saw these qualities in England, his model commercial republic,[16] so Tocqueville saw them in America, his model commercial republic. Again and again he remarked on "the soaring spirit of enterprise"—a product in part of peculiarly American conditions, to be sure, but at a deeper level a natural consequence of man's freedom to indulge in "a kind of decent materialism." Restlessness goaded men on, and the prospect of happiness, like the horizon, beckoned and receded before them. Life itself became a thrilling gamble as greed and everchanging desires elicited efforts of heroic proportions from unheroic men for unheroic objectives.[17]

No sketch of the commercial republic should neglect to stress that, as a model both for a national polity and for the entire trading world, it tended to ignore or transcend the conventional divisions within nations and among them. Its eighteenth-century proponents could realistically urge men to consider their larger interdependence without expecting (or even desiring) the neglect of national interest and identity, for commerce, properly understood and reasonably conducted, would serve both man and citizen. Commerce inclined men to consider one another primarily as demanders and suppliers, to consider the world as constituting "but a single state, of which all the [particular] societies are members."[18] Commerce was preeminently traffic in movables—things that have little if any identification with a particular state of the kind real property necessarily has. In what Adam Smith called "the great mercantile republic"—by which he meant all producers and traders of movables—the owners and employers of capital stock were properly citizens of the world and "not necessarily attached to any particular country."[19] What began as a simple recognition of our separate and common needs would end in a complex, ever-changing interdependence. Even as each labored intently to satisfy his own wants, men would become commercial cousins, cool fellow-citizens of a universal republic.

A MORE HUMAN ALTERNATIVE

This was the world—part vision, part fact—that these eighteenthcentury advocates pronounced good. If others were to judge likewise, they had to understand why the commercial republicans preferred the market regime: they had to see that, better than any of its predecessors and alternatives, this regime suited human nature because, more than any of its predecessors and alternatives, it could be realized taking men as they are.

The contrast with and opposition to the Christian and Greek worlds could hardly have been greater. In Montesquieu's analysis it was the Christian Schoolmen—and not the commercial practices they condemned—that deserved the label criminal. In condemning something "naturally permitted or necessary," the doctrinaire and unworldly Scholastics set in train a series of misfortunes, most immediately for the Jews, more generally for Europe. Gradually, however, princes had learned to be more politic; experience taught them that toleration paid. "Happy is it for men to be in a situation in which, while their passions inspire in them the thought of being wicked, it is, nevertheless, to their interest not to be." The calculation prompted by nature or necessity overpowered the passion prompted by religion and corrected the enthusiastic excesses of those professing it.

For Montesquieu, the reliance of Greek thinkers on virtue as the support of popular government displayed an equal disregard for how men are. Political thinkers of his own time, in contrast, "speak to us only of manufacture, commerce, finance, opulence, and even of luxury." This was not a change that Montesquieu regretted.[20] According to the commercial republicans, the ancient polity rested on a distortion of almost every quality of human nature. Nowhere was this seen more clearly than in the case of Sparta. The Spartan's heroic virtue and his indifference to his own well-being were almost perfectly antithetical to the cast of the commercial republican. John Adams's characterization could serve as the verdict of all the commercial republicans: "Separated from the rest of mankind, [the Spartans] lived together, destitute of all business, pleasure, and amusement, but war and politics, pride and ambition; . . . as if fighting and intriguing, and not life and happiness, were the end of man and society. . . . Human nature perished under this frigid system of national and family pride."[21] This attack on Sparta (an extreme case if ever there was one) may be seen as a rejection of that primary reliance on virtue placed not only by the ancients but by latter-day men who drew their inspiration from classical models. Commercial republicans could reject the ancient premises even while admiring some ancient accomplishments.[22] In so doing, some may have been unaware or perplexed, and others torn between zealous wishes and sober doubts, but the foremost of them were, for these purposes, concerned less with the rare excellence of a rare individual than with what might ordinarily be expected of the generality of men.

Sparta, and the ancient world generally, accomplished astonishing feats, astonishing because they defied "the more natural and usual course of things." For Hume and his fellows, Sparta was a "prodigy," less a model than a freak.

The ancient policy of preferring the greatness of the state to the happiness of the subject was "violent"; recurrence to that policy in modern times was "almost impossible." But beyond that, what sense did such a policy make? The sovereign who heeded Hume's counsel would know that "it is his best policy to comply with the common bent of mankind, and give it all the improvements of which it is susceptible. Now, according to the most natural course of things, industry, and arts, and trade, increase the power of the sovereign, as well as the happiness of the subjects." Far from being tempted to deal harshly with his subject to compel him to produce a surplus, the modern sovereign would take care to "furnish him with manufactures and commodities, [so that] he will do it of himself." This sovereign would take to heart Hume's lesson that "our passions are the only causes of labour"; he would appreciate and use the mighty engine of covetousness. And let it even be granted that the ancient policy of infusing each citizen-soldier with a passion for the public good might not be utterly futile, for it is at least conceivable that a community might be converted temporarily into a camp of lean and dedicated citizens. "But as these principles [of ancient citizenship] are too disinterested, and too difficult to support, it is requisite to govern men by other passions, and animate them with a spirit of avarice and industry, art and luxury."[23] With less pain—and less nobility—commercial republican principles could lead to a strong, secure polity.

American commercial republicans did not promote this new policy with quite the breezy equanimity of Hume. The groping, hesitation, and even anguish catalogued by Gordon Wood amply document that fact.[24] But neither did the leading Americans reject Hume's premises. In the long run, perhaps, the corruption of the republic was inevitable. Precautions might be taken to postpone that day, but the foundations were not themselves in question.[25] Again, we find in Tocqueville a distillation of what most Americans were not yet able or willing to state for themselves. The generalized expression of the commercial republican view of man and of human association was what Tocqueville called "the doctrine of self-interest properly understood," the fusing of public interest and private profit to the point where "a sort of selfishness makes [the individual] care for the state." The result was a kind of patriotism in no way to be confused with the ardent love of the ancient citizen for his city; it was less a public passion than a private conviction, a conviction arising out of private passions. Each man would come to recognize his need for involvement with others; he might even learn to temper his selfishness. Whatever else might be said of his frame of mind, there was no denying that it sustained and was sustained by commercial activity. Even as commerce reminded men of their common needs and made them more like one another and more aware of that likeness, the doctrine of self-interest properly understood taught them simply and plainly to give the dictates of "nature and necessity" their due. Human nature stood stripped of the pretensions that had kept earlier men from satisfying their natural wants.[26]

MILD AMBITIONS AND WILD ONES

Though some might well prefer the commercial republic because it better suited men as they are, they had to look still further. Were the political ills that had beset men and nations from time out of mind less likely under the new dispensation? To what extent would the commercial republic ameliorate the self-induced miseries of political life? Its eighteenth-century proponents had high but not excessive hopes that men and nations would live in greater security as more of mankind adopted the market model. They believed that, on the whole, men would find it easier to be less cruel toward one another as they came to care more about their own safety and comfort.

Montesquieu clearly expected this to be the case in relations among the nations. "Commerce cures destructive prejudices"; it "polishes and softens barbaric morals." In making men more aware of both human variety and sameness, commerce made them less provincial and in a sense more humane. "The spirit of commerce unites nations." Driven by their mutual needs, trading partners entered into a symbiosis they could ill afford to wreck by war. They would learn how to subordinate disruptive political interests to those of commerce. Such nations, devoting themselves to a "commerce of economy," had, so to speak, a necessity to be faithful; since their object was gain, not conquest, they would be "pacific from principle."[27]

American variations on these themes were both more and less sober than the Montesquieuan original. Writing in the nonage of the American nation, Thomas Paine noted with seeming indifference that the preoccupation with commerce "diminishes the spirit both of patriotism and military defence." He could accept this diminution (once the times that tried men's souls were past) because "our plan is commerce," not "setting the world at defiance."[28] For John Jay and Alexander Hamilton, however, a reliance on the presumed pacific genius of commercial republics would be "visionary." If anything, commerce—especially when conducted in the forward American manner—would create its own occasions for aggrandizement and warfare.[29] Thus, according to Hamilton, the proposition that the people of a commercial republic, under the influence of the new prevailing modes of thought, had to grow less martial would not, even if true, entail a belief in an end to war. It was more likely that where the business of the people was business, the economic objections to a citizen army would be "conclusive" and war would be left to the professionals.[30] Generally, however, European and American commercial republicans believed that commerce gave promise of influencing international relations for the better. Like Benjamin Rush, they viewed commerce as "the means of uniting the different nations of the world together by the ties of mutual wants and obligations," as an instrument for "humanizing mankind."[31] Hamilton was the outstanding demurrer.

Even greater than these transnational benefits was the anticipated dividend in increased domestic security.[32] For Hume, the simultaneous indulgence and tempering of men's passions was almost a matter of course. Men would continue to be instructed in "the advantages of human[e] maxims above rigour and severity." Relieved of the distortions imposed by ignorance and superstition, political life would come more and more to wear a human face. "Factions are then less inveterate, revolutions less tragical, authority less severe, and seditions less frequent." Free to pursue happiness as each individual saw it, men would be able to continue to rise above their ancestors' ferocity and brutishness. Furthermore, the development of commerce and industry drew "authority and consideration to that middling rank of men, who are the best and firmest basis of public liberty."[33] Smith seconded Hume's observation, pronouncing this effect the most important of all those stemming from commerce and manufacturing. Where before men had "lived almost in a continual state of war with their neighbours, and of servile dependency upon their superiors," now they increasingly had "order and good government, and, with them, the liberty and security of individuals." The self-regarding actions of a part had led to the gradual elevation of the whole.[34]

The turmoils and revolutions of the seventeenth and eighteenth centuries demonstrated that the monopoly of public service enjoyed by the great could be broken. They also suggested how even the humblest man, by adopting and acting on commercial maxims, might serve himself and thereby the public good.[35] These lessons were not lost upon a newly emancipated order of men, whose typical member (in Smith's sketch) was an impatient "man of spirit and ambition, who is depressed by his situation." For him and his kind, escape from the mediocrity of one's station was the first order of business.[36] In principle he would stick at nothing to accomplish this. "He even looks forward with satisfaction to the prospect of foreign war or civil dissension," the attendant confusion and bloodshed creating opportunities for him to cut a figure. In the old regime such a frustrated man would have been ridiculous and might have been dangerous, but in the commercial republic he came into his own—and without having to take to the barricades. For it was above all in the world of commerce and in the polity devoted to commerce that this new man enjoyed a comparative advantage over the conventional aristocrat, over "the man of rank and distinction." The latter "shudders with horror at the thought of any situation which demands the continual and long exertion of patience, industry, fortitude, and application of thought." For the new man, however, such humdrum exertions afforded the likeliest escape from detested obscurity and insignificance. His prudence consisted of a blend of foresight and self-command with a view to private advantage. His road to fame and fortune was straight and narrow; he respected the conventions of society "with an almost religious scrupulosity," of which Smith deemed him a much better example than that frequently set by "men of much more splendid talents and virtues." His virtues, indeed, were closer to the virtues of "the inferior ranks of people" than to those of the great. They were emphatically private virtues. Needless to say, they would have been altogether unfashionable in the reign of Charles II.[37]

Where such burghers were preponderant, civil life took on a distinctive coloration. The private preoccupations, the quiet virtues, the insistent passions of commercial individuals became the core of an entire system of honor. When Tocqueville looked at the Americans more than half a century later, he thought he saw a people who carried the "patient, supple, and insinuating" habits of traders into political life. He was struck by their love of order, regard for conventional morality, distrust of genius, and preference for the practical over the theoretical. He offered what he thought a sufficient explanation: "Violent political passions have little hold on men whose whole thoughts are bent on the pursuit of well-being. Their excitement about small matters makes them calm about great ones."[38] It would not be hard to regard this broad characterization of American life as at best fanciful and tendentious. But any such quick dismissal probably says more about differing understandings of "great" and "small" than about the validity of Tocqueville's explanation.

Whatever else it is, this prosaic, politically cautious people was anything but sluggish. Its tastes and feelings were intense but well channeled. Thus the natural taste for comfort became an all-consuming passion, filling the imaginations and thoughts of all ranks of the people with middling expectations. "It is as hard for vices as for virtues to slip through the net of common standards." Tocqueville saw democratic ambition as "both eager and constant," but generally confined to "coveting small prizes within reach." Selfmade men found it hard to shake off the prudent habits of a lifetime: "a mind cannot be gradually enlarged, like a house." Courage and heroism, too, were present, but again with a difference. Trade and navigation and colonization were with the Americans a surrogate for war. The ordeals they endured, the dangers they braved, the defeats they shrugged off were astonishing, not least because the coveted laurel was, more often than not, something comparable to being able to "sell tea a farthing cheaper than an English merchant can." From such a man of commerce, who treated all of life "like a game of chance, a time of revolution, or the day of a battle," much was to be expected and little feared.[39] American experience confirmed Hamilton's observation that "the love of wealth [is] as domineering and enterprising a passion as that of power or glory." But it also showed that the effects of that passion could go beyond avaricious accumulation. John Adams maintained that "there is no people on earth so ambitious as the people of America." Whereas in other lands, he thought, "ambition and all its hopes are extinct," in America, where competition was free, where every office—even the highest—seemed within one's grasp, the ardor for distinction was stimulated and became general. In America "the lowest can aspire as freely as the highest." The farmer and tradesman pursued their dream of happiness as intensely as any man. Most revealing, however, were the objects of those dreams. "The post of clerk, sergeant, corporal, and even drummer and fifer, is coveted as earnestly as the best gift of major-general." No man was so humble but a passion for distinction was aroused; no object so small but it excited somebody's emulation. In Adams's Arcadian vision the general emulation taking place in a properly constituted, balanced government "makes the common people brave and enterprising" and—thanks to their ambition—"sober, industrious, and frugal. You will find among them some elegance, perhaps, but more solidity; a little pleasure, but a great deal of business."[40] The commercial republicans could, in good conscience, recommend the unleashing of men's ambition because they saw how, in the case of the Many (even including most of the traditional Few), that ambition would be tame. Political checks, powerfully supported by new social and economic aspirations, would keep men busy, wary, and safe.

What, though, of the problem posed by the others, those whom James Madison in *The Federalist* noted as "a few aspiring characters"? A philosopher or statesman concerned with promoting and sustaining a commercial republic had to be mindful of the political threat likely to arise from such individuals. What, Hamilton asked, was to be done about men whose aspirations fell only sometimes within the ordinary system of rewards held out by a republic—men of "irregular ambition," intent on seizing or even creating chances for self-promotion?[41] To this challenge the commercial republicans responded with counsel and modest hopes, but no sure solution. The limits of the market model were in sight.

John Adams's lifetime of rumination on this theme testifies to its importance—and its intractability. There was, he thought at age twenty-six, no "source of greater Evils, than the Tendency of great Parts and Genius, to imprudent sallies and a Wrong Biass." It was to "the giddy Rashness and Extravagance of the sublimest Minds" that man's bloody and tumultuous past was owed. Popular government, far from being immune, was more vulnerable to this danger than any other form. The proper course to follow was not "the general Method in Use among Persons in Power of treating such spirits." Experience indicated, rather, that "unskilfull and rough Usage" only succeeded in making genius more desperate and troublesome. Treated differently, "with a wise and delicate Management," such minds might be made into "ornaments and Blessings."[42]

Would an example of a beneficent management be Smith's proposal, in *The Wealth of Nations*, for dealing with the "ambitious and high-spirited men" of British America? Smith's premise was that free government could endure, and endure well, only if "the greater part of the leading men, the natural aristocracy of every country," had it within their power to gratify their sense of self-importance. He went on to make a suggestion that seemed to him "obvious." Present those colonial worthies with "a new and more dazzling object of ambition"; raise their sights from "piddling for the little prizes" offered by "the paltry raffle of colony faction" to "the great prizes which sometimes come from the wheel of the great state lottery of British politics"; direct their hopes and abilities to the imperial seat of "the great scramble."[43] Smith's was a more politic proposal than those brought forward by successive ministries and privy councils after 1763. But was it enough? A wearier and less sanguine Adams might doubt that. Among men of spirit, whose private interest could be enlisted chiefly or only through noncommercial appeals, he knew there were some few—the extreme and practically most important cases—who insisted on engrossing all the coin of pride. "This . . . is the tribe out of which proceed your patriots and heroes, and most of the great benefactors to mankind." As he confided to his old comrade, Benjamin Rush, "there is in some souls a principle of absolute levity that buoys them irresistibly into the clouds."[44] Just as prudential investments held little charm for the likes of these, so would honors shared with others not satisfy. The threat and the problem remained. In the last analysis, the only safeguard against a dangerously overreaching ambition was what Hume called the "watchful jealousy" of the people.[45]

Consider this modestly elevated multitude on whom the shapers of the commercial republic placed their hopes.[46] At the end, they soberly expected, ordinary farmers, mechanics, and tradesmen would remain just that—and voters as well—busy with their own affairs, forever preoccupied with the economic side of life and without more vaulting ambition. But that did not exhaust the matter. Though the ordinary work of society remained to be done by ordinary men, the commercial republic promised these citizens literally a new birth of freedom and invested them with a new sense of selfesteem. For now, as these men collectively and for the first time assumed decisive political and social significance, they found their aspirations raised, their energies stirred and directed, their capacities enlarged.[47] They would move forward with confidence, believing that "one Man of tolerable Abilities may work great Changes, and accomplish great Affairs among Mankind" if only he brought the proper method and diligence to his task. They would move forward with no apology to those who might view their concerns as "trifling Matters not worth minding or relating," for a "seemingly low" or trivial matter, when recurring frequently, gained "Weight and Consequence." They would act on the belief that "Human Felicity is produc'd not so much by great Pieces of good Fortune that seldom happen, as by little Advantages that occur every Day."[48] Thus, in promoting their private affairs and tending to their public business—however slight or narrow—they could look forward to physical gratification, enhanced social standing, and the satisfaction of performing an acknowledged public service. Even their notions of what is their business grew; they would come to take a selfish interest in the public weal. This, then, was the electorate that, freed of the benighting miseries of the past, might yet be alert enough in their own interests to keep the threatening natural aristocracy in check. Given a properly contrived constitution, they might even employ that aristocracy's talents to advantage.

The commercial republicans were cautiously hopeful that the emancipation promised by their new regime would not be self-destructive. Tocqueville, taking in the scene at a later date and from a different perspective, was somewhat less hopeful. Looking beyond the jarring wishes and fears of Jacksonian America,[49] he thought he saw how a preoccupied electorate might turn into an indifferent crowd, how a "people passionately bent on physical pleasures" might come to regard the exercise of their political rights as "a tiresome inconvenience," a trivial distraction from "the serious business of life." He thought he saw how, with their anxieties fueled by a self-contradictory hedonism, such a people might readily hand over their liberties to whatever able and ambitious man promised them the untroubled enjoyment of their private pursuits.[50] Alternatively, they might slide—quietly, mindlessly—into a bondage altogether new, where "not a person, or a class ... , but society itself holds the end of the chain." Either way they would lose their liberty and their very character as men and citizens.[51] It was in anticipation of this Tocquevillean nightmare that Rousseau inveighed against those who would rather hire a representative than spare the time to govern themselves, and rather pay taxes than serve the community with their bodies. Absorbed in their ledgers and accounts, they stood to lose all. "The word 'finance,'" Rousseau wrote, "is slave language; it has no place in the city's lexicon."[52]

ASSESSING BENEFITS AND COSTS

Although the founding fathers of commercial republicanism were neither money-grubbers nor philistines nor indifferent citizens, Rousseau's statement could not be farther from their conclusion. In the last analysis, commerce commended itself to them because it promised a cure for destructive prejudices and irrational enthusiasms, many of them clerically inspired. Commerce was an engine that would assault and level the remaining outposts of pride in all its forms: family pride, aristocratic pride, pride that concealed from "mankind that they were children of the same father, and members of one great family," pride in "learning" (which Rush distinguished sharply from "useful knowledge"), pride in whatever led men to believe that they could rise above the workaday world. Commerce, like the plain teachings of the Gospels, like useful knowledge, would humble the mind, soften the heart, help bring "the ancient citizen to a level with the men of [only] yesterday," and assimilate all men everywhere to one another.[53] If, in a sense, commerce imposed a ceiling upon some men's aspirations, it more significantly also supplied most men with a floor to stand on. Commercial men would come at last to regard themselves and their societies as members of a single universal state, a brotherhood of demanders and suppliers.

That this triumph of commerce would entail significant human losses was a foregone conclusion for these commercial republicans. Nonetheless, they were prepared to accept those losses, even as they sought ways to mitigate them. For Montesquieu, a regime dedicated to commerce partook less of a union of fellow citizens, bound together by ties of friendship, than of an alliance of contracting parties, intent on maximizing their freedom of choice through a confederation of convenience. It was in this character of an alliance that men found themselves cut off from one another or, rather, linked to one another principally through a market mechanism. It was a world in which everything had its price—and, accordingly, its sellers and buyers. Not surprisingly, the habits of close calculation and "exact justice" appropriate to one kind of activity were extended to all kinds, and political community was replaced by a marketplace of arm's-length transactions.[54]

Smith was even more explicit and detailed than Montesquieu in assessing "the disadvantages of a commercial spirit." He saw it as bringing about a narrowing and demeaning of men's souls, with the "heroic spirit" being "almost entirely extinguished." As in his discussion of the effects of the division of labor upon "the great body of the people," Smith squarely faced the debasement implicit in his scheme of civilization. Whether his proposals for public education would forfend the predicted "mental mutilation," "gross ignorance and stupidity," and corruption of "all the nobler parts of the human character," is not my present question. I note here only that Smith recognized the need that civilized society had for civilized men, a kind that his society normally would not nurture.[55]

The American commercial republicans who struggled with this problem sought a solution in some passion or pride that might vie with the love of wealth. For them, America's dedication to commerce was both fitting and frightening. On the one hand, it would take commerce and all the energies it could command to exploit the opportunities offered by the new land.[56] Modern statesmen, such as Hamilton, were mindful of how effectively commerce moved men. "By multiplying the means of gratification, by promoting the introduction and circulation of the precious metals, those darling objects of human avarice and enterprise, it [that is, commercial prosperity] serves to vivify and invigorate the channels of industry, and to make them flow with greater activity and copiousness. The assiduous merchant, the laborious husbandman, the active mechanic, and the industrious manufacturer, all orders of men look forward with eager expectation and growing alacrity to this pleasing reward of their toils."[57] Discerning statesmen, such as Adams, also understood how, in certain European lands, it was in the general interest for the nobility to affect "that kind of pride, which looks down on commerce and manufactures as degrading." Reinforced by "the pompous trumpery of ensigns, armorials, and escutcheons," "the proud frivolities of heraldry," aristocratic prejudice might retard "the whole nation from being entirely delivered up to the spirit of avarice." Though these particular pretensions could only be considered mischievous and ridiculous in America,[58] the need for some countermeasures persisted. For in this respect America was no exception: an unrestrained indulgence in the passion for wealth would lead only to "cowardice, and a selfish, unsocial meanness," "a sordid scramble for money." To save "our bedollared country" from "the universal gangrene of avarice," Adams suggested making republican use of the rivals of ambition and pride of birth, thereby employing "one prejudice to counteract another."[59] All this befitted a man who knew something of himself and had hopes for his son. Individuals and indeed families might reasonably cherish qualities that set them apart and above—for example, a deserved reputation for public service in war and peace.[60] In a commercial republic such pretensions would be manageable, even indispensable. The solution, however, remained an uneasy one, and Adams himself wavered between hope and despair for his country.

Benjamin Rush's ambivalence toward commercialism is especially revealing. Though he did not think commercial wealth was necessarily fatal to republican liberty, he hastened to add parenthetically, "provided that commerce is not in the souls of men." For commerce, "when pursued closely, sinks the man into a machine."[61] And yet when considering the mode of education proper in a republic, he exalted commerce as right for America and for mankind. However much his taste as a private man was offended by a merchant class who "have little relish for the 'feast of reason and the flow of soul,'"[62] as a public man Rush could only be pleased by the promotion and triumph of the commercial mode of thought. "I consider commerce in a much higher light [than as a means of promoting public prosperity] when I recommend the study of it in republican seminaries. I view it as the best security against the influence of hereditary monopolies of land, and therefore, the surest protection against aristocracy."[63] In this perspective, the costs of commerce could be borne gladly.

THE AMERICAN TERMINUS

In the beginning, Locke asserted, all the world was America. In the end, Tocqueville predicted, all the world would be American. To speak of America, then, was to speak of man's fate, perhaps even of a divine decree. This country's rapid passage from a Lockean state of nature to a Tocquevillean democracy instructively telescoped the creation or emergence of the new man of commerce. The American democrat was the man of the future, an exemplar for humanity. He had adopted habits of mind and action that could not fail to be intelligible and attractive to most men everywhere. So, at any rate, Tocqueville thought; and in this he was not alone. In setting forth the American commercial republican as the new-model man, Tocqueville was simultaneously predicting and prescribing. In each case, however, he was beset by foreseeable certainties and by a sense that "the spirit of man walks through the night."[64] If we draw back from the margin of the providentially predestined circle and confine our speculations to things we can see with our own eyes, the reasons for his prescription emerge clearly enough.

Consider the spectacle of a united people spreading relentlessly over the land, a people who for all their present or future diversities and divisions were made one and kept one by their social state and by their habits, manners, and opinions. Whatever the future might bring, "the great AngloAmerican family" would remain kinsmen by virtue of their equality of social condition, their taste for physical well-being, and their single-minded enterprise in seeking to gratify that taste. That much, at least, would remain both common and constant; "all else is doubtful, but that is sure."[65] Lifting our gaze above the fortuitous and peculiarly American features of this scene, we can detect what Tocqueville deemed fundamental for all men and all places in the new world aborning. As "the great bond of humanity is drawn tighter . . . men would become more equal, more comfortable, and more alike in conforming to some middling Standard. Much of what set people against people and country against country would loosen its grip; all men, in a sense, would become votaries at the same shrine."[66] To this extent, the realm of freedom would be constricted. But though we are fated to live our lives as members of the new egalitarian cosmopolitan regime, we are not without choices, choices that tax to the limit our strength, our will, and our art.[67] The province of statesmanship or of political science is preserved with Tocqueville's assurance (at the end of the second volume of *Democracy in America*) that it is up to us "whether equality is to lead to servitude or freedom, knowledge or barbarism, prosperity or wretchedness."[68] It is in the light of that choice that Tocqueville's recommendations are to be understood: a recommendation of the commercial republic, and a recommendation of those means consistent with the regime that are most likely to foster freedom, knowledge, and prosperity.

There was much in the commercial republic that Tocqueville found distasteful: its discreet sensualism, the counting-house character of its politics, the stifling of public spirit by the petty concerns of private life. But beyond the commercial republic, beyond "America," was the alternative: not Greece or Rome, not "China,"[69] but "Russia." The grand and awesome alternatives with which Tocqueville ended *Democracy in America* were prefigured (at the conclusion of the first volume) by the contrast between "Russia" and "America." He insisted that the servitude and centralization of the one were as compatible with egalitarianism as were the freedom and individualism of the other.[70] Indeed, that equality of condition which Tocqueville would have us regard as a providential fact, a fated certainty, might more easily be manifest in servitude than in the kind of independence that crumbles into anarchy.[71] If, in one sense, "Russia" is literally Russia—a harsh, barbarous despotism, an atavism totally apart from the modern egalitarian tendency—in another sense it may be Tocqueville's relevant cautionary example of the vast and terrible power that can be generated by uniformity and concentration. The saving grace of "America," then, and of the commercial republic for which it stands, is the way in which it "relies on personal interest and gives free scope to the unguided strength and common sense of individuals."[72] "Trade makes men independent of one another and gives them a high idea of their personal importance; it leads them to want to manage their own affairs and teaches them how to succeed therein."[73] But for all its utility, even necessity, commerce may not be sufficient. For though commerce was part of Tocqueville's solution, it also was part of Tocqueville's problem. To counter the forces that press in on modern men and narrow their souls, Tocqueville looked to the commercial man's predisposition to liberty. Yet commerce may also predispose men to acquiesce in a new type of oppression—not the naked personal power of a Muscovite czar, but the gloved and masked impersonal power of a modern "sovereign, whatever its origin or constitution or name." Faced with an alternative that would degrade men into "a flock of timid and hard-working animals,"[74] Tocqueville searched for the highest grounds on which he could justify men's "strongest remaining guarantee against themselves."[75]

That search led him to "the doctrine of self-interest as preached in America." Most generally stated, men are more preoccupied with wants they feel than with needs they must reason about. And oddly enough, a system that frees men to try to satisfy their physical wants is more apt than any likely alternative to lead them to see their need for liberty. More apt, that is, if their egoism were enlightened, if each (as with the Americans) "has the sense to sacrifice some of his private interests to save the rest." But where a political system failed to instruct and encourage men in this calculated self-restraint and failed to show them that what is right may also be useful, there could be neither freedom nor public peace nor social stability. Where each (as with the Europeans) insisted on keeping the lot for himself, he often ended up losing the lot.[76] Tocqueville, like some predecessors of his, could praise and recommend the commercial republican way of life because it can go beyond accommodating itself to our weaknesses. It also invites us to "try to attain that form of greatness and of happiness which is proper to ourselves."[77] Tocqueville, like a successor of his, might well have called this the last, best hope of earth.

NOTES

1. Mr. Lerner is a member of the Collegiate Division of the Social Sciences at the University of Chicago. He wishes to thank especially Marvin Meyers and Thomas S. Sehrock for criticism and suggestions.

In proposing to treat the advocates of commercial republicanism as a conscious collectivity I run the risk of asserting what cannot be proved for the sake of emphasizing what tends to be neglected. It was their shared commitment to ordered liberty and their desire to promote it by emancipating men from many of the modes of thought of the past that led these thinkers to commend the commercial republic in the first place. What was a republic might, in this sense, be ascertained better by regarding the sphere of liberty rather than the formal organization of a state. Thus, for Montesquieu, England was a republic masquerading as a monarchy; for Smith, the trading world as a whole was a mercantile republic. Compare Albert O. Hirschman, *The Passions and the Interests: Political Arguments for Capitalism before Its Triumph* (Princeton, NJ, 1977), esp. 100–112, for an argument that differs from the one offered here by (among other things) seeing greater significance in Smith's divergences from his predecessors and less significance in Smith's political intentions and expectations.

2. For a recent analysis of the economic category as presupposing an emancipation from the political domain and the general run of morality, "only at the price of assuming a normative character of its own," see Louis Dumont, *From Mandeville to Marx: The Genesis and Triumph of Economic Ideology* (Chicago, 1977), esp. 26, 36, 61, 67, 106–108. A parallel treatment of this "isolation of the economic impulse" traces the Anglo-Americans' break with traditional morality but, unlike my analysis in this essay, views the result as simply amoral or morally neutral. See J. E. Crowley, *This Sheba, Self: The Conceptualization of Economic Life in Eighteenth-Century America*, Johns Hopkins University Studies in Historical and Political Science, 92d ser., no. 2 (Baltimore, 1974), 34–49, 123–124.

3. Alexis de Tocqueville, *Democracy in America*, ed. J. P. Mayer and Max Lerner (New York, 1966), 497; hereafter cited as Tocqueville, *Democracy in America*.

4. Montesquieu, *De L'Esprit des Lois*, III, 7, IV, 2, XIII, 1.

5. Jean-Jacques Rousseau, *Du contrat social*, IV, 8; "Of Commerce," in David Hume, *Essays Moral, Political and Literary* (Oxford, 1963), 264–266, 268–269.

6. Adam Smith, *The Theory of Moral Sentiments* (Indianapolis, 1976), 127, 235, 405–409. 416, 420–421. See also D. D. Raphael, "The Impartial Spectator," in Andrew S. Skinner and Thomas Wilson, eds., *Essays on Adam Smith* (Oxford, 1975), 86–94; Arthur O. Lovejoy, *Reflections on Human Nature* (Baltimore, 1961), 247–264; and Joseph Cropsey, *Polity and Economy: An Interpretation of the Principles of Adam Smith* (The Hague, 1957), 18–19.

7. "Of the Balance of Power," in Hume, *Essays*, 347–348; "Of the Populousness of Ancient Nations," Hume, 405; "Of Parties in General," Hume, 57–61; "Of the Coalition of Parties," Hume, 484–485.

8. Adam Smith, *An Inquiry into the Nature and Causes of the Wealth of Nations*, ed. Edwin Cannan (New York, 1937), 541, 742; hereafter cited as Smith, *Wealth of Nations*. See Cropsey, *Polity and Economy*, 33–34, on the luxury of benevolence.

9. The distinction between these forms of excessive self-esteem is critical for Montesquieu's analysis, but the reader is left to define them for himself (*Esprit des lois*, XIX, 9–11, XX, 22). Lovejoy's attempt to impose terminological order on 18thcentury discussions of the passions (*Reflections on Human Nature*, 87–117) was in the end frustrated by his many authors' "exceedingly variable and confused" usage (p. 129). Here I follow Smith in treating vanity as a man's ostentatious display undertaken in the hope that others would regard him as more splendid than he really is at the moment; and pride as the self-satisfied and severely independent behavior of a man sincerely convinced of his own superiority (*Theory of Moral Sentiments*, 410–421). See the cogent analysis of Smith's doctrine concerning pride in Cropsey, *Polity and Economy*, 49–53.

10. Smith, *Wealth of Nations*, 362–364.

11. Smith, *Wealth of Nations*, 572, 14, 717; Smith, *Theory of Moral Sentiments*, 487–494, 417; "Of the Dignity or Meanness of Human Nature," in Hume, *Essays*, 87–88; Thomas Hobbes, *Leviathan; or the Matter, Forms and Power of a Commonwealth, Ecclesiasticall and Civil*, ed. Michael Oakeshott (Oxford, 1946), 6, 98, 138–139.

12. Smith, *Theory of Moral Sentiments*, 350–353. See also Montesquieu, *Esprit des lois*, XX, 4.

13. Tocqueville, *Democracy in America*, 45–46, 372, 433–434, 591.

14. Tocqueville, 405, 424–425, 428–429, 501.

15. Tocqueville, 573, 585. See especially his fine contrast of the effects of slavery's presence or absence on the mores of southerners and northerners. Ibid., 344–345.

16. Montesquieu, *Esprit des lois*, XIX, 27; XX, 4.

17. Tocqueville, *Democracy in America*, 148, 225, 260–262, 319, 504–505, 633, 707. See also Marvin Meyers, *The Jacksonian Persuasion: Politics and Belief* (Stanford, CA, 1957), 31–41.

18. Montesquieu, *Esprit des lois*, XX, 23. See the interpretation of this attenuation of parochial passions in J. G. A. Pocock, *The Machiavellian Moment: Florentine Political Thought and the Atlantic Republican Tradition* (Princeton, NJ, 1975), 492–493.

19. Smith, *Wealth of Nations*, 412, 800; see also 345–346, 395, 858, 880. The point is nicely illustrated by the political neutrality or indifference of late 18thcentury Nantucket whalemen. See the editorial discussion and Jefferson's echoing of Smith's characterization of merchants in Julian P. Boyd et al., eds., *The Papers of Thomas Jefferson*, XIV (Princeton, NJ, 1958), 220–221.

20. Montesquieu, *Esprit des lois*, XXI, 20, III, 3.

21. Charles Francis Adams, ed., *The Works of John Adams, Second President of the United States, with a Life of the Author, Notes and Illustrations* (Boston, 1850–1856), IV, 554.

22. See the pithy analysis in Gerald Stourzh, *Alexander Hamilton and the Idea of Republican Government* (Stanford, CA, 1970), 63–75, and the extensive documentation in Pocock, *Machiavellian Moment*, chaps. 14–15. Whether "the founders of Federalism were not fully aware of the extent to which their thinking involved an abandonment of the paradigm of virtue" (ibid., 525) is a question that cannot be answered while dealing with aggregates.

23. "Of Commerce," in Hume, *Essays*, 262–269.

24. Gordon S. Wood, *The Creation of the American Republic, 1776–1787* (Chapel Hill, NC, 1969).

25. Gerald Stourzh, "Die tugendhafte Republik—Montesquieus Begriff der 'vertu' und die Anfänge der Vereinjgten Staaten von Amerika," in Heinrich Fichtenau and Hermann Peichl, eds., *Österreich und Europa* (Graz, Austria, 1965), 247–267, esp. 260–262.

26. Tocqueville, *Democracy in America*, 85, 217, 481–482, 497–499, 524–525, 602. Compare Melvin Richter's interpretation in "The Uses of Theory: Tocqueville's Adaptation of Montesquieu," in Richter, ed., *Essays in Theory and History: An Approach to the Social Sciences* (Cambridge, Mass., 1970), 95–97.

27. Montesquieu, *Esprit de lois*, XX, 1, 2, 7, 8. See Thomas L. Pangle, *Montesquieu's Philosophy of Liberalism: A Commentary on "The Spirit of the Laws"* (Chicago, 1973), 203–209. See also "Of the Jealousy of Trade," in Hume, *Essays*, 338, and the discussion by Paul E. Chamley, "The Conflict between Montesquieu and Hume," in Skinner and Wilson, eds., *Essays on Adam Smith*, 303–304.

28. Thomas Paine, "Common Sense," in Philip S. Foner, ed., *The Life and Major Writings of Thomas Paine* (New York, 1961), 36, 20.

29. Jacob E. Cooke, ed., *The Federalist* (Middleton, Conn., 1961), No. 4, 19–20, No. 6,

31–32, No. 11, 66; hereafter cited as *Federalist*. See Stourzh, *Hamilton and the Idea of Republican Government*, 140–150.

30. *Federalist*, No. 24, 156–157, No. 25, 162, No. 29, 183–184.

31. Benjamin Rush, "Of the Mode of Education Proper in a Republic," in Dagobert D. Runes, ed., *The Selected Writings of Benjamin Rush* (New York, 1947), 94.

32. Pangle, *Montesquieu's Philosophy of Liberalism*, 114–117, 125–130, 147–150, 197–199.

33. "Of Refinement in the Arts," in Hume, *Essays*, 280–281, 283–284.

34. Smith, *Wealth of Nations*, 385.

35. Harvey C. Mansfield Jr., "Party Government and the Settlement of 1688," *American Political Science Review*, LVIII (1964): 933–946, esp. 936, 944–945.

36. See Harold C. Syrett and Jacob E. Cooke, eds., *The Papers of Alexander Hamilton*, I (New York, 1961), 4.

37. Smith, *Theory of Moral Sentiments*, 52–53, 167, 188–191, 177–178.

38. Tocqueville, *Democracy in America*, 262–263, 612–613, 617.

39. Tocqueville, 502–505, 598, 604–605, 368–370.

40. *Federalist*, No. 6, 32; Adams, ed., *Works of John Adams*, IX, 633–634, IV, 199–200.

41. *Federalist*, No. 57, 386, No. 59, 402, No. 72, 491–492.

42. L. H. Butterfield et al., eds., *Diary and Autobiography of John Adams* (Cambridge, Mass., 1961), 221–222.

43. Smith, *Wealth of Nations*, 586–588, 898.

44. Adams, ed., *Works of John Adams*, VI, 248–249; John Adams to Benjamin Rush, Apr. 12, 1807, in John A. Schutz and Douglass Adair, eds., *The Spur of Fame: Dialogues of John Adams and Benjamin Rush, 1805–1813* (San Marino, Calif., 1966), 78.

45. "Of the Liberty of the Press," in Hume, *Essays*, 10–11. This was a common theme in the period under discussion, and one on which many changes were rung. In a class apart, though, is the profound—and profoundly disquieting—discussion in Lincoln's "Young Men's Lyceum Address," Jan. 27, 1838, in Roy P. Basler et al., eds., *The Collected Works of Abraham Lincoln*, I (New Brunswick, NJ, 1953), 108–115. See the interpretations by Gerald Stourzh, "Alexander Hamilton: The Theory of Empire Building" (paper delivered at the American Historical Association meeting, New York, Dec. 30, 1957); Stourzh, *Hamilton and the Idea of Republican Government*, 204–205; and Harry V. Jaffa, *Crisis of the House Divided: An Interpretation of the Issues in the Lincoln-Douglas Debates* (Garden City, NY, 1959), 182–232.

46. With these commercial republicans we ought to include even Jefferson while he was extolling the chosen people of God who labor in the earth. The commercial character of agriculture in the Jeffersonian vision deserves emphasis. The rising nation spreading over a wide and fruitful land, which he contemplated, was not an agglomeration of peasants eking out a living, indifferent to the economic implications of the latest discoveries of scientific husbandry. For all his urging of household self-sufficiency, cottage industry, and the like, Jefferson thought of American agriculture clearly as a business and as a part of a world economy.

47. In reading the history of the life of "the youngest Son of the youngest Son for 5 Generations back" of an "obscure Family," they would learn how little ashamed he was of

having no distinguished ancestry; they would have a vivid demonstration of "how little necessary all origin is to happiness, virtue, or greatness" (Leonard W. Labaree et al., eds., *The Autobiography of Benjamin Franklin* [New Haven, CT, 1964] 46, 50, 137). In the details of this individual's career they might easily glimpse their own career, "the manners and situation of a rising people" (ibid., 135). The last two quotations are from a letter by Benjamin Vaughan, Jan. 31, 1783, which Franklin intended to insert in his autobiography.

48. Ibid., 163, 207.
49. Meyers, *Jacksonian Persuasion*, 4–23, 92–107.
50. Tocqueville, *Democracy in America*, 503, 508–509, 511–512, 613.
51. Tocqueville, 667–668; and see 641–680, passim.
52. Rousseau, *Contrat social*, III, 15.
53. Rush, "Of the Mode of Education," in Runes, ed., *Selected Writings of Rush*, 94; "Observations upon the Study of the Latin and Greek Languages," in Benjamin Rush, *Essays, Literary, Moral and Philosophical*, 2d ed. (Philadelphia, 1806), 43; "Leonidas" [Benjamin Rush], "The Subject of an American Navy," *Pennsylvania Gazette*, July 31, 1782.
54. Montesquieu, *Esprit des lois*, XIX, 27, XX, 2; Aristotle, *Politics*, 3–9. 1280b, 6–11. See also Richard Jackson to Benjamin Franklin, June 17, 1755, in Leonard W. Labaree et al., eds., *The Papers of Benjamin Franklin*, VI (New Haven, CT, 1963), 81.
55. Edwin Cannan, ed., *Lectures on Justice, Police, Revenue and Arms, Delivered at the University of Glasgow by Adam Smith, Reported by a Student in 1763* (Oxford, 1896), 259; Smith, *Wealth of Nations*, 734–740, 744–748. See Cropsey, *Polity and Economy*, 88–95.
56. "We occupy a new country. Our principal business should be to explore and apply its resources, all of which press us to enterprise and haste. Under these circumstances, to spend four or five years in learning two dead languages, is to turn our backs upon a gold mine, in order to amuse ourselves in catching butterflies" ("Observations upon the Study of the Latin and Greek Languages," in Rush, *Essays*, 39).
57. *Federalist*, No. 12, 73–74.
58. Adams, ed., *Works of John Adams*, IV, 395. See also John Adams to James Warren, July 4, 1786, in Worthington C. Ford, ed., *Warren-Adams Letters: Being Chiefly a Correspondence among John Adams, Samuel Adams, and James Warren*, II (Massachusetts Historical Society, Collections, LXXIII [Boston, 1925]), 277.
59. Adams, ed., *Works of John Adams*, VI, 270–271; Adams to Rush, June 20, 1808, in Schutz and Adair, eds., *Spur of Fame*, 110–111. See Mercy Warren, *History of the Rise, Progress and Termination of the American Revolution, Interspersed with Biographical, Political and Moral Observations*, III (Boston, 1804), 415.
60. Peter Shaw, *The Character of John Adams* (Chapel Hill, NC, 1976), 198–199, 232–235, 241, 315–316.
61. L. H. Butterfield, ed., *Letters of Benjamin Rush*, I (Princeton, NJ, 1951), 285, 85. See also Crowley, *This Sheba, Self*, 99, 152.
62. Butterfield, ed., *Letters of Rush*, I, 85. Rush was quoting from Pope's *Imitations of Horace: Satires*, bk. 2, sat. 1, line 127.
63. Rush, "Of the Mode of Education," in Runes, ed., *Selected Writings of Rush*, 94.
64. Tocqueville, *Democracy in America*, 677.

65. Tocqueville, 376–378.
66. Tocqueville, 678–679.
67. Tocqueville, 679–680, 649, and cf. 55.
68. Tocqueville, 680.
69. A code-word for the limp, prosperous barbarism that a civilized people can impose on itself. Tocqueville, 82, n. 50, 431, 512, 605–606.
70. Consider an analogous kind of equality of condition that Tocqueville saw as having prevailed in the Roman empire at the time of Christianity's origin. Tocqueville, 411.
71. Tocqueville, 643.
72. Tocqueville, 378–379.
73. Tocqueville, 612.
74. Tocqueville, 675.
75. Tocqueville, 499.
76. Tocqueville, 499.
77. Tocqueville, 679.

CHAPTER 1

Locke, Hume, and Property: On the Philosophical Foundations of Capitalism

Michael Zuckert

In the late seventeenth and early to mid-eighteenth centuries philosophers began to think seriously about the mode of economy or social organization we have come to call capitalism. They did not use that name, but they recognized the emergence of a relatively new kind of social order that they called "commercial society." As philosophers, their chief response was to question the legitimacy or goodness of this new type of order. Among other things, they asked what justifies property ownership and what justifies the kind of inequalities that capitalism and markets produce?

John Locke and David Hume were both defenders of the emerging order, and they approached the issue in terms of property's status, nature, and justification. Locke, like most philosophers, wrote in a context set by earlier thinkers. Foremost among them was Aristotle. Unlike his teacher Plato, Aristotle favored private property, but in a form and with a rationale quite different from what Locke would develop. In the second book of his treatise on politics Aristotle raised the question "whether possessions should be common or not." Plato had recommended communism of property holdings for the rulers of the city.[1] Aristotle's recommendation was different, for he favored private property: people take care of what is theirs, and that, he thought, is more conducive to the public good. But he also called for public use of this property, in recognition of the principle that property should serve the common good of the community. Therefore, he endorsed the formula "private ownership, public use."[2]

Aristotle's argument against communism was confirmed two thousand years later by the American Pilgrims, who, in the first flush of their ambition to found a truly Christian community, decreed what they called a "common course," whereby all worked on land held in common, with the fruits divided according to need. Reflecting later on their experience, Governor William Bradford concluded that it showed

> the vanity of that conceit of Plato's . . . that the taking away of property and bringing in community [of property] would make [the citizens] happy and flourishing. For this community (of property) was found to breed much confusion and discontent and retard much employment that would have been to their benefit and comfort. For the young men, that were most able and fit for labour and service, did repine that they should spend their time and strength to work for other men's wives and children without any recompense. The strong had no more of victuals and clothes than he that was weak and not able to do a quarter the other could; this was thought injustice. And for men's wives to be commanded to do service for other men, as dressing their meat, washing their clothes, etc., they deemed it a kind of slavery, neither could many husbands well brook it.[3]

In response to these problems, the Pilgrims soon changed their system to one of private ownership.

LOCKE

Locke appreciated the lesson taught by Aristotle and the Pilgrims, but he went much further. He made two innovations that were crucial for the development of the theory of capitalism. First, he presented a new basis for understanding the foundation of property. Second, he clarified the nature of property rights. Both these innovations led to the further development of commercial society.

Locke's greatest innovation was his development of the case for a natural right to property. At the time, there were two dominant views regarding the origin of property: some held that it was of divine origin, while others argued it was of human origin. Particularly germane to Locke was the argument of Sir Robert Filmer, whose book *Patriarcha* he subjected to a stinging critique. Filmer was the most extreme champion of the doctrine of the divine right of kings in seventeenth-century England. He held that in the beginning God gave the entire earth to Adam as his property when He blessed Adam and said: "Be fruitful and increase in number; fill the earth and subdue it. Rule over the fish in the sea and the birds in the sky, and over every living creature that moves on the ground." Filmer took this to mean that God had granted Adam all the land on the earth, and all the animals were his private property.[4]

The theory of the divine source of property rights was a minority view among theologians and philosophers, however. More common was the theory that property rights originated in human law, through some sort of ordinance or agreement among human beings. Thus, William of Ockham asserted that in the "state of innocence," before the fall, there was no private property.[5] Human beings originally held the world in common, by which he meant that all were free to use the things of the world as they needed, but nobody owned any of it. Ownership, in contrast to the freedom to use something, includes the right to exclude others from using or possessing the item owned. Consider a public beach. All have the right to use a public beach, to spread their beach towels on the sand, to enjoy the sun, to build sand castles. But the right to use this public land does not equal ownership. Thus, none of the beachgoers has the right to exclude others from using the beach; nor do they have the right to remove sand from the beach or to construct a permanent edifice on the beach. As Ockham, Thomas Aquinas, and most seventeenth-century thinkers saw it, the world as a whole was originally like one huge public beach.

One way these thinkers expressed this view was to say that originally, under the law of nature, the entire world was common. However, few maintained that this common possession of the world could last. Thinkers such as the Dutch philosopher Hugo Grotius saw population growth and the accretions of time as sufficient to work a change. As more human beings competed for access to the same resources, or as they made permanent improvements on the commons, such as by building shelters for themselves and their families, it became clear that rules were needed to allocate rights over the parts and possession of the world. Human beings developed conventions or agreements establishing property rights for the purpose of keeping the peace and maintaining good order among themselves. Therefore, although the natural law's original mandate was that the world was held in common, it was possible to add to the natural law by introducing or allowing private property.[6]

Locke rejects both the positions sketched here. He summarily dismisses Filmer's notion that God granted the world and everything in it to Adam, so that no one, not even Eve and their children, could eat any plant or make a wrap from an animal skin without Adam's express permission. Locke rejoins that much better scriptural evidence is required to make us believe that God would put all his creatures at the mercy of one man as sole owner of the entire world.[7]

Locke's response to the other position is more subtle. He begins with what he calls the state of nature—a state in which none of the external world is owned, as the earlier thinkers had held. However, unlike them, Locke insists that property does not arise from human agreement, consent, or law. Property arises, rather, by natural right (II:25–26). Locke develops his account of the origin of property in two steps.

Locke's predecessors argued that in the original commons individuals had the right to use the things of the world, but no one could claim ownership of them. This meant, for example, that one could eat what one needed today, but one could not lay claim to foodstuffs for tomorrow's dinner. That kind of exclusive possession did not exist. Locke first challenges this view by noting that "the Fruit or venison, which nourishes" a resident of the original commons, "must be his, and so his, i.e., a part of him, that another can no longer have a right to it, before it can do him any good for the support of his life" (II:26). If our primary interaction with the external world is the consumption of the fruits of nature, then that exclusive aspect of property existed prior to any agreement or law: to eat is to ingest and use in such a way as to establish an exclusive and excluding claim. The original situation is shot through with this aspect of property in the full sense.

But Locke recognizes that to eat and thus make food exclusively one's own does not constitute property in the full sense. Animals eat, digest, and assimilate food in the same way, yet they do not possess property or property rights. There must be something unique about human beings that produces property in the full sense. Locke identifies this something as follows: "Though the earth and all inferior creatures be common to all men, yet every man has a property in his own person. This nobody has a right to but himself" (II:27). According to Locke, human beings are self-owners. This is a basic fact, as witnessed by the aspect of human consciousness that claims one's body, one's thoughts, one's hopes, and one's fears as one's own. What is it that claims self-possession but the self itself? Locke is evoking that center of consciousness, the human ego or the "I," that stands both above and outside its experiences and at the same time finds itself within all of them—the characteristic that makes those experiences "mine" without them being exhaustively "me."

Locke sometimes uses a shorthand expression for this uniquely human character by saying that we are persons. Personhood figures in his theory of property in a simple yet profoundly important way. "The labor of his body, and the work of his hands, we may say, are properly his"—that is, they fully and exclusively belong to him (II:27). They have the character of exclusivity that marks off ownership from common use. Given this signally important fact, "whatsoever . . . he removes out of that state nature hath provided, and left it in, he hath mixed his labour with, and joyned to it something that is his own, and thereby makes it his property" (II:27). When one mixes something that is one's own property (one's labor) with something completely unowned (the common external world), the new entity—the labored-over world—now embodies something that is one's own. This, says Locke, "excludes the common right of other men" to that object. The character of human beings as self-owning persons grounds property as natural. One has a natural right to what one has annexed in this way, by which Locke means that others now have a moral obligation to respect an individual's exclusive claim to the goods in question. This means, as a moral matter, that if one gathers nuts and berries for tomorrow's dinner as well as today's, one has an exclusive right to save that food until needed; others no longer have a right to treat those nuts and berries as part of the commons.

The process of providing for the morrow not only accords with human personhood but also corresponds to the temporal structure of human beings, another trait that tends to distinguish us from other animals. We are future-oriented beings; we live in awareness of and pointedness toward the future. We know that tomorrow we will be hungry again; thus, unlike the lilies of the field, we rationally attempt to provide for that anticipated event. Only if there is natural property can we fulfill our nature as temporal beings.

It might be objected that this is unfair, for if an individual can unilaterally remove from the commons certain goods to which all have an original right of access, making those goods exclusive, have not the others lost their valuable right to access the commons? Locke thinks not, at least under certain conditions. If there is no real scarcity, others have the right to do exactly the same. If there is scarcity, Locke insists that each appropriator recognize the limitations on their right of appropriation, such that nothing they take spoils before it can be used (II:31). One has a right to provide for one's own sustenance, now and in the future, but one does not have the right to harm others by wasting goods that others could use. They too have self-ownership rights that must be respected.

In addition to being a moral limitation, the proscription against spoilage is largely self-enforcing, for with some experience of the world, individuals learn that collecting and hoarding materials that will spoil before they can be used is wasted labor. However, the real answer to the problem of scarcity is the development of agriculture. Human beings learn that enclosing and cultivating land makes it much more productive. Locke estimates that cultivated land is initially ten times, then a hundred times, and finally a thousand times more productive than uncultivated land (II:37).

Just as mixing one's labor with the unowned fruits of the earth creates property, so does mixing labor with unowned land. But by making private and exclusive what was once public and open to all, ownership seems to leave some individuals without productive resources. Locke denies this. Given the immense increase in productivity, he concludes that the one who appropriates and cultivates the land is actually a benefactor of the others. Rather than taking an acre out of common use, he is creating the equivalent of 999 extra acres for the others.

Something like the spoilage limitation applies to land, too. One cannot rightly appropriate more land than one can "till, plant, improve, cultivate, and use the product of" (II:32). Given the limits of human labor and consumption, the amount of land appropriated by any one individual would perforce be small. The great productivity of cultivated land produces a potential surplus, but much of what is grown can also spoil, so unless the owner can find a way to use the excess before it spoils, the incentive to labor to produce that surplus does not materialize. The problem of spoilage is partially overcome through barter exchanges. If one can trade the surplus for something else one lacks, that creates the incentive to produce more. The process of incentivizing labor is greatly increased when money is discovered or invented, for it is a nonspoiling item that stores value indefinitely and flexibly (II:47).

Locke's two fundamental insights here involve the self as future-oriented self-owner and nature as the source of, at best, "almost worthless material." Human labor supplies most of what is considered valuable through its power to transform that which is given by nature and make it both more plentiful and more suited to human use. The solution to the human problem, to the extent there is a solution, lies in unleashing the power of human labor to overcome the various forms of penury that human beings face in the world.

When all land is owned, labor is no longer a title to property, but it remains a source of value, though not of market value. Locke acknowledges that prices are the result of market forces and are not related directly to the labor invested in goods; nor should they be. Market price—what people in general are willing to pay for goods—signals how the labor of individuals can be coordinated to produce goods that serve the public good; individual labor uncoordinated with the labor and desires of others presents no guarantee of serving the public good.

With the disappearance of the commons there is no longer unowned land on which individuals can hunt and gather for subsistence. The new system of private property greatly favors some over others; some own land, while others are reduced to dependence on their self-owned bodies and labor power, which they must sell in order to survive. Locke sees this arrangement as justified by the rights of the owners and also by its service to all, including the nonowners. The creation of a society with a complex division of labor and great productive power is of benefit to all because, as Locke observes, "a king of a large and fruitful territory [in America, where there is no private property] feeds, lodges, and is clad worse than a day labourer in England" (II:41).

To the extent that some do not benefit from the system of private property, Locke affirms a "right to charity," which "gives every Man a Title to so much out of another's Plenty as will keep him from extreme want, where he has no means to subsist otherwise" (I:42). In support of this lingering natural right Locke proposed a poor law, a limited safety net to provide social support and the means of subsistence to which the unemployed have a right without sapping incentives to labor by creating dependency.

The system of private ownership serves the public good so far as it allows the freedom to acquire and use property. More or less everyone is better off under this system than they would be without it, but the benefits are apportioned differentially throughout society, giving the system a class character. Some own a lot and can hire others to do the labor that produces value; others must sell their labor to survive. As a result, great inequality comes to characterize society.

Locke affirms owners' almost unlimited power to determine the uses of property—a freedom implicit in the very idea of property but also, on the whole, necessary to the adjustment of property uses to markets and thus to the public good. But Locke does not concede complete freedom. The natural law prohibition on harming others always remains in effect; hence, property is subject to regulation. The great inequality concomitant with the property system also introduces the strong possibility of class conflict in which some (owners) may possess the resources to oppress others (nonowners). In other words, the owners may threaten the nonowners' property in themselves; conversely, the nonowners may try to dispossess the owners or redistribute their property. Claims of both individual natural right and the public good speak against these outcomes and lead Locke to affirm that the purpose of political power is the "Preserving of Property," by which he means the property of all and in both the narrow and broad senses of property, in light of the potential conflict between the two (II:3). Without a government to regulate and preserve both sorts of property, the institution of property, which is of great value to humankind, is vulnerable to abuses from the two great classes formed around ownership.

In Locke's account we see the main prerequisites of capitalism as an economic and social system: the right to and role of private property, the reliance on markets to coordinate the use of resources and to set prices, the acceptance of class inequalities resulting from differential ownership and market power, and the emphasis on economic growth based on the idea that a "rising tide raises all boats." Most important of all, Locke gives us a moral justification of capitalism as consistent with both natural rights and the common good.

Locke's doctrine was tremendously influential in encouraging and rationalizing the growth of capitalist economies in Britain, America, France, and elsewhere in Europe. But there was also resistance to Locke's theory, some of it very practical, and the rest more philosophical. Next I examine an example of the latter.

HUME

Today, Locke's idea of a natural property right is not as powerful as it once was, and it has been replaced by something like a utilitarian theory. The causes of the waning of the Lockean theory are several, but an extremely important one was the philosophical work of David Hume. Hume took aim at Locke's natural right to property, substituting the alternative theory that property is based entirely on human convention, agreement, or law and rests solely on its utility, that is, on its tendency to contribute to the "well-being of mankind and existence of society."[8] Hume was nonetheless just as committed as Locke—perhaps more so—to the idea that property relations, contracts, and other appurtenances of the market must be recognized and strictly enforced, even when doing so appears to result in hardship or injustice in certain cases, for the system of laws regulating the economy is what ensures a secure, stable, and prosperous society. Since the system of laws must be maintained, Hume is unsympathetic to exceptions based on need or compassion. Unlike Locke, he does not speak of a safety net for those who do not benefit from or are unable to participate in the market economy.

Hume took particular issue with Locke's notion of a natural right to property. As he says in his *Treatise of Human Nature*, "our property is nothing but those goods, whose constant possession is established by the laws of society; that is, by the laws of justice. Those, therefore, who make use of the word 'property' or 'right,' or 'obligation' before they have explained the origin of justice ... are guilty of a very gross fallacy and can never reason upon any solid foundation. The origin of justice explains that of property."[9] This passage is aimed at Locke (although it does not name him), and Hume's point is that Locke got things backward. Locke held that first there is natural property, then there is justice as the honoring of the claims of that property.

For Hume, human-made rules of justice come first, and property assignments are made according to and under the rules of justice. Thus, positive law tells us how property may be acquired, held, transferred, passed on, and so forth. Hume's most insistent claim is that the rules of justice are made for the sake of social utility, that is, to promote "the interest and happiness of human society" (*ECPM*, 30). For Hume, both the origin and the end of property are society, whereas for Locke, the origin or "fountain" of property is the individual. Hume has excised the individual dimension of the Lockean property right, a move with momentous consequences.

Hume does not confront Locke's natural right to property head-on but approaches it indirectly. He asks his readers to imagine a number of hypothetical situations that differ a good deal from the world in which we live. In one of these hypothetical states, Hume posits that there is such plenty that human beings never feel the sting of scarcity. The goods needed for a comfortable existence are readily accessible to all. There is little or no need for the exertions of labor or competition for goods. In such a situation, Hume asks, would rules of justice ever arise?

> It seems evident that, in such a happy state, every other social virtue would flourish, and receive ten-fold increase; but the cautious jealous virtue of justice would never once have been dreamed of. For what purpose make a partition of goods, where everyone has already more than enough? ... Why call this object

mine when, upon the seizing of it by another, I need but stretch out my hand to possess myself of what is equally valuable? (*ECPM*, 21)

Hume also posits a number of other hypothetical situations—for example, that human beings are so benevolent that they consider benefiting others just as valuable as benefiting themselves, or a world in which scarcity forces everyone to prioritize the mere right of self-preservation and to have no regard for so-called property rights. In all these cases, he asserts, there would be no use for the rules of justice by which property is defined. "Thus," he concludes, "the rules of justice depend entirely on the particular state and condition in which men are placed, and owe their origin and existence to the *utility*, which results to the public from their strict and regular observance" (*ECPM*, 25).

Hume's argument is both very clever and very simple: only under certain conditions—those that actually obtain in our world—are the rules of justice useful and likely to arise. Therefore, he concludes, the only basis and point of justice and property is social utility. There is no need and no room for a natural individual right to property—it does no real work in explaining the existence of a system of private property and market exchange.

Hume is a careful philosopher, but his argument about the origin and basis of property rests on a number of confusions and conceptual omissions. In two places Hume's argument is particularly vulnerable to a Lockean rejoinder. First, Locke might say that Hume has confused the occasions for justice and property with the bases for justice and property. For example, consider a family held together by love. Each member values the good of the other members as much as or even more than his or her own good. In this situation, rules of mine and thine might not arise. Property would be held in common within the family, especially between the husband and wife. But what if the relationship sours and the partners contemplate divorce or separation? Under this condition, utility would indeed dictate the fashioning of some rule for dividing the common family goods among the individual members. Would there be no *basis* now for generating such a rule? Would there not be some notion of fairness or dueness to guide the parties or a neutral observer in devising a rule of partition? Even if there were no *occasion* for justice and property in the past, would we not see that there was a *basis* for justice all along, even if the occasion did not arise to appeal to it? Thus, Hume's hypotheticals do not touch the claim Locke raises.

Second, Hume has no compunction in appealing to a right of self-preservation in his scenario of extreme penury. But what is this right if not an aspect of justice and, in Locke's terms, a claim to self-ownership? Indeed, even in Hume's hypothesized state of plenty, are there not many occasions for appeal to a more primitive personal right of property? External goods are not the only objects of human desire, after all. What about sexual desire? Humans desire the bodies of others, and they even desire the bodies of particular others. Would a superfluity of external goods eliminate such desires? Is there no basis in Hume's projected state of plenty to conclude that rape is an injustice, a violation of the rights of others? What Hume misses, in essence, is the existence of more primitive rights such as the right over one's own body and the correlative immunity from the violence of others. In other words, Hume fails to notice or respond to Locke's claim that the natural right to property rests on humans' prior right to themselves.

At bottom, what Hume misses is Lockean self-ownership as grounded in the Lockean theory of the self. This is no accident, for Hume is well known for his skepticism regarding the idea of the self.[10] Rather than examining the issues raised by Locke's theory and Hume's perplexity about the self, our topic requires us to turn to the implications of their theories of property for commercial society.

COMMERCIAL SOCIETY

What real difference does it make whether we adhere to one theory or the other? It might appear that, on practical grounds, the advantage clearly shifts toward Hume, for to affirm a natural right to property seems to leave us in a situation where an absolute property right could be invoked to resist all attempts to regulate and control property in the public interest. For Hume, property relations exist for the sake of social utility, so there seems to be no barrier to social and political control of property for the common good. Locke's position might be attractive to libertarians and robber barons, but not to those who see the need for (some) social control over property.

Locke does not endorse the robber baron position, however, for he concludes his discussion of the right to property with the assertion that "in governments the laws regulate the right of property, and the possession of land is determined by positive [laws]" (II:50). That is, the natural right to property prevails in the so-called state of nature and serves to validate individuals' original right to appropriate. But in society—in the condition actually relevant to all of us—civil law prevails and both regulates and sets forth the terms of ownership. It seems, then, that the alleged natural right to property exists in a fictitious or quasi-fictitious state where no one lives, and it fades away where it might have some real relevance.

It is certainly true that the Lockean natural right to property does not stand as an absolute barrier to the social regulation and control of property, but it is not true that the natural right to property has no lingering significance in political society. As Locke puts it, upon the formation of government, a person gives up "the power of doing whatsoever he thought fit for the preservation of himself, and the rest of mankind, . . . to be regulated by the laws made by the society, so far forth as the preservation of himself, and the rest of the society shall require; which law of society in many things confine the liberty he had by the law of nature" (II:129). However, despite this cession of right, the original natural right remains present and morally potent in society. First, the individual surrenders the right to do whatever he or she judges to be conducive to the preservation of property in the broad sense of life, liberty, and estate but does not in any way divest of self-ownership. Second, such surrender of rights and liberty is done for the sake of securing other rights, including the right to property. Third, the surrender occurs only to the extent necessary to achieve the larger protection of rights and the public good. For Locke, the unsurrendered rights are not side constraints, as they are for libertarian philosopher Robert Nozick; nor are they absolute limitations on what government may rightly do. Locke, to repeat, is not a libertarian.

The boundaries of the state's permissible dealings with property are admittedly uncertain in Locke's schema. Locke himself seems to favor some mercantilist policies and a tight monetary policy that some would not consider proper to capitalism. Nonetheless, I try to flesh out those boundaries by raising two questions against which to measure Locke and Hume: Which is more supportive of free enterprise? Which is better overall for achieving the public good?

Hume himself interprets his utility-based property regime as pointing toward the strict honoring of the property system, contracts, and so on. On the whole, and as interpreted by Hume himself, that system supports property, free enterprise, and commercial activity. It thus seems very compatible with capitalism. Locke, affirming a natural right to property, favors the same sort of property-preserving and -fostering laws and practices as Hume but makes the stronger claim that these practices are not only for the public benefit, as Hume asserts, but also expressive and protective of individual rights.

In their Humean form, then, utilitarian practices are favorable to capitalism, but that compatibility is contingent. It depends on the conviction that the protection of property and property exchange is most conducive to "the greatest good of the greatest number," as measured by some standard of "greater good." But this means that attacks on capitalist-type property relations can readily occur within the Humean utilitarian rationale. Thus, many welfare state or even socialist theories find justification in Hume-type utilitarian arguments.

Locke's rationale for property allows state intervention in economic relations, but it is more precise in specifying the justification for that intervention and more preservative of the basic property right than Hume's theory. Thus, given the right to property, there is always a presumption in favor of property rights, including laborers' right to their property in their lives and liberties. The state may therefore intervene to protect against the misuse of property and to secure the basic rights to life and liberty of the otherwise unpropertied.

Moreover, the Lockean rationale for political action relative to property carries strong implications for the kind of political practices and institutions that can rightly regulate property. For instance, the property owners themselves must be represented in the lawmaking body. Given that all individuals have property in themselves, this means that the Lockean system points toward a fully democratic system: there are no "experts" claiming to know what is for the "benefit of society," and no vanguard party or bureaucracy can replace the democratic legislature as the source of valid regulations. Among other things, that limitation reinforces Locke's observation that the legislature may not delegate its legislative power. The Lockean state would not be a bureaucratic state with extensive rule making (i.e., legislative power) vested in irresponsible bureaucrats. In principle, then, the Lockean understanding of property produces a state supportive of capitalist property arrangements yet morally capable of resisting, in a focused and effective manner, the abuses of property and of respecting the claims of those who possess only property in themselves.

Overall, Lockean property may be more favorable to private enterprise than Humean property, but is it more likely to serve the public good? This is a large topic encompassing the multifarious dimensions of the public good and the many contingencies involved in achieving it. Therefore, I must limit this discussion to just a few considerations. One aspect of the public good is the ability to meet the legitimate needs of those for whom the reigning economic system does not well provide. Hume's system seems unable to provide for unfortunates who are not taken care of in the prevailing system. His emphasis is on the utility of the overall system and strict respect for property and contract, so that ameliorative measures are discouraged because they violate the rigorous system allegedly productive of public benefit.

Locke's more rights-oriented system is better able to respond to the needs of those left out of the regular economy. Because all have a right deriving from self-ownership of life and liberty, those who are, for example, unemployed in a less than full-employment economy possess a right to social support, for they have, in effect, traded their right to access the commons for a system in which all property is held by relatively few private individuals and those without property may sell their labor, perhaps ending up better off economically than if the land had remained in common. Those without external property possess, in the first instance, a right to be part of the labor market; thus the state can rightly intervene to guarantee access to all by preventing discrimination or denial of employment on the basis of race, religion, or any other extrinsic quality. But in addition to that, if there is not a full-employment economy, the state is obliged to provide some sort of safety net for the unemployed.

To formulate this point more generally, the Lockean rationale for a natural right to property builds on an understanding of the human person that recognizes the inherent equality, liberty, and dignity of each and every individual. The Humean rationale for property does not and thus leaves us with a theory of property that, strangely, arms property with either too much or not enough protection.

NOTES

This chapter was originally prepared as a public address delivered at Holy Cross College on the topic of the foundations of capitalism.

1. Plato, *Republic*, bk. 5.
2. Aristotle, *Politics*, 1263a38–40.
3. William Bradford, *Of Plymouth Plantation, 1620–1647*, ed. Samuel Eliot Morison (New York: Modern Library, 1967).
4. Robert Filmer, *Patriarcha*, in *Patriarcha and Other Writings*, ed. Johann Sommerville (Cambridge: Cambridge University Press, 1991), 7.
5. William of Ockham, "The Work of Ninety Days," in *A Letter to the Friars Minor and Other Writings*, ed. Arthur McGrade and John Kilcullen (Cambridge: Cambridge University Press, 1995), 34–35.

6. Hugo Grotius, *The Rights of War and Peace*, ed. Richard Tuck (Indianapolis: Liberty Fund, 2005), 420–427.

7. John Locke, *Two Treatises of Government*, ed. Peter Laslett (Cambridge: Cambridge University Press, 1960), I:21–43; hereafter cited parenthetically in text.

8. David Hume, *Enquiry Concerning the Principles of Morals* (Oxford: Oxford University Press, 1975), 31; hereafter cited in text as *ECPM*.

9. David Hume, *Treatise of Human Nature* (Oxford: Oxford University Press, 2011), 491.

10. Hume, bk. 1, pt. 4, sec. 6.

CHAPTER 2

Montesquieu: Commerce and Character

Paul A. Rahe

> The Greek statesmen and political writers who lived under popular government knew of no force able to sustain them other than virtue. Those of today speak only of manufactures, of commerce, of finance, of wealth, and of luxury itself.
> —Charles-Louis de Secondat, baron de La Brède et de Montesquieu

In 1748, when, in stages, Montesquieu dispatched the manuscript of *The Spirit of the Laws* to his editorial coordinator Jacob Vernet in Geneva so that it could be published there by Barrillot et Fils, he specified that the work be divided into parts. At first, there were supposed to be five parts and then, after he had added a discussion of the evolution of French and Roman law, there were to be six parts—with anywhere from three to eight of the work's thirty-one books assigned to each.

There was a logic to this arrangement. The groupings made sense. But Vernet failed to see the point and chose not to distinguish the parts.[1] Montesquieu responded by making sure that the parts were clearly distinguished in the "corrected" and "augmented" edition of the book published in Paris by Huart under a false imprint in 1750. It was this version that he described to a correspondent as "the edition" of *The Spirit of the Laws* that was "the most exact."[2]

Organizing the various books in this fashion was also important to the larger meaning of Montesquieu's magnum opus, which was written in a dialectical manner. Each part was intended as a corrective to what had come before. The first part, which consists of the work's first eight books, specifies what Montesquieu calls "the nature" of the democratic and the aristocratic republic, of monarchy, and of despotism; it describes "the principle"—which is to say "the passion"—that sets each of these "in motion"; it explores "the laws" to which "the nature" and "the principle" of each form of government are apt to give rise; and it sketches the species of "corruption" to which "the principle" of each is prone (*EL*, 1.1–8). This analysis is vulnerable to one insuperable objection: it, for the most part, ignores the constraints faced by the lawgiver—above all, the virtual certainty that these polities will be confronted with war.

In the work's second part, Montesquieu takes up this question and examines the capacity of each species of government to come to grips with the need for defensive and offensive force (*EL*, 2.9–10). Then he complicates matters further by reporting that different polities, including some with the same form of government, pursue different "objects" and by introducing yet another species of government, exemplified by England, which has as its "direct" object "liberty." And it is political liberty—which Montesquieu defines from two different perspectives as the rule of law and as "that tranquility of spirit (*esprit*) which comes from the opinion that each has of his own security"—that now becomes thematic (2.11.3, 6, p. 397). For Montesquieu devotes the remainder of the second part of his *Spirit of the Laws* to considering the laws favorable to and unfavorable to liberty's promotion (2.11–13). It is only later, at the very end of the third part of the work, that one is allowed to see the connection between this species of "liberty" and the effective use of defensive and offensive force—for it is only there that we learn that, in the circumstances pertaining in Montesquieu's own time, the polity devoted to "liberty" understood in this peculiar fashion is the form of government best suited to the deployment of defensive and offensive force (3.19.27).

War is by no means the only constraint faced by the lawgiver. As Montesquieu intimates in the last book of the first part of his *Spirit of the Laws* (*EL*, 1.8.16–21), geography can be decisive, and we learn in the first four books of the third part of that work that climate matters enormously as well (3.14–17).

The themes taken up by Montesquieu in the first three parts of his magnum opus resemble those addressed by Plato in his *Republic* and *Laws* and by Aristotle in his *Politics*. The latter two figures had focused their attention on different forms of government, and they had touched on the various constraints on legislative action explored by Montesquieu: the prospect of war, geography, climate, and the mode by which the population subsists. There is, of course, this difference. Aristotle makes *lógos*—rational speech—and the political opinions to which reasoning gives rise thematic. It is rational or quasi-rational principle that distinguishes the various regimes. Each is set in motion by a conviction regarding justice. By way of contrast, Montesquieu's political science resembles that of Plato's *Republic* in distinguishing the various polities with an eye to the political psychology each fosters and depends upon. His "principles" are in no sense rational. They are, as he makes abundantly clear, "passions." In consequence, the French philosophe devotes much more space to the constraints on lawgiving than does his peripatetic predecessor.[3]

This is one part of the story. There is another dimension to Montesquieu's political science as well, and it is arguably even more significant. For the most part, Aristotle averts his gaze from the larger currents of change over time; and Plato, in dealing with change over time, focuses narrowly on the weakness inherent in each of the particular political regimes and on the manner in which each tends to dissolve and be replaced by another of the polities on his list.[4] In the first three parts of his great work, Montesquieu for the most part does the like. It is only in parts four, five, and six that he makes history in the broad sense thematic. It is only there that he forcefully brings home to his readers something that he has in the work's first three parts only touched on in passing: the fact that the setting within which legislation takes place is itself in motion—that commerce and technology are undergoing a revolution, that religions come and go, and that, under their influence, the laws evolve.[5]

Montesquieu's *Spirit of the Laws* is a gigantic work. In the eighteenth century, it was always published in more than one volume. The edition ushered into print in Paris by Huart under a false imprint in 1750 contained three volumes—in which Montesquieu paired parts one and two, parts three and four, and parts five and six. This made a certain amount of sense. Parts one and two have forms of government as a focus, and the discussion of commerce and technology in part four suggests ways in which the geographical terrain discussed in the penultimate book of part three (*EL*, 3.18) may cease to be as determinative as it was in the past.

We do not know whether Jacob Vernet and the printer in Geneva were following Montesquieu's instructions when, in 1748, Barrillot et Fils published the work in two volumes—each consisting of three of the six parts the author had marked out. But it does seem likely—for, in the two-volume edition, also said to have been "corrected" and "augmented" by the author, that Huart brought out under the same imprint in 1749, a sharp division is marked out between what had in the 1748 edition been called the "*Tome Premier*" and the "*Tome Second*," with the former redescribed as the "*Première Partie*" and the latter as the "*Seconde Partie*." Moreover, on the title page of the *Seconde Partie* we find the epigraph originally printed on the title page of the second volume of the 1748 edition.

The bipartite division, evident in the 1748 edition and in this particular

1749 edition, makes excellent sense—for it sets the books focused on change over time off from those which for the most part presuppose that the broader conditions constraining the efforts of lawgivers are unchanging. Moreover, Montesquieu underlined the importance of the radical shift in perspective that takes place between the first three and the second three parts by adding to the editions that were published late in 1749 and thereafter a map of the world designed to make "the chapters on commerce intelligible." This he tells us on the covers of the two-volume 1749 edition published in Paris by Huart and again on the cover of each of the three volumes in Huart's 1750 edition.[6]

By means of this map and the chapters on commerce that it adorns, the French philosophe makes it abundantly clear that, thanks to the technological changes that produced the age of sail and thereby laid the foundation for the voyages of discovery that followed, there was now, for the very first time in the history of humankind, a global order tied together by transport and trade. In reading *The Spirit of the Laws* and in pondering its division in these early editions into volumes, parts, books, and chapters, we must never forget Montesquieu's observation in the preface that its "author's design" could only be discovered by studying "the design of the work." It is to the books and chapters on commerce and to the passing remarks foreshadowing their theme that one must most closely attend if one wishes to fathom what, in Montesquieu's estimation, was in the offing of profound interest to those in his own time who aspired to be lawgivers.

A TORRENT

For the most part, Montesquieu, in the first three parts of his magnum opus, treats commerce in much the same fashion as Plato, Aristotle, and the ancient Greek writers more generally—as a solvent apt, if given free rein, to loosen the ties of friendship and solidarity that inspire civic virtue and public-spiritedness more generally (*EL*, 1.4.6–7; 2.12.30, p. 458 n. a). At the beginning of his twentieth book (the first book in part four), however, he hints that, in the long run, commerce cannot be denied free rein and that, as a force, it deserves much closer scrutiny than it was accorded by these earlier writers. "I would like," he cries out, "to drift along a tranquil river. I am swept on by a torrent" (4.20.1).

What Montesquieu means by describing commerce as "a torrent" is not, however, immediately evident. His readers have to wait for his twenty-first book to find out. For there he denies the ultimate effectiveness of political restrictions, suggesting that commerce is a force in its own right, asserting that it is subject to "revolutions," and intimating that it has already produced in the political sphere what we today would call revolutions. "Sometimes destroyed by conquerors," he writes, "sometimes obstructed by monarchs, commerce wanders the earth, flees from where it is oppressed, takes its repose where one lets it breathe again: it reigns today where once one saw only deserts, seas, and rocks; there where it once reigned, there are only deserts now." If commerce has a "history," he explains, this history is indistinguishable from "that of the communication of peoples. Their various destructions and a certain ebb and flow of populations and devastations form its greatest events" (*EL*, 4.21.5).

To a degree, the ancient Greeks and Romans relied on commerce. But, at the same time, they regarded it and its practitioners—artisans and merchants alike—as vile; and, except where and when they needed to import a strategic substance, they generally did nothing to promote it. Moreover, as a consequence of Aristotle's influence, Western Christendom in the High Middle Ages outlawed on the part of Christians the issuance of loans at interest, and rulers had no qualms about pillaging the Jews in their midst who were left free to perform that necessary function and did so, thanks to the political risks they incurred, at usurious rates. What it took to liberate commerce from political oversight and to lower the rate of interest was a simple invention.

If trade and moneylending ceased to be "covered in infamy" and to be indistinguishable from "the most horrid usury, from monopolies, from the levy of subsidies, and all dishonest means of acquiring silver," if these activities eventually emerged from "the bosom of vexation and despair," it was, we are told, because the Jews, "proscribed by each country in turn, found the means for saving their effects. By this they rendered their retreats forever fixed—since . . . a prince, who wanted very much to get rid of them, would not for all that be in a humor to be rid of their money as well." This these moneylenders achieved by the simple expedient of making their money vanish. Thanks to their invention of letters of exchange, "commerce was able to elude violence and to maintain itself everywhere," for "the richest trader had nothing but invisible goods, which could be conveyed everywhere and leave not a trace in any place." According to Montesquieu, this invention obliged the neo-Aristotelian theologians "to rein in their principles." As a result, "commerce, which had been linked by violence with bad faith, returned, so to speak, to the bosom of probity" (*EL*, 4.21.20).

The ruling order within late medieval and early modern Europe may have shared with the Greeks and Romans a contempt for trade and a profound dislike for those who secured their livelihood in this fashion, but this no longer mattered. From the moment when these bankers introduced the letter of exchange, "it became necessary for princes" to exercise self-restraint in their dealings with these moneylenders and to "govern themselves with greater sagacity than they would themselves have thought possible." If scholastic speculation was responsible for "all the evils that accompanied the destruction of commerce," it was, Montesquieu asserts, "to the avarice of princes" that Europe owed "the establishment of a thing which places commerce in a certain fashion beyond their power" (*EL*, 4.21.20).

There were two other inventions that contributed greatly to the commercial revolution that serves as a background to Montesquieu's ruminations: the invention of deep-hulled ships and of sailing rigs that allowed these vessels to sail into the wind, and the invention of the compass. Both are mentioned in *The Spirit of the Laws*, and it is to the latter that the work's author most closely attends—for, in tandem with dead reckoning, the compass made it possible for a ship to venture with some confidence far from shore, and this enabled the Portuguese to sail deep into the Atlantic in the direction of Brazil where, in the appropriate season, they could catch prevailing winds enabling them to reach the Cape of Good Hope and circumnavigate Africa (*EL*, 4.21.6, 10, 21). It was this and the voyages of discovery to the New World mounted by Christopher Columbus and others that justified the addition of a map of the world within the later editions Montesquieu's magnum opus.[7]

To grasp the significance of the commercial revolution, one need only contrast agriculture as a mode of subsistence with trade. Real estate, such as the land worked by cultivators of the soil, is national in character: as a "species of wealth," Montesquieu notes, it "belongs to each state in its particularity," and it fosters "dependency." For where the countryside is "fertile," there will be "plains" from which "one cannot in any way mount a contest against the man with the greatest power"; and once one adopts a posture of submissiveness "the spirit of liberty" will abate and not be apt to return. Moreover, the distinct territories farmed by the cultivators of the soil distinguish the peoples of the earth, set them apart, and provide occasions for their wars.

"The spirit of commerce" has the opposite effect: it is, as we have seen, at odds with arbitrary rule. It is incompatible with "despotism" and "servitude," and it promotes what Montesquieu calls liberty as well as "moderate government." Moreover, it "unites the nations" even though "it does not unite individuals at the same time." The ordinary objects of commerce, "movable effects, such as silver, bank notes, letters of exchange, company shares, ships, and every form of merchandise, belong to the entire world, which, in this respect, composes but a single state of which all the societies are members" (*EL*, 1.5.15; 3.18.1–2; 4.20.2, 4, 23; 4.22.2, 14).

THE SINEWS OF WAR

There were various ways in which the ongoing commercial revolution had by Montesquieu's time reshaped the foundations on which governments had to be constructed. The most significant of these had to do with defensive and offensive force. By the late seventeenth century, if not before, money had become the sinews of war. This was brought home to the young Montesquieu, then fifteen years old, not long after August 13, 1704—the day when John Churchill, soon to be the duke of Marlborough, and Prince Eugene of Savoy annihilated a French army in the Battle of Blenheim. Years later, looking back, Montesquieu remarked:

> Before the battle of Blenheim, France had risen to a time of greatness that one regarded as immutable, although the country was then on the verge of decline (*touche au moment de la décadence*). It is certain that the league [of those allied against Louis XIV] was in despair. That day at Blenheim, we lost the confidence that we had acquired by thirty years of victories.... Whole battalions gave themselves up as prisoners of war; we regretted their being alive, as we would have regretted their deaths.[8]

It seems to have been this formative experience, which was reinforced by subsequent victories on the part of Marlborough at Ramillies, Oudenarde, and Lille, that occasioned Montesquieu's lengthy sojourn in England from October 1728 to the spring of 1731. It was during this sojourn that Montesquieu acquired a copy of, read, or at least heard a summary of the argument advanced in a little pamphlet, entitled *A Discourse of Trade*, that had been published in London in 1690 by Nicholas Barbon, son of the Puritan firebrand Praise-God Barebones.[9]

There is no entry for this slender volume in the catalog of Montesquieu's library at La Brède.[10] In his published works and in what survives of his commonplace books he nowhere cites the book, and in the secondary literature on the French philosophe Barbon passes almost unmentioned.[11] While in England, however, Montesquieu must have perused *A Discourse of Trade* or listened to its argument rehearsed in detail, for the analysis that he set out to present in his *Reflections on Universal Monarchy in Europe* and restated in his *Spirit of the Laws* echoes Barbon's account of the obstacles he thought likely to prevent Louis XIV from establishing a universal dominion on the continent of Europe, as well as the Englishman's careful examination of the economic and institutional foundations of his own country's strength. What Montesquieu argued in retrospect Barbon had described in prospect.

Barbon began his argument with the Venetians and the Dutch, noting the degree to which these two commercial polities possessed a political weight far greater than the size of their territory would suggest possible. Then he turned to the manner in which technology—the invention of gunpowder, in particular—had transformed the character of war and made commerce "as necessary to Preserve Governments, as it is useful to make them Rich." In his view, this rendered an anachronism what Livy and the other ancient writers had written concerning "the Causes of the Rise and Fall of Governments," and the same criticism could be applied to the writings of Niccolò Machiavelli, who had inexcusably ignored the revolution being effected by the commerce carried on with great verve all around him in Florence. As Barbon put it, "*until* Trade became *necessary to provide Weapons of War, it was always thought Prejudicial to the Growth of Empire, as too much softening the People by Ease and Luxury, which made their Bodies unfit to Endure the Labour and Hardships of War.*" In antiquity, he added, this conviction had made good sense, for the fact that "Trade *was not in those days useful to provide Magazines for Wars*" explains how it was that "*the Romans . . . in the almost Infancy of their State*, managed to *Conquer that Rich and* Trading *City of* Carthage, *though Defended by* Hannibal *their General, one of the greatest Captains in the World.*"[12]

In Barbon's judgment, England, the modern Carthage, and its allies were apt to thwart the attempt of Louis XIV's modern Rome "to Raise Empire in *Europe.*" The latter, which was not a great trading power, lacked the wherewithal with which to conquer that continent, while England possessed the resources requisite for France's defeat. Even more to the point, Barbon thought that his native land—blessed, as it was, with what he called "*Gothick* Government," with a distant and detached situation as an island, and with a trading tradition—had the means with which to establish a great empire at sea. As a naval commercial power it could, he claimed, enjoy "an Empire, not less Glorious, and of a much larger Extent than either *Alexander's* or *Caesar's*."[13]

When he returned from England to France, Montesquieu set out to pen a tripartite work in which he adopted Barbon's argument and refined it. In his *Considerations on the Causes of the Greatness of the Romans and Their Decline*, he pondered Rome's rise to what Europeans in his time and earlier called "universal monarchy," and he considered the ultimate collapse of that dominion. Then, in his *Reflections on Universal Monarchy in Europe*, he examined the history of Western Christendom and the situation in his own time.[14] To the latter task he brought two advantages that Barbon had lacked: he knew the outcome of Louis XIV's quest, and he had studied law. It was his contention that conditions had changed and that it was no longer "possible for a People" in Europe "to maintain over the other peoples" on that continent "an unceasing superiority, as the [ancient] Romans did." Montesquieu thought this achievement "*moralement impossible*"—morally or completely impossible. In support of this assertion, he contends that "innovations in the art of war," such as the introduction of artillery and firearms, "have equalized the strength of all men and consequently that of all Nations," and he picks up on an observation made by Machiavelli in his *Art of War* and argues that "the *Ius Gentium* [Law of Nations] has changed" and that it is no longer possible for a conqueror to massacre or enslave those defeated and seize and sell their moveable goods and land. In consequence, he adds, "under today's Laws war is conducted in such a manner that by bankruptcy it ruins above all others those who [initially] possess the greatest advantages." Put simply, "we ruin ourselves [financially] in capturing places which capitulate, which we preserve intact, and which most of the time we return" (*RMU*, 1.1–19).[15]

In short, it was Montesquieu's view that universal monarchy can no longer be achieved. To reinforce his argument, he adds "that in Europe prosperity cannot be permanent anywhere, and . . . that there is a continual variation in [the distribution of] power, which, in the three other parts of the world, is, so to speak, fixed." In his opinion, Europe differs from the rest of the world in one crucial particular: "at present," it "is responsible for all the Commerce in the Universe and for the Carrying Trade (*Navigation*) in its entirety." Like Barbon, he was persuaded as well that in his own day, at least in Europe, Machiavelli's famous dictum had been proven wrong and that money really had become the sinews of war—so that, "to the extent to which a State takes a greater or lesser part in Commerce or in the Carrying Trade, its power necessarily grows or diminishes." In consequence, he contends, since war gets in the way of trade, "a State which appears to be victorious abroad ruins itself [financially] at home, while states which remain neutral augment their strength." It can even happen that "those conquered regain their strength." In fact, "decline (*décadence*) generally sets in at the time of the greatest successes, for these can neither be achieved nor sustained except by violent means" (*RMU*, 2.28–39).[16]

Poverty was once, Montesquieu acknowledges, an advantage in war. In antiquity, when citizen armies were predominant, those from wealthy communities "were made up of men lost to flabbiness, idleness, and pleasure," and "for that reason" these cities "were often destroyed by the armies of neighbors accustomed to a life both painful and harsh, who were better suited to the war and military exercises of that time." In his own day, however, "the situation is not the same since no one group of Soldiers, the vilest part of every Nation, has a share in luxury greater than that of any other group, since in military exercises there is no longer need for the same strength and skill, and since it is now easier to form armies of regulars" (*RMU*, 2.45–54).

THE POLICY OF ENGLAND

Montesquieu's tripartite work never appeared. For a variety of reasons particular to the reign of Louis XV, he came to think it impolitic to be so frank. So he set aside what he had already written on the English form of government; and, in 1734, he reluctantly suppressed his *Reflections on Universal Monarchy in Europe* and published his ruminations on Rome as a free-standing book entitled *Considerations on the Causes of the Greatness of the Romans and Their Decline*.[17]

Though checked, Montesquieu was undaunted; and soon thereafter he set out to compose *The Spirit of the Laws*, wherein he discreetly inserted the argument of his *Universal Monarchy*. Therein, moreover, in the two longest chapters of the work (*EL*, 2.11.6, 3.19.27), he added the detailed discussion of the English form of government and of the policy to which it naturally gives rise that he had begun writing in 1734.[18]

In his magnum opus, Montesquieu draws a sharp distinction between modern European monarchy and despotism. The difference flows from the fact that they differ in "nature," which is to say structure—above all, because of the existence of a landed aristocracy in the former that does not derive its status or property from the passing whim of the ruler. What follows from this are intermediary powers, a quasi-independent judiciary, the rule of law, and an ethos of honor that serves as a check on everyone's conduct—above all, on that of the king himself—which is favorable to what Montesquieu calls liberty (*EL*, 1.2.1, 45; 3.1, 5–10; 5.9–16). This is the upside.

There is also a downside—part of which stems from the fact, wholly consistent with the manner in which the existence of a hierarchy of ranks transforms ordinary human vanity into a deep longing for honor, that monarchy's aim (*but*) is glory. In consequence, "the spirit of monarchy is war and aggrandizement," for, as Montesquieu makes clear, glory can be attained only in a deplorable fashion through success on the battlefield (*EL*, 1.5.19; 9.2, 7; 10.2; 2.11.5, 7; 3.13.1, 17; 4.20.22). In a sense, then, monarchy is at odds with itself. For success of the sort sought, were it to reach completion and eventuate in universal monarchy, would—as he had made clear in sections of his *Reflections on Universal Monarchy in Europe* that he later inserted into his *Spirit of the Laws*—be fatal to the monarchy as a monarchy by transforming it into an enormous polity governable only via despotism (*RMU*, 17; *EL*, 1.8.8, 15–17, 19–20; 2.9.6–7; 10.9, 16).

Even more to the point, Montesquieu contends that, in a world gone commercial, monarchy is at a great disadvantage—since, given the nature of the government and the political psychology to which it gives rise, that form of government is not fully compatible with the commercial spirit. Monarchy does give rise to what the French philosophe calls a "commerce of luxury." This is a given. But it does not favor the emergence of what he calls a "commerce of economy" of the sort practiced with such great vigor by the Venetians, the Dutch, the English, and the other peoples engaged in the carrying trade; and it is incompatible with the institutions that enabled these peoples to succeed in trade and become inordinately rich (*EL*, 1.5.9; 4.20.4–5, 7–8, 10–14, 21–22). In practice, then, the French monarchy is condemned to a pursuit of glory and conquest that the French economy can no longer properly sustain.[19]

By way of contrast, the English polity imagined by Montesquieu, who tends to speak of it in the conditional, would suffer neither of the disadvantages attendant on monarchy. In a chapter of *The Spirit of the Laws* entitled "How the Laws Can Contribute to the Formation of the Mores, Manners, and Character of a Nation," Montesquieu shows us how and why a well-ordered Carthage, such as England, "whose principal strength consists in her credit and commerce," was able to "render fictive wealth real," equip "her Hannibal" with "as many men as she could buy," and "send them into combat," while Louis XIV's ill-ordered French Rome, "in a spirit of vertigo," patiently awaited "the blows" solely "in order to receive them" and fielded "great armies" only "to see [her] fortresses taken" and her "garrisons deprived of courage, and to languish in a defensive war for which" she had "no capacity at all" (*MP*, 645).

In this chapter, Montesquieu refrains from intimating, as he does repeatedly elsewhere (*EL*, 2.13.17; 4.20.4–5, 10), that the monarchies on the European continent find it well-nigh impossible to inspire the confidence necessary to enable them to borrow the immense sums of money needed for the conduct of war in modern times. It suffices for him pointedly to remark that, given its laws, England should have little difficulty in sustaining the credit required. It could, after all,

> borrow from itself and pay itself as well. It would, then, undertake enterprises beyond its natural strength and deploy against its enemies immense fictional riches, which the confidence it would inspire and the nature of the government would render real.
>
> For the purpose of preserving its liberty, it would borrow from its subjects; and its subjects, seeing that its credit would be lost if it was conquered, would have yet another motive for exerting themselves in defense of its liberty.[20] (*EL*, 3.19.27, p. 577)

England could borrow from its subjects because, under the constitution that Montesquieu has in mind, its subjects would not, in fact, be subjects at all. They would be citizens, as Montesquieu quickly acknowledges (*EL*, 3.19.27, p. 577), in what he has already alluded to elsewhere in *The Spirit of the Laws* as "a republic" and as "a republic concealed under the form of a monarchy" (1.5.19, p. 304, with 6.3). And, as citizens, they could see to the payment of the debts that they owed themselves.

Though inclined, like Rome, to defend itself with resoluteness and vigor, this England would by no means be a nation intent on conquest. If it occupied an island, as it might, it would recognize that "conquests abroad" on the continent of Europe or elsewhere would serve only to "weaken it." If this island were blessed, as also it might be, with good soil, this nation "would have no need for war as a means for enriching itself." And since its laws would guarantee that "no citizen would be dependent on another, each would take his liberty more seriously than the glory reserved for a few citizens or one." In consequence, although the soldierly profession might be deemed useful and would no doubt often be dangerous, its members would be regarded as "persons whose services are burdensome (*laborieux*) for the nation itself, and civil status would be accorded greater regard."

The reason why the England imagined by Montesquieu would in this particular be so unlike Rome is simple. Situated, as it would be, on an island and blessed with the farmland and constitution with which it would be blessed, it would quite naturally be a seat of "peace and liberty"; and, when "liberated from destructive prejudices"—such as those rooted in the otherworldliness to which the Christian religion gives rise—it "would be inclined to become commercial" and to exploit to the limit the capacity of its "workers" to fashion from its natural resources objects of "great price." It would be inclined to carry on a great trade with those nations to the south that require its commodities and have much to offer that the English could not provide for themselves; and in flight from the heavy taxes that it would impose, many of its citizens, on the pretext of travel or health, would seek their fortunes abroad, "even in the lands of servitude itself" (*EL*, 3.19.27, pp. 577–578).

Commerce these Englishmen would conduct as other nations conduct war. This people would have "a prodigious number of petty, particular interests." There would be "an infinity of ways" in which it could do and receive harm (*choquer et être choqué*). "It would become sovereignly jealous, and it would be more distressed by the prosperity of others than it would rejoice at its own." Its laws, "in other respects gentle and easy, would be so rigid with regard to commerce and the carrying trade . . . that it would seem to do business with none but enemies" (*EL*, 3.19.27, p. 578, with 4.20.12).

Commerce would, in fact, be dominant in every sphere. "Other nations," Montesquieu remarks elsewhere, "have made their commercial interests give way to their political interests: this one has always made its political interests give way to the interests of its commerce" (*EL*, 4.20.7). If England, he tells us, were to send out colonies far and wide, to places such as North America, "it would do so," precisely as ancient Carthage had, "more to extend the reach of its commerce than its sphere of domination" (3.19.27, p. 578, with 4.21.21). With these colonies, in keeping with its aim, it would be generous, as the Carthaginians had been, conferring on them "its own form of government," which would bring "with it prosperity" so that "one would see great peoples take shape in the forests which they were sent to inhabit" (3.19.27, p. 578).

As an island nation possessed of "a great commerce," Montesquieu's

England "would have every sort of facility for fielding maritime forces." Safeguarding "its liberty would not require that it possess strongholds (*places*), fortresses, and armies on land," but "it would have need of an army at sea to guarantee it against invasion, and its navy would be superior to that of all the other powers, which, needing to employ their finances for war on land, would not have enough for war at sea."

England's supremacy at sea would not be without effect. "The empire of the sea has always given those peoples who possessed it a natural pride. Sensing themselves capable of insulting anyone anywhere," the English "would believe their power as unlimited as the ocean," and they would be inclined to exercise it when circumstances warranted. In consequence, "this nation would have a great influence on the affairs of its neighbors. Because it would not employ its power for conquest, they would be more inclined to seek its friendship, and they would fear its hatred more than the inconstancy of its government and its internal agitation would appear to justify." In consequence, although "it would be the fate of its executive power almost always to be uneasy at home," it would nearly always be "respected abroad" (*EL*, 3.19.27, pp. 579–580, with 4.20.8, 4.21.7). In short, thanks to changes in the *ius gentium* and to the great commercial revolution that had also taken place, the tables had been turned, and Carthage now had the advantage over Rome.

THE DEMISE OF THE REPUBLIC OF VIRTUE

I have frequently used the phrase "for the most part" in this essay, and for the introduction of that qualification there is a reason. Montesquieu is an exceedingly playful writer; and, although the world he depicts in the first three parts of his magnum opus would appear to be static and, in effect, stagnant, every once in a while he drops a cryptic remark that suggests the contrary.

Early in part one, for example, in alluding to modes of subsistence, he mentions hunters, herders, and farmers. Later, in part three, he adds, without fanfare, those who engage in maritime commerce (*EL*, 1.1.3, p. 9, with 3.18.8), and he makes no further mention of this mode of subsistence until the last chapter of what would be the first volume of the 1748 edition of *The Spirit of the Laws*, where he describes England as "*une nation commerçante*"—a commercial nation (3.19.27, pp. 578–579). This is all a tease, designed to encourage curiosity on the part of those who read with care.

Montesquieu does the like in his discussion of the changes that have taken place in the *ius gentium*, which he attributes in part to "today's religion" (*EL*, 2.10.3, with 6.29.14). And he does so again in the midst of his discussion of democratic republicanism in part one. There he argues that "the principle" of "democracy" is "virtue" understood as "a renunciation of self" grounded in a "love of the laws and the fatherland" and in a "love of equality." There, he asserts that this virtue requires "a continual preference for the public interest over one's own" and a restriction of "ambition to a single desire, to the sole happiness of rendering to the fatherland greater services than the other citizens." And there, after acknowledging that virtue is "a very painful thing," he observes that it does not arise naturally, that it has to be inculcated, and that this requires what he calls "singular institutions" designed to make outsiders seem as alien as possible.

These institutions, he later explains, "shock all the received usages by confounding all the virtues" as well as "things naturally separate," such as "laws, mores, and manners." In this particular, the exemplary lawgiver was the Spartan Lycurgus:

> By mixing larceny with the spirit of justice, the harshest slavery with extreme liberty, the most dreadful sentiments with the greatest moderation, he gave stability to the city. He seemed to deprive it of all resources—the arts, commerce, silver, walls: there, one had ambition without the hope of improvement; there, one possessed the natural sentiments without being a child, husband, or father; modesty itself was denied to chastity.

It was by means of these "harsh institutions" that this Lycurgus instilled a "warlike spirit" into the Lacedaemonians, rendered them "grave, serious, dry, taciturn," and produced a "people always correcting or being corrected, always giving instruction or being instructed, equally simple and rigid."

Within a republic, Montesquieu adds, when virtue dissolves, a different species of "ambition" rears its head, "and avarice enters every heart." At this point, "the desires change their objects: that which one loved, one loves no longer; one was free under the laws and wishes to be free against them."

> Each citizen is like a slave who has escaped from the house of his master: what was a maxim, one calls rigor; what was a rule, one calls an awkwardness; what was watchfulness, one calls fear. There it is frugality that passes as avarice, and not

the desire to possess. Beforehand the wealth of particular citizens made up the public treasury, but now the public treasury becomes the patrimony of particular citizens. The republic is a layer of skin sloughed off (*dépouille*), and its force is no more than the power of a few citizens and the license of all.

In the midst of this discussion, which strongly suggests that the commercial revolution is apt to be fatal to virtuous republicanism, Montesquieu suddenly and without warning introduces what seems like a contradiction in terms: "a democracy based on commerce." Therein, he tells us, "it can very easily happen that particular individuals have great wealth and that the mores there are not corrupted" (*EL*, 1.3.3; 4.5–8; 5.2–7; 7.2; 8.2–3, 16; 3.19.7, 16, 21).

This, too, is a tease—for it will not be until part four in the second of the two volumes of the work's first edition that Montesquieu makes commerce thematic. And the same can be said for the claim that the French philosophe advances early in part two when he asserts that "the spirit of republics is peace and moderation" (*EL*, 2.9.2)—a claim in no way compatible with what he has earlier said regarding the martial character of Rome and the cities of ancient Greece (1.4.8) and that makes sense only if he is describing commercial republics (4.20.2).

For the time being, however, readers who have not reached part four and who are sympathetic to republican government may regard these asides as a consolation of sorts. For shortly before he first alludes to the commercial republic, Montesquieu drops yet another cryptic remark suggesting that the world is by no means as static as he has made it seem. The virtue of the ancients, he intimates, is no longer "in full force." When it was, however, "they did things that we no longer see and which astonish our little souls." If his contemporaries are unable to rise to the same level, it is, he adds, because the "education" given the ancients "never suffered contradiction," while "we receive three educations different" from and even "contrary" to one another: "that of our fathers, that of our schoolmasters, that of the world. What we are told in the last overthrows the ideas imparted by the first two." In short, there is now "a contrast between the engagements" which arise "from religion" and "those" which arise "from the world" that "the ancients knew nothing of." This would appear to be why the moderns possess such "little souls," and it explains the absence of republics of virtue in Montesquieu's own time (*EL*, 1.4.4). Thanks, then, to the great revolution that occurred when Christianity, with its supracommunal and otherworldly orientation, replaced the resolutely civic religions of the classical world, virtuous republicanism is no longer available as an alternative to despotism. Given the fact that in the age in which the French philosophe lived European monarchy appears no longer to be viable, the only available bulwark against despotism would appear to be this apparent contradiction in terms: the "democracy based on commerce."

THE SPIRIT OF THE COMMERCIAL REPUBLIC

It is by no means obvious to the unsuspecting glance how the "democracy based on commerce" can escape corruption. After all, Montesquieu makes a point of insisting that the republics devoted to virtue proscribed "silver, whose effect is to fatten the fortunes of men beyond the limits that nature has set for them, to teach men to conserve uselessly that which they have amassed in the same fashion, to multiply infinitely their desires, and to supplant (*suppléer*) nature, which has given us very limited means for irritating our passions and for corrupting one another" (*EL*, 1.4.6). Moreover, in the very first chapter of his twentieth book, he bluntly tells us, "Commerce corrupts pure mores" (4.20.1).

Montesquieu points to the solution to this quandary when he asserts that we must always keep in mind the fact that "not all political vices are moral vices and that not all moral vices are political vices" (*EL*, 3.19.11). As he later explains, "one can say that the laws of commerce perfect mores for the same reason that they destroy mores. Commerce corrupts pure mores: this is the subject of Plato's complaints; it polishes and softens barbarous mores, as we see all the days" of our lives (4.20.1).

In endorsing this paradox—that private vices can promote the public good and that the progression from barbarism to civilization is grounded in moral corruption—Montesquieu is following the lead of and even borrowing language from the Jansenist Pierre Nicole, the Huguenot savant Pierre Bayle, and Bernard Mandeville (*MP*, 1553), a Dutch immigrant to England whose book *The Fable of the Bees: or, Private Vices, Publick Benefits* had enjoyed a grand *succès de scandale* in the early decades of the eighteenth century.[21] In this notorious and highly influential work, Mandeville not only defended vanity as a spur to commercial growth and to progress in the sciences and the arts; like Nicole and Bayle, he contended that "self-liking" is at the root of all the splendid, external qualities that men justly admire.

To begin with, Mandeville stoutly denied that human beings are by nature "sociable"; the origins of human association he attributed to the fear of wild beasts. For the cooperative capacity of his contemporaries, he had a simple explanation: in the course of time, "by living together in Society," men underwent a process akin to the fermentation of grapes. Painful experience slowly taught them that it is in every man's interest to accommodate himself to his fellows, and "good Manners or Politeness came into the World." This attitude actually supplanted brutishness when the canniest human beings acquired the civilizing art of subterfuge and learned "to be proud of hiding their Pride." "The nearer we search into human Nature," the Dutch-born satirist argued, "the more we shall be convinced that the Moral Virtues are the Political Offspring which Flattery begot upon Pride."[22]

When Montesquieu suggests "that when democracy is based on commerce, it can very easily happen that particular individuals have great wealth and that the mores there are not corrupted," he provides an explanation in keeping with the observations of Nicole, Bayle, and Mandeville. This odd and unforeseen result comes about because "the spirit of commerce" quite often "carries with it a spirit of frugality, economy, moderation, industry, wisdom, tranquility, orderliness, and regularity (*règle*). In this fashion, as long as this spirit subsists, the wealth that it produces has no bad effect. The evil arrives when an excess of wealth destroys this spirit of commerce; suddenly one sees born the disorders of inequality, which had not yet made themselves felt" (*EL*, 1.5.6).

Within such a republic, Montesquieu adds, one can best sustain "the spirit of commerce" if one makes arrangements to ensure that "the principal citizens engage in commerce themselves." And he tellingly indicates that this works best where "this spirit reigns alone and is crossed by no other," where "the laws favor it," and where "the same laws, by their dispositions, divide fortunes in proportion to their increase through commerce and thereby place each poor citizen in a condition of ease sufficient that he can work as others do and each rich citizen in a condition of mediocrity sufficient (*dans une telle médiocrité*) that he has need of work if he is to preserve what he has or acquire more." In "a commercial republic," Montesquieu concludes, the statute which "gives to all children an equal proportion in succession to their fathers" is "a very good law." Where partitive inheritance is the norm, it makes no difference "what fortune the father has made," since "his children, always less rich than he was" at the time of his death, "will be induced to flee luxury and to work as he did" (*EL*, 1.5.6).

When Montesquieu constructs a list of republics based on commerce, he mentions not only Tyre, Carthage, Corinth, Marseilles, and Rhodes, but also Florence, Venice, and Holland, indicating that such republics did exist in classical antiquity and, more to the point, that they still exist in modern times. Although commercial republics were evidently marginal in antiquity, they survived Christianity's victory over paganism for the same reason that despotism did: they are founded on a phenomenon no less cosmopolitan and no less alien to the spirit of particularism required by virtuous republics than is Christianity itself. Thus, while "the Greek statesmen and political writers (*les politiques grecs*) who lived under popular government knew of no force able to sustain them other than virtue," their counterparts in the republics of Montesquieu's day "speak only of manufactures, of commerce, of finance, of wealth, and of luxury itself" (*EL*, 1.3.3).

When Montesquieu first indicates that "democracy" can be "based on commerce," he lists as an example Athens alone (*EL*, 1.5.6). When he first introduces the notion of a "commerce of economy," specifying that it tends to be practiced under popular governments (*le gouvernement par plusieurs*), he mentions Athens among its aficionados (4.20.4). Much later, when he once again singles out Athens with an eye to her commercial character, he places great emphasis on her possession of an "empire over the sea"—an empire imperfect in one particular, which was identified by the author of *The Constitution of the Athenians* found among the works of Xenophon. Because "Attica belongs to the mainland (*tient à la terre*)," Montesquieu quotes from this tract, Athens' "enemies ravage" her territory when "she makes expeditions abroad." Her leading men then "let their farms (*terres*) be destroyed and place their goods in security on some isle. The people, who have no farms, live without uneasiness (*inquiétude*)." If only, the tract's author wistfully adds, "the Athenians inhabited an island and, besides this, possessed an empire over the sea, so long as they remained masters of the sea, they would have the power to injure others without being subject to injury themselves." At this juncture, Montesquieu feels compelled to chime in, "You could say that Xenophon wanted to speak of England" (4.21.7).[23]

Here is a case in which Montesquieu expects his more attentive readers to recall to mind the substance of his claim that "antiquity" has its own peculiar "*esprit*" and to take care lest they "miss the differences distinguishing cases that seem similar" (*EL*, preface). For, from his perspective, modern England was everything that ancient Athens might have been and was not. The Athenians

Montesquieu describes as a "commercial nation," but he quickly concedes that they succumbed to the spirit of war and aggrandizement: as he puts it, they were "more attentive to extending their maritime empire than to using it." Athens was, in fact, so "full of projects for glory" that she never "achieved the great commerce promised by the working of her mines, the multitude of her slaves, the number of her sailors, her authority over the Greek towns, and, more than all this, the fine institutions of Solon." In effect, then, Athens sacrificed economic to political and imperial concerns (4.21.7). England, though far better situated for war and aggrandizement, tended to do the opposite (4.20.7). England really was a democracy based on commerce, and as such, it exemplified the spirit of "peace and moderation."

THE VERY MODEL OF A MODERN COMMERCIAL REPUBLIC

England was, in fact, everyone's ideal trading partner. It was, as Montesquieu puts it, "a nation which demands little and which the requirements of commerce render to some degree dependent; a nation which, as a consequence of the breadth of its vision and the extent of its business, knows where to place all superfluous merchandise." England was "rich and able to take on much in the way of produce (*denrées*)." It tended "to pay for this promptly." It had, "so to speak, a need to be faithful." It was "pacific on principle" and inclined to "seek gain and not conquest" (*EL*, 4.20.8). One consequence was that, in modern times, the English tended not to be a threat to the territorial integrity of the nearby states on the European continent. "Politics" Montesquieu describes as "a dull file": it "achieves its end slowly by wearing away." The English lack the patience for this. They "would be unable to endure the delays, the details, the cold-bloodedness (*sang-froid*) of negotiations; in these they would often be less successful than every other nation; and they would lose, by their treaties, that which they had obtained by their arms." Their inability to attend to high politics may have had another root as well. While "other nations made the interests of commerce give way to political interests," Montesquieu tells us, England "always made its political interests give way to the interests of its commerce" (3.14.13, 4.20.7).

To suppose, however, that their commercial orientation was somehow damaging to the English would be a considerable blunder. "This is the people in the world," Montesquieu emphasizes, "who have known best how to take advantage of these three great things at the same time: religion, commerce, and liberty" (*EL*, 4.20.7). The Englishmen that Montesquieu encountered when he sojourned in Great Britain from November 1729 to May 1731 struck him as more like "kings" than subjects. In their dealings with one another, they comported themselves as "confederates rather than fellow citizens." They were "haughty (*fière*)," and they were "proud (*superbe*)." But, unlike their neighbors the French, they were neither sociable nor "vain." In England, there were "many people" who cared not a whit "to please anyone" and who abandoned "themselves to their own humors" (3.19.5, 9, 27, pp. 582–583). If the English lacked the "greatness of soul" sometimes elicited from France's nobility by its monarchy, they possessed in its place a profound "independence" of both spirit and mind. One might describe them as *"recueillis"*—collected within themselves, contemplative, and even withdrawn—but, in their customary state of "retirement (*retraite*) [from] society," they could be relied on to "do their thinking each and every one entirely on his own." The citizens of a polity like the one in England would be, as Montesquieu puts it, "at all times independent." Each would have "his own will" and value "his independence according to his pleasure." Each would follow "his caprices and his fantasies in matters public as well as private" (1.5.12; 3.19.27, pp. 575, 583).

The laws of the English would favor no individual in preference to another; no citizen there would fear another citizen; and none would depend on any other. In Montesquieu's England, since the enjoyment and preservation of liberty would require freedom of the press, everyone would be able to say what he thought—to "say and write everything that the laws did not expressly prohibit his saying and writing"—and this everyone would do. It goes almost without saying that every citizen within such a state would also be inclined to make much more of "his own liberty than of the glory belonging to a few citizens or one" (*EL*, 3.19.27, pp. 575, 577).

"With regard to religion," Montesquieu tells us that the same spirit of fierce independence was apt to reign. "Since, within the state, each citizen would possess his own will and would in consequence be conducted by his own illumination (*lumières*) or fantasies, it would come to pass that" many "would display a great indifference with regard to every sort of religion of whatever type," and the clergy would be given "so little credit that the other citizens would have more." The clergy would be mindful of this fact and, instead of forming a separate order, its members would prefer to "bear the same burdens as the laity." In an attempt "to attract respect from the people, they would distinguish themselves by a retired life, by conduct more reserved, and mores more pure." Aware that they lacked the means with which to constrain and that they could neither protect religion nor expect that it would protect them, they would opt for persuasion, take up the pen, and produce "works" of genuine merit "proving revelation and the providence" of God (*EL*, 3.19.27, pp. 580–581).

As a consequence of the reigning indifference, Montesquieu notes, nearly everyone would be "inclined to embrace the dominant religion"—although, of course, some in their capriciousness would be "zealous for religion in general," and "the sects would multiply." It would not be "impossible," he adds in an especially revealing aside, "that there would be in this nation people who had no religion and who would nevertheless be unwilling to endure being obliged to change the religion that they would have had if they had had one," for the sort of men formed by a species of government which takes political liberty as its direct object "would sense right away that their lives and property were no more theirs than their manner of thinking and that he who is able to rob them of the one would be better able yet to deprive them of the other" (*EL*, 3.19.27, p. 580).

Those who governed in the England that Montesquieu constructed on the basis of observation and reflection were dependent on public opinion. Theirs would be "a power which is replenished (*se remonte*), so to speak, and remade every day." They would tend, therefore, to pay "greater regard to those who were useful than to those who might divert them." There would be in evidence, Montesquieu adds, "fewer courtiers, flatterers, pleasers" and fewer of "the types who draw advantage from the emptiness of spirit" that afflicts "the great." Precisely because they would be so unlike their neighbors the French, the English would be "emancipated from destructive prejudices." They would judge men simply as men: hardly at all with reference to "their frivolous talents and attributes," and almost solely in terms of their "real qualities"—their "personal merit" and their "wealth" (*EL*, 3.19.27, pp. 578, 581).

The laws of Montesquieu's England left "all the passions" there "free." The consequences were everywhere to be seen. "Hatred, envy, [and] jealousy" appeared "in their full extent," and these all seem to have found expression in "the ardor to enrich and distinguish oneself" (*EL*, 3.19.27, p. 575). As one would then imagine, Montesquieu's Englishmen were to be "always preoccupied with their interests." In consequence, they would lack "that politeness that is founded on idleness (*oisiveté*)," for they "really would not have the time."

This species of politeness he associated with "the establishment of arbitrary power," arguing that "absolute government produces idleness" and that "idleness causes the birth of politeness." Nonetheless, the very fact that the populace in England would be sizable and that men would "need to do business (*d'avoir des ménagements*) with one another and not displease" meant that among the English "there would be politeness" of a sort (3.19.27, pp. 581–582).

There was, Montesquieu intimates, much to be said for this particular species of politesse. The politeness nourished in monarchies was a politeness of manners rooted in rivalry (*EL*, 1.4.2, p. 263), and, as a consequence, it was a mode of conduct wholly external, which "flatters the vices of others" (3.19.16). In their solitude, the English might be relatively insensitive to "ridicule" of the sort associated with courts, but they were in no way oblivious to "vice," and the politeness that they would be most likely to display was, he implies, a "politeness of morals (*moeurs*)," a species of conduct genuine and internal, rooted in a sense of obligation. "That which ought to distinguish us from barbarous peoples," he explains, is more closely bound up with "the politeness of morals than with the politeness of manners" (3.19.16, 27, pp. 582–583).

Largely because of their lack of pretensions, the English would possess "a solid luxury," which would be founded on "real needs" and "not on the refinements of vanity." Many would enjoy "a great superfluity" and, since "frivolous things" would, in effect, be "proscribed," they would have "more wealth than occasion for expense" (*EL*, 3.19.27, p. 581).

Commerce promised to cure any "destructive prejudices" to which the English might in the future be inclined to fall prey (*EL*, 4.20.1). And it no doubt contributed to the process by which a people, once inclined to "fanaticism and enthusiasm," who had become "indignant against the laws themselves," eventually settled into a mood of religious indifference. Montesquieu is obviously alluding to the effects of England's turn to commerce when he later remarks that "as a general rule invitations contribute more forcefully to changing religion than do penalties" and adds that it is a surer strategy "to attack religion by favor, by the conveniences (*commodités*) of life, by the hope of fortune; not by that which warns one of one's mortality but by that which makes one forget it; not by that which provokes indignation but by that which casts one into a disposition lukewarm (*qui jette dans la tiédeur*) so that other passions act on our souls and those which religion inspires fall silent" (5.25.12). Such are the effects of "solid luxury" among a commercial people "always occupied with their own interests" (3.19.27, p. 581).

Of course, there were drawbacks to the emerging commercial order explored by Montesquieu. It promoted "gentle mores." It encouraged reciprocal dependence among nations and thereby favored peace. But it did so at a price. It loosened ties between individuals. It disaggregated human communities. It turned men into "confederates" who otherwise would have been "fellow citizens," as we have seen. Moreover, "in the countries, where one is affected by nothing but the spirit of commerce," Montesquieu observes, "we see that one traffics in all human activities and in all the moral virtues: the smallest things, which humanity demands, are done there or given for money." This is due to the fact that "the spirit of commerce produces in human beings a certain sentiment of exact justice, opposed on the one side to brigandage and on the other to the moral virtues which cause one to not always restrict one's discussion rigidly to one's own interests, and which enable one to neglect one's interests for those of others" (*EL*, 4.20.2).

In so unsociable an environment, men would be virtually immune to the charm of sexual difference, and there would be very little social intercourse between the two sexes. "Women would be modest—which is to say, timid: this timidity would constitute their virtue while the men, lacking gallantry, would hurl themselves into debauchery" (*EL*, 3.19.27, p. 582). Moreover, "the majority of those who possess intelligence and wit (*esprit*) would be tormented by that very *esprit*: in the disdain or disgust" that they would feel with regard "to all things, they would be unhappy with so many reasons (*sujets*) not to be so" (3.19.27, pp. 576, 582).

In the England imagined by Montesquieu, the rule of law would be established. No citizen would fear another. But the Englishman would not enjoy a "tranquility of spirit." In part because the English are a "people collected within themselves" who are inclined to "think each entirely on his own," they are a solitary lot. That a man as solitary as the Englishman should have an "uneasy spirit (*esprit inquiet*)" stands to reason (*EL*, 3.19.27, p. 582). Nor is it surprising that, unprompted by genuine peril or even by false alarm, he should nonetheless "fear (*craint*) the escape of a good" that he "feels," that he "hardly knows," and that "can be hidden from us," and that this "fear (*crainte*)" should "always magnify objects" and render him "uneasy (*inquiet*) in his situation" and inclined to "believe" that he is "in danger even in those moments when [he is] most secure." In consequence, "uneasiness (*inquiétude*)" without "a certain object" would appear to be the Englishman's normal state of mind (3.19.27, pp. 575–576).

There is, moreover, something about commerce that is undignified and utterly grim. As Montesquieu puts it, "This commerce is a species of lottery, and each is seduced by the hope of a black ticket. Everyone loves to play, and the wisest people play willingly, when its character as gambling, its obsessiveness (*ses égarements*), its violence, its dissipation, the loss of time, and even of one's whole life, is not apparent" (*EL*, 4.20.6). If men in the modern world possess such "little souls" (1.4.4), it is not solely or, perhaps, even primarily because of the Christian religion.

Across the English Channel, there was a reminder that what later came to be called the ancien régime had its charms. For there, Montesquieu intimates, we might encounter "a nation which possessed a sociable humor, an openness of heart, a joy in living, a taste, a facility for communicating its thoughts, which was lively, agreeable, playful, sometimes imprudent, often indiscreet; and which had along with this courage, generosity, frankness, a certain sensitivity to honor." Not surprisingly, such a nation would foster a "taste for the world and for commerce with women above all else" (*EL*, 3.19.5–6). Monarchies may not have liberty as their "direct object." They pursue "glory" instead. But, we are told, this pursuit of glory gives rise to "a spirit of liberty" which "may contribute as much to happiness as liberty itself" (2.11.7). It is no wonder that—when Montesquieu remarked that "Germany was made to travel in, Italy to sojourn in, [and] England to think in"—he added, regarding the "France" of his own time, that it was made "to live in."[24]

This should give us pause. For we in the West live in Montesquieu's "democracy based on commerce," and it exhibits all the qualities—both good and bad—that he identified. Among these qualities there is an *inquiétude* that drives a quest for public provision requiring a degree of administrative centralization that threatens liberty.[25] And within these commercial republics there has long been endemic a species of seething discontent, to which "those who possess intelligence and wit" are especially prone—which has over and over again engendered sociopolitical movements of a quasi-religious nature profoundly hostile to what, in imitation of Jean-Jacques Rousseau, they denounce as "bourgeois society." Tranquil in spirit we are not.

NOTES

1. [Charles-Louis de Secondat, baron de la Brède et de Montesquieu], *De l'esprit des loix* (Geneva: Barrillot & Fils, [1748]). See also letters from Jacob Vernet, July and August 1748,

September 4, 1748, in Charles-Louis de Secondat, baron de La Brède et de Montesquieu, *Oeuvres complètes de Montesquieu*, ed. André Masson (Paris: Les Éditions Nagel, 1950–55), vol. 3, 1121–1122, 1130–1132; hereafter cited as Nagel. Evidence from these letters allows one to infer that Vernet bore responsibility for the omission of the parts.

2. [Charles-Louis de Secondat, baron de la Brède et de Montesquieu], *De l'esprit des loix*, nouvelle édition (Geneva: Barrillot & Fils, 1750). Letter to Pierre-Jean Grosley, April 8, 1750, in Nagel, 3:1297. There are good reasons for rejecting the long-dominant scholarly presumption that the posthumous edition best reflects the author's intentions. See Albert Postigliola, "Editer L'Esprit des lois," in *Editer Montesquieu, Publicare Montesquieu*, ed. Alberto Postigliola (Naples: Liguori Editore, 1998), 65–77. For further discussion of the early editions and a full list, see Cecil Patrick Courtney, "Montesquieu et les imprimeurs de *L'Esprit des lois* (1748–1758)," in *L'Écrivain et l'imprimeur*, ed. Alain Riffaud (Rennes, France: Presses Universitaires de Rennes, 2010), 193–216. Hereafter, I cite Montesquieu's *De l'esprit des lois* parenthetically in text as *EL*, using the divisions provided by the author (part, book, and, where pertinent, chapter); I sometimes include a page number from the second volume of Charles-Louis de Secondat, baron de La Brède et de Montesquieu, *Œuvres complètes de Montesquieu*, ed. Roger Caillois (Paris: Bibliothèque de la Pléiade, 1949–51). All translations in this chapter are my own.

3. See Plato, *Republic* 8.543c–9.580a and *Laws* 3.676a–5.747e, as well as Aristotle, *Politics* 1252a1–1288b6, 1324a35–1331b18. In assessing Plato's position, one must keep in mind the way in which he brings rational principles into play in his *Laws* 3.690a–d.

4. See Plato, *Republic* 8.543c–9.580a.

5. In this connection, see Paul A. Rahe, "Was Montesquieu a Philosopher of History?" in *Montesquieu et les philosophies de l'histoire au XVIIIe siècle*, ed. Lorenzo Bianchi and Rolando Minuti (Naples: Liguori Editore, 2013), 71–86.

6. Cf. the two-volume edition published by Huart in Paris in 1749—[Charles-Louis de Secondat, baron de la Brède et de Montesquieu], *De l'esprit des loix*, nouvelle édition (Geneva: Barrillot & Fils, 1749)—with the 1748 edition cited in note 1, above, and with the three-volume 1750 edition cited in note 2, above. I erred in an earlier publication in claiming that the map was present in the original edition: Paul A. Rahe, *Montesquieu and the Logic of Liberty: War, Religion, Commerce, Climate, Terrain, Technology, Uneasiness of Mind, the Spirit of Political Vigilance, and the Foundations of the Modern Republic* (New Haven, CT: Yale University Press, 2009), 169. I became aware of my error thanks to the extraordinary generosity of Stuart Warner, who gave me some years ago a facsimile edition of the 1748 edition of Montesquieu's magnum opus.

7. If Montesquieu does not mention the sextant, it is presumably because it was not deployed until 1731 and he was unaware of its importance.

8. Charles-Louis de Secondat, baron de La Brède et de Montesquieu, *Pensées, le Spicilège*, ed. Louis Desgraves (Paris: Robert Laffont, 1991), 1306; hereafter cited in the text as *MP* (referring to the notebooks Montesquieu entitled *Mes pensées*), followed by the entry number.

9. See Nicholas Barbon, *A Discourse of Trade* (London: Thomas Milbourn, 1690), reprinted in *Commerce, Culture and Liberty: Readings on Capitalism before Adam Smith*, ed. Henry C. Clark (Indianapolis: Liberty Fund, 2003), 66–99.

10. See Louis Desgraves and Catherine Volpilhac-Auger, *Catalogue de la bibliothèque de Montesquieu à La Brède* (Naples: Liguori Editore, 1999).

11. This omission I tried to rectify in Paul A. Rahe, "Carthage Can Now Defeat Rome: Political Order, Seaborne Commerce, and the Projection of Power in Barbon & Montesquieu," in *Applied History and Contemporary Policymaking: School of Statecraft*, ed. Robert Crowcroft (London: Bloomsbury, 2022), 53–66.

12. Barbon, *Discourse of Trade*, A1–4.14.

13. Barbon, A1–4.40–61.

14. Charles-Louis de Secondat, baron de La Brède et de Montesquieu, *Réflexions sur la monarchie universelle en Europe*, in *Œuvres complètes de Montesquieu*, ed. Jean Ehrard, Catherine Volpilhac-Auger, et al. (Oxford: Voltaire Foundation, 1998–2008; Paris: Éditions Classiques Garnier, 2010–), vol. 2, 339–364; hereafter cited in the text as *RMU*, followed by chapter and line. An English edition of this important work, translated by David W. Carrithers, can now be found in Montesquieu, *Discourses, Dissertations, and Dialogues on Politics, Science, and Religion*, ed. and trans. David W. Carrithers and Philip Stewart (Cambridge: Cambridge University Press, 2020), 170–187.

15. Cf. Niccolò Machiavelli, *Dell'arte della guerra* 2, 5, in Machiavelli, *Tutte le opere*, ed. Mario Martelli (Florence: G. C. Sansoni, 1971), 332–333, 359–360. Note also Machiavelli, *Istorie fiorentine* 5.1, 6.1, in *Tutte le opere*, 738–739, 765–766; Machiavelli, *Discorsi sopra la prima deca di Tito Livio* 2.6, in *Tutte le opere*, 155–156.

16. Cf. Machiavelli, *Discorsi sopra la prima deca de Tito Livio* 2.10 and *Dell'arte della guerra* 7, in *Tutte le opere*, 159–160, 386.

17. For the details, see Paul A. Rahe, "The Book that Never Was: Montesquieu's *Considerations on the Romans* in Historical Context," *History of Political Thought* 26, 1 (Spring 2005): 43–89, reprinted in a French translation by Céline Spector as "Le Livre qui ne vit jamais le jour: les *Considerations sur les Romains* et leur contexte historique," *Revue Montesquieu* 8 (2006): 67–79; Rahe, *Montesquieu and the Logic of Liberty*, 1–60.

18. For a much more detailed discussion of the argument advanced in *The Spirit of the Laws* than it is possible for me to articulate here, see Rahe, *Montesquieu and the Logic of Liberty*, 61–238.

19. Rahe, *Montesquieu and the Logic of Liberty*, 186–211 (with 31–45). See also Paul A. Rahe, "Montesquieu's Critique of Monarchy: A Self-Destructive Anachronism," in *Montesquieu et la civilité, Annuaire de l'Institut Michel Villey* 2010, 2 (2011): 209–228.

20. This passage should be read in light of *EL*, 4.22.17–18.

21. For a more extensive discussion than there is space for here, see Paul A. Rahe, "Blaise Pascal, Pierre Nicole, and the Origins of Liberal Sociology," in *Enlightenment and Secularism: Essays on the Mobilization of Reason*, ed. Christopher Nadon (Lanham, MD: Lexington Books, 2013), 129–140; Paul A. Rahe, "Beyond Confessional Paradigms: Re-grounding Virtue on Secular Calculation Alone," in *Recht, Konfession und Verfassung im 17. Jahrhundert*, ed. Mathias Schmoeckel and Robert von Friedeburg (Berlin: Duncker & Humblot, 2015), 269–283.

22. Consider Bernard Mandeville, *The Fable of the Bees: or, Private Vices, Publick Benefits*, ed. F. B. Kaye (Oxford: Clarendon Press, 1924), vol. 1, 47, 51, 78–80, 342–344, 369; vol.

2, 128–134, 147, 188–189, 268, in light of Kaye's introduction in vol. 1, xxxiii–cxlvi, and Ronald Hamowy, *The Scottish Enlightenment and the Theory of Spontaneous Order* (Carbondale: Southern Illinois University Press, 1987). See also Mandeville, *Fable of the Bees*, 1:41–57, 323–369.

23. Cf. Xenophon, *Athenaion Politeia* 2.14–16.

24. [Jean le Rond d'Alembert], "Éloge de M. le President de Montesquieu," in *Encyclopédie, ou Dictionnaire raisonné des sciences, des arts, et des métiers*, ed. Denis Diderot and Jean le Rond d'Alembert (Paris: Briasson, 1751–72; Neufchâtel: S. Faulche, 1765; Amsterdam: M. M. Rey, 1776–77; Paris: Panckoucke, 1777–80), vol. 5, vii.

25. See Paul A. Rahe, *Soft Despotism, Democracy's Drift: Montesquieu, Rousseau, Tocqueville and the Modern Prospect* (New Haven, CT: Yale University Press, 2009).

CHAPTER 3

The Commercial Republic and Adam Smith's *The Theory of Moral Sentiments*

Ann Charney Colmo

Adam Smith changed the world of economics with the publication of *The Wealth of Nations* (1776). This might have caused a moral dilemma, but it was a dilemma Smith had foreseen and resolved in his earlier work *The Theory of Moral Sentiments* (1759), no doubt after reflecting on the character of modernity.

With the "modern turn" taken by Hobbes and Locke, the primary focus of political thought became the individual and the individual's right to self-preservation. But this raised a problem: what was the basis of morality for the individual? Prior to this modern turn, the cornerstone of morality was society. Morality, in all its contexts, was based on the notion that humans are social beings.

This problem was exacerbated by the rise of the "commercial republic," for which Smith was largely responsible. The founders of the commercial republic provided a basis to "assimilate all men everywhere to one another," sloughing off the previous distinctions of church and state that gave superiority and freedom to only a few.[1] Tocqueville saw the commercial republic as a means for individuals to "try to attain that form of greatness and happiness which is proper to ourselves." In such a republic, the highest task of government is to "instruct and encourage men in ... calculation of self-restraint and ... to show that what is right may also be useful."[2] The republic is *commercial*, which "frees man to try to satisfy their physical wants, not conscious of the superstructure of economics"—the "invisible hand," as set out by Smith in *The Wealth of Nations*.[3]

Tocqueville later developed a notion of morality that could be derived from the self: "self-interest properly understood" became the watchword of morality.[4] But for Smith, self-interest (or as he called it, "self-love") was a shaky basis.

How could self-interest provide a firm morality? And how was "properly understood" to be determined? At best, it was a circular morality. It was the self judging itself, confused and unable to get outside of the self.[5] However, Smith believed there was another part of human nature, a part that could supply the morality needed.[6] He expressed this at the beginning of *The Theory of Moral Sentiments*: "How selfish soever man may be supposed, there are evidently some principles in his nature, which interest him in the fortune of others, and render their happiness necessary to him, though he derives nothing from it except the pleasure of seeing it" (*TMS*, I.I.i).[7] This quote may be surprising to those who know Smith only from *The Wealth of Nations*, with its emphasis on the form of economics now known as capitalism. But it seems undeniable that Smith cannot simply be called an economist in the present-day sense of the term, and even to call him the "father of economics" is to adopt the novel doctrine that paternity is determined by the desires of the child. One might even argue that "economics"—whether capitalist or Marxist—was what Smith was trying to protect humankind from, in part by making its harsh requirements clear, and in part by indicating the path to its transcendence.[8]

By accepting that Smith was writing about politics, the student of his works is able to avoid the embarrassment that plagues economic interpreters of Smith: what to do with *The Theory of Moral Sentiments*. From an economic point of view, this work seems like a gentle digression from the real matters of life. Viewed politically, however, it is a stern warning about the limits of economics and an ennobling promise of the possibilities in the modern universe.[9] In this work, we find such important notions as the "invisible hand" (prior to its use in *The Wealth of Nations*) and the view that the irregularities of nature that cause human beings to "approve" or "disapprove" of actions that are not reasonably worthy of approbation or disapproval have a beneficial influence on the whole tapestry of natural morality. Although Smith did not particularly admire "men of system" who made no compromise with the practical, it is a great injustice to accuse him of not recognizing an essential connection between *The Theory of Moral Sentiments* and *The Wealth of Nations*. If there is such a connection, a consideration of the former will shed light on the latter, allowing us to better judge the intentions of Smith's works as a whole and thus judge the results in the light of those intentions.

THE THEORY OF MORAL SENTIMENTS

As the title of the work indicates, Smith views certain sentiments or passions as moral or leading to the foundation of morality in human beings' passionate nature. The importance of this assertion is readily apparent to those familiar with the difficulties stemming from the natural rights doctrines of Hobbes and Locke. Although Hobbes asserts the existence of natural rights and natural law, he also emphatically states that there can be neither law nor justice in the state of nature. It is clear that the existence of rights in the state of nature precludes their enjoyment there and that the law of nature requires a civil sovereign for its promulgation. Within the commonwealth, the sovereign is the standard of the just and the unjust. Even the standards of equity and iniquity are given no substantive character but are merely the formal and evident criteria of peace.[10]

The strength this particularizing of the standard of justice gives to society, however, proves to be the Achilles' heel of morality, a weakness that has been a prime cause of the subsequent modern political philosophy movement. Certainly it is a major force in the direction and character of the argument in *The Theory of Moral Sentiments*.[11] Smith is trying to find a basis for morality that runs deeper than the will of the sovereign or the requirements of peace—deeper than individualism or the self. His insistence that intention is the primary basis of humans' moral being is a sign of his dissatisfaction with the Hobbesian scheme.[12] Although Smith allies himself with certain ancient views of virtue and restores to prominence ends that were extolled in the ancient as opposed to the Hobbesian teachings, he departs from the older doctrines at exactly the place where Hobbes goes his separate way.

Smith's critiques of Hobbes are both explicit and implicit. Decrying a political doctrine based too much on self-love or self-interest (e.g., *TMS*, VII.iii.1), Smith resorts to the springs of fellow feeling that seem to be generated by association with others. Nature itself leads people to desire the approbation of others, and this desire is the platform of morality. Smith's critique of the modern systems of Clark and Shaftesbury—that is, their views that beneficent action is embodied in propriety—might be made against that of Hobbes as well: "None of those systems account either easily or sufficiently . . . for that diversity of sentiment which they naturally excite. Neither is the description of vice more complete. . . . [N]one of those systems easily and sufficiently account for that superior degree of detestation which we feel for such action" (VII.ii.1.50). The proper passion to associate with morality, the precise or distinct measure of the fitness of the passions, is sympathy, not self-interest (VII.iii.3).

Dismayed by a politics and a morality of self and utility, Smith seeks another basis for morality. He searches in the same location, however, where the modern men of system found such a rich matrix: the passions. Smith's promotion of sympathy is due to his belief that people judge the propriety or impropriety of the passions of others by comparing them with their own.[13]

It is important to note, however, that the approbation or disapproval we feel for others' passions is due not to our supposition of what we would do in similar circumstances but to our imagining that we *are* the other person. Thus, morality is determined by passion or sympathy, not by calculation and not by selfish passion, for by becoming the other for the sake of judgment, we are no longer considering ourselves. In this way, Smith goes beyond the merely utilitarian calculation that offends him in Hobbes's and Mandeville's theories. Smith abjures the systems of private prudence or self-love, whether those of the Epicureans in ancient times or Hobbes and company in modern times. His theory, in contrast, allows for the noble character of public prudence—more akin to the prudence described by Aristotle than that defined by Hobbes. It is a system "which bases morality on propriety"—a categorization that allies Smith with the ranks of Plato, Aristotle, Zeno, and the Stoics (*TMS*, VI.I, VII. ii.1).

Yet Smith's morality begins and remains in the sentiments, or the passions, and their "natural" objects, rather than in reason or reasoned habits. In this sense, he maintains the modern emphasis on passion or intention (will). It is true that the passions cannot be compared without the imagination, but the imagination itself is more closely related to passion than to reason. The passions of others are naturally compared by putting oneself in their place. Smith shows this by explaining how knowledge of the fear of violent death is acquired. That knowledge *cannot* come from one's own personal experience of violent death; it must therefore come from putting oneself in another's place (*TMS*, I.i.1).

Smith is so far from basing morality on the individual's calculation of self-interest that he exempts responses to one's own circumstances from the standard for approbation. In our own case, we are without a lodestone for judgment. Our response to another's situation constitutes the true sentiments of morality, which we then generalize to rules of conduct we may eventually apply to ourselves. Only then do we arrive at an awareness of our own duties, those we must follow to be decent. We must see ourselves not as we believe ourselves to be but as our neighbors see us. We must feel much for others and little for ourselves. These duties of beneficence or altruism predominate because the mainspring of morality is the natural impulse—probably spontaneous and inescapable—to put ourselves in another's place, to sympathize (*TMS*, I.i.4, II.ii).

Smith believes an unbiased judgment by the passions is possible—and it seems absolutely necessary to the solidity of his moral system—as shown by his repeated asseveration that judgments should be made by the "impartial spectator," that is, someone removed from the eye of publicity and thus from the temptation to make self-serving judgments, if only to gain the approbation of another (*TMS*, III.ii.32, III.iii.4). Judgment by the impartial spectator has the additional advantage of avoiding the preaching of morality—once its true source and therefore its true content have been discovered—to a world that must allow the individual the freedom to judge his own good but, at the same time, must protect itself from the potentially harmful effects of that judgment.

This might seem to require a great deal of self-forgetfulness to arise from the passions, but Smith claims to be building on those passions that are "perhaps the strongest of our desires": the desire for the sympathy, approbation, and respect of others, which are "among the strongest which stir men." Passion predominates—even law is the result of will—making Smith's moral system compatible with the modern view of nature (*TMS*, I.2.v, III.vi, VI.1, III.v).[14]

THE SYSTEM AND ITS IRREGULARITIES

The act of sympathizing puts us in another's place and, by use of the imagination, allows us to feel what another feels. To repeat, this is not merely *imagining* ourselves in the other's place—imagination comes into play after we are impelled to transport ourselves. It is *transforming* ourselves completely into the other being. Furthermore, we do not sympathize or desire sympathy from others out of motives of self-interest: we do not give sympathy for the sake of a reward, and we do not desire sympathy because we believe help will follow. Rather, sympathy occurs spontaneously when we see another's passion; when we experience others' passions, such as sorrow, our overburdened hearts receive "almost the only agreeable sensation which it is [at a time of distress] capable of receiving." Our original acceptance of another's sentiment derives not from utility but from its rightness, its appropriateness, and its agreeableness to truth (*TMS*, I.i.2, I.i.4).

The morality of an action is judged from two vantage points: the cause of the passion that initiates the action, and the "end which [the passion] proposes, or the effect which it tends to produce" (*TMS*, I.i.3.5). The first vantage point forms the basis for judging the action's *propriety*: if the passion is suitable (the degree of passion is included in this judgment of suitability) to the object that excited it, the subsequent action is proper or decent. The second vantage point determines the appropriate reward or punishment for the action: if the effect the action aims or tends to produce is beneficial, the action has *merit* (I.i.3).[15] Propriety, or the suitability of the passion to its object, is an approvable sentiment within the reach of all humankind. Virtue goes beyond propriety and is not available to all; it is to be admired and celebrated. The major portion of Smith's work is concerned with propriety, which *is* within the purview of all.

Smith discusses a variety of passions—those stemming directly from the body and those coming from the imagination—and the natural sentimental reaction to them. In each case, there is a necessary moderation whereby the sufferer tries to mute his passion and the spectator tries to arouse his, resulting in the harmonious sharing that is the core of sympathy and our desire for it (*TMS*, I.i.4). Smith enunciates a moral system that almost perfectly articulates the private and the public good, the self and society.

But there are irregularities in matters of propriety. The remarkable conjunction of what we are disposed to sympathize with and what is good is not uniformly present in human beings' actions or propensities. The doctrine of nature runs counter to the doctrine of reason and philosophy with respect to the relative merits of wealth and high rank, on the one hand, and wisdom and virtue, on the other. Nature inclines the passions in general to admire the former for the same reasons that those of a philosophical nature admire the latter: wealth and rank seem to be concomitants of happiness, freedom, and peace of mind, and the possession of these characteristics evokes sympathy and approbation (*TMS*, I.iii.2–3, VI.iii.30). Although Smith first mentions these "irregularities" in his discussion of propriety (proper reaction) in part I, he resolves their apparent disturbance of his system only in part IV when he undertakes an extended discussion of the relation between the sentiments of approbation and utility.

The second aspect of morality—proper reward and punishment—Smith calls merit. If the merit of an action is found in "the beneficial . . . nature of the effects which the affection aims at, or tends to produce," what is the basis for judging that benefit? Smith suggests a twofold connection: direct sympathy with the sentiments of the agent, and indirect sympathy with the gratitude of the benefited. This seems to make the merit of an action dependent on the gratitude of the person who is its intended beneficiary. We do not need to be well versed in testimonials of literature—or real life, for that matter—to see the difficulty with this criterion, and in fact Smith retracts it in a lengthy footnote at the end of the discussion on merit and demerit (part II). We sympathize with the individual's gratitude *as if he were* grateful. In many respects, morality is not what people feel but what they ought to feel (*TMS*, II.1.v, note; II.i.2).

It is only with the discussion of merit and demerit that Smith introduces the impartial spectator as the appropriate judge of virtue. Smith seems to be signaling that merit is an aspect of virtue that is problematic to discuss in terms of sentiment. Something more—one is tempted to say something more discerning—is needed to judge merit accurately. At this point, however, the impartial spectator seems to be an outside spectator (*TMS*, I.i.5.). The proper objects of gratitude and resentment are those that "the heart of every impartial spectator entirely sympathizes with," those actions that everybody who knows of them would wish to either reward or see punished (II.i.2). This apparent harmony between the impartial spectator and "everybody" is mentioned in the context of the "sacred and necessary law of retaliation," which "Nature, antecedent to all reflections upon the utility of punishment, has . . . stamped upon the human heart, in the strongest and most indelible characters." Yet Smith affirms that resentment seems odious, and its excess, revenge, "appears to be the most detestable of all the passions, and is the object of the horror and imagination of every body" (II.i.5, note). His solution is twofold. Smith applies the rule of the mean and infers that there must be a mean that evokes esteem and admiration, although it is difficult for those who feel resentment to moderate that passion. Moreover, resentment is a necessary condition for the existence of society, the animating principle in justice, and the negative but required virtue of not harming others. The harshness of punishment, and even the intent of harsh punishment, must be considered in light of its end: the preservation and welfare of society. "When the preservation of an individual is inconsistent with the safety of a multitude, nothing can be more just than that the many should be preferred to the one" (II.ii.3.11). Lest this argument seem too close to the calculating and utilitarian morality Smith wishes to avoid, he notes that the welfare of society "is seldom [the] consideration which first animates us against [licentious practices]. All men, even the most stupid and unthinking, abhor fraud, perfidy, and injustice, and delight to see them punished." The reasoning person must use the notion of the welfare of society to console himself when confronted with the injury a single individual receives through punishment (II.ii.3.9, 11). People are naturally inclined to vindictiveness and revenge, so the introduction of the impartial spectator can be explained on these grounds alone.

With regard to matters of propriety, there is an irregularity of sentiment related to the judgment of character, so there is an irregularity in matters of merit. Although the proper locus of responsibility for action lies in the intention, we cannot help—here, "we" includes even the impartial spectator—wishing to reward or punish, to be grateful or resentful, because of the action's result. That is, we hold the actor responsible for his conduct, even those aspects that chance may entirely remove from his hands. So pervasive is this connection that the actor himself feels it. The law, too, operates in this manner to a great extent: an involuntary homicide is still a homicide, and attempted crimes are not treated as accomplished ones (*TMS*, II.3.ii).

Smith explains this irregularity by recourse to nature, with respect to humankind's happiness and perfection. Attempts to delve into the minds of others result only in the inquisitorial law; the judgment of intention belongs only to "the great Judge of hearts." The usefulness of this irregularity is undeniable: people are spurred to better themselves and others in an effort to demonstrate their virtue and goodwill. The happiness of our fellow human beings through our mediation becomes a sign of virtue, and because they are judged by results, people are impelled to vindicate themselves even when they have unintentionally caused harm (*TMS*, II.iii.2).

Smith insists that intention accounts for the entirety of the possession of morality and that intention is confined to the initial sentiment preceding the action. As a result, he is required to exonerate the tendency to judge by results and to insist on the need for such exoneration. In addition, he is forced to admit that the general good is achieved not by a virtuous intention but by chance and an irregularity in the natural human sentiments. No one can accuse Smith of propounding a utilitarian morality. But it remains to be seen whether we can fathom the intention that underlies these unusual results.

The first two parts of *The Theory of Moral Sentiments*—on propriety, or the virtue of the sentiments, and on merit, or the reward of actions—concern judgment of the virtue of others. The virtues are not so much described as they are deduced from the sentiments that Smith says cause us to approve them. But the difficulties raised by the irregular sentiments' interference in the operation of both propriety and merit, and the need to introduce the impartial spectator into the judgment of merit, signal that the discussion of one's own actions cannot be postponed. In part III, then, Smith reflects on the basis of judging our own sentiments and conduct and explores the source of our sense of duty.

With regard to how accurately we judge our own conduct, Smith inserts a barrier of self-preoccupation that seems to preclude any objective judgment and thus shut out the possibility of self-improvement and hinder the sense of duty. "We can never survey our own sentiments and motives, we can never form any judgement concerning them; unless we remove ourselves, as it were, from our own natural station, and endeavour to view them as at a certain distance from us" (*TMS*, III.i.2). But through a seeming inversion of the usual depiction of the natural course of the moral virtues, Smith describes self-judgment as dependent on the opinion of others. "We either approve or disapprove of our own conduct, according as we feel that, when we place ourselves in the situation of another man, and view it, as it were, with his eyes and from his situation, we either can or cannot entirely enter into and sympathise with the sentiments and motives which influenced it" (III.i.2).

Thus Smith uses our inability to judge ourselves to deduce the need for others. The morality of one's own conduct, then, depends decisively on getting outside oneself. Like most of Smith's arrangements, this occurs almost automatically. Underlying this idea of putting oneself in another's place, however, are stronger and more autonomous passions: the desire for praise and for praiseworthiness.

If Smith had stopped here, his theory would have been open to the objection that it delineates a morality based on honor or the desire for honor, which not only makes goodness dependent on something external to the actor but also makes it dependent, to a certain extent, on a fundamental lack of self-knowledge. But there is an *internal* tribunal that oversees the honors others bestow on us or even the honors we believe others would bestow. That tribunal is, of course, the impartial spectator, the conscience. Moreover, conscience is the source of the generosity and nobility that make us benevolent toward others.[16]

True to the requirements of this benign but stern standard, Smith admits it is not the province of every individual. The mechanics of comparison and approbation, which work so well when we judge others and discern the appropriate standard with respect to their actions and rewards, do not operate so automatically on our own behalf: the path to achieving clarity about ourselves is circuitous.

> This self-deceit [in judging our own actions], this fatal weakness of mankind, is the source of half the disorders of human life.... Nature, however, has not left this weakness, which is of so much importance, altogether without a remedy; nor has she abandoned us entirely to the delusions of self-love. Our continual observations upon the conduct of others insensibly lead us to form to ourselves certain general rules concerning what is fit and proper either to be done or to be avoided.... We do not originally approve or condemn particular actions, because, upon examination, they appear to be agreeable or inconsistent with a certain general rule. The general rule, on the contrary, is formed by finding from experience that all actions of a certain kind, or circumstanced in a certain manner, are approved or disapproved of. (*TMS*, III.iv.6–8)

General rules seem at first to obviate the need for the impartial spectator. But they change character on further investigation, when it becomes clear that general rules substitute for the lack of an internal spectator capable of making precise judgments on each occasion. General rules are the calculating or reasoned substitute for the correct emotional response to a given set of circumstances. Perhaps not surprisingly, it transpires that the general rules have been devised by someone other than the one who needs them most (*TMS*, III.iv, III.v).

As Smith admits, the operation of "the sentiment upon the propriety of which we found our approbation of [the conduct of others]" is not so effective in terms of our own actions. Its fortification, however, comes from God and nature, which reward—in heaven and on earth—the conduct the impartial spectator ought to commend. Nature is the intermediary, evoking sentiments of God by drawing on natural hopes and fears (perhaps especially fears) and opening our hearts to the thought of divine punishment and reward. Nature itself punishes or rewards the neglect or fulfillment of our duties, and this is beneficial: "the works of Nature ... seem all intended to promote happiness, and to guard against misery" (*TMS*, III.v.7). The irregularities that immediately spring to mind in this case are not truly irregularities, as Smith explains.

The just man unjustly accused is exonerated by his lifelong conduct. We may want the industrious knave to be confounded and the indolent but decent citizen to prosper, but we are wishing against nature and its regular consequences. The industrious knave will naturally be rewarded by prosperity but punished for his knavery, perhaps by his conscience or perhaps by the ostracism of his neighbors. By not prospering, the indolent but decent man may be encouraged to be a bit more diligent, but he will no doubt be succored by his appreciative neighbors. The neighbors' actions demonstrate that "man is by Nature directed to correct, in some measure, that distribution of things which she herself would otherwise have made" by precisely meting out reward or punishment. Even when people are powerless to redress the excesses of nature's strict justice, a benefit ensues: they are reminded of one who is mighty enough to counteract the ordinances of nature, even though the correction may take place in a "future state." Moreover, the assurance of God as the fortification of nature strengthens the entire moral edifice. When "our regard to the will of the Deity [is] the supreme rule of our conduct . . . the sense of propriety is . . . well supported by the strongest motives of self-interest" (III.v).

By the end of part III, "On Duty," the suggested bases for judging and directing the morality of our own actions—the impartial spectator as conscience, nature's sanctions, and religion's threats and promises—have become so tenuous as to require immediate shoring up. The impartial spectator is too infrequent a visitor to the hearts of humankind, the sanctions of nature do not seem designed to inculcate rules of morality, and "false notions of religion are almost the only cause which can occasion any very gross perversion of our natural sentiments," where we believe we are doing right but in fact are doing wrong.

Smith's next section is devoted to a discussion of utility. He emphasizes that utility is a false standard because we mistake contrivance for convenience. Much of what we seek in the name of utility is just the illusion of utility given off by ingenious, orderly, or great objects. To base a moral or political system on utility, then, is to base it on opinion rather than human nature. Smith even raises the possibility that there is no utility outside opinion. This makes plausible a morality based on passion and self-interest but not subject to deterioration into the expedient or the instrumental. It is then necessary only to show that self-interest depends on the opinions of others, which he argues later in part V.

Our delusion about the usefulness of material objects is nevertheless a useful delusion. It is in fact the usefulness of the system of capitalism. Smith at this juncture explains the benefits arising from the irregularity of the objects of approbation he spoke of in connection with propriety. The chimera of utility is another aberration by which nature has provided a benefit that humankind might not have enjoyed by the operation of more regular sentiments.

> We are ... charmed with the beauty of that accommodation which reigns in the palaces and economy of the great.... If we consider the real satisfaction which all these things are capable of affording, by itself and separated from the beauty of that arrangement which is fitted to promote it, it will always appear in the highest degree contemptible and trifling....
>
> And it is well that nature imposes upon us in this manner. It is this deception which rouses and keeps in continual motion the industry of mankind ... to cultivate the ground, to build houses, to found cities and commonwealths, and to invent and improve all the sciences and arts, which ennoble and embellish human life.... The earth, by these labors of mankind, has been obliged to redouble her natural fertility, and to maintain a greater multitude of inhabitants. It is to no purpose that the proud and unfeeling landlord views his extensive fields, and without a thought for the wants of his brethren, in imagination consumes himself the whole harvest that grows upon them.... The rich only select from the heap what is most precious and agreeable. They consume little more than the poor; and in spite of their natural selfishness and rapacity, though they mean only their own conveniency, though the sole end which they propose from the labors of all the thousands who they employ be the gratification of their own vain and insatiable desires, they divide with the poor the produce of all their improvements. They are led by an invisible hand to make nearly the same distribution of the necessaries of life which would have been made had the earth been divided into equal portions among all its inhabitants; and thus, without intending it, without knowing it, advance the interest of the society, and afford means to the multiplication of the species. (*TMS*, IV.i.9–10)[17]

Like the pursuit of wealth, the pursuit of rank offers oblique benefits. The degree of beauty of character lies in the extent to which that character promotes the happiness of the individual or society. The end of government is also the well-being of the governed. Yet those who aim at rule are likely to do so from a desire for glory or admiration. Moreover, instead of possessing complete virtue, the "splendid characters of history" who are revered are marked by an excess of self-admiration; they have been guided not so much by the intention to promote the happiness of society as by the desire for public esteem and rank. Yet the result has been public betterment deserving of esteem. As with prosperity, both the doer and the benefited are led to their own good by mistaken passions or objects of passion. Even those in government who intend to work for the good of society look not so much toward the humane outcomes of their actions as toward the "beautiful and orderly system"—for example, the perfection of police or the extension of trade and manufacture they will facilitate. Yet what surer way to bring about humane objectives?[18] Utility, then, is not virtuous, but it accords with virtue, almost in spite of itself. One cannot deny that virtue and the promotion of happiness seem to be concentric circles.

Smith moves to a discussion of the virtues in part VI, "Of the Character of Virtue." It is natural to admire the virtues, but is it because their practice, whether by ourselves or others, has agreeable consequences? According to Smith, this is only accidental, or secondary. Consider the things we most admire. What could be less useful than mathematics? Yet it stands among the greatest and most admired faculties. Part VI is divided into three sections: one on the connection between an individual's morality and happiness, one on an individual's morality in relation to the happiness of others, and a concluding section on self-command. The subject of the first section is prudence, and that of the second is beneficence and justice. Self-command seems to be a substitute for the petty and utilitarian character of private prudence.

The virtue conducive to one's own happiness is divided into two parts. Private prudence, though regular, orderly, and respected, is neither endearing, ennobling, nor admired. The second kind of prudence is broader in scope, akin to public-spiritedness (*TMS*, VI.ii).

Any postponement of the attainment of present goods for the sake of future ones appears profitless to others; yet our self-command in declining the immediate pleasures is admired. Furthermore, the usefulness of the deferment is apparently not sufficient to cause the actor himself to choose it; he acts rather on the thought that his action will be praiseworthy. This type of virtue is prudence (*TMS*, IV.ii).

Emphasizing self-command is a way to bolster the respectable virtues, which tend to be eroded by advances in civilization (*TMS*, I.i.5). The objects of the amiable virtues, the pleasures, are also erosive (VI.i.7). One might therefore conclude that the desire for ease constitutes the driving force of civilization (V.i, VI.iii; cf. I.i.5).[19]

In the middle section, beneficence and justice are, not surprisingly, connected to Smith's morality. As he prepares to emphasize the true grounds of morality, his discussion turns to the distinction between self-preservation and morality. The former is, as one might expect, the first "object which nature recommends to the case of every individual." But self-preservation is not the direct impetus to morality. Even this primary desire seems to lead to "perhaps the strongest of all our desires," the desire to be respected for one's external fortune (*TMS*, VI.i).

Yet self-preservation plays a role in morality and in sociality. Self-preservation requires care, which begins with the self, since "every man is certainly, in every respect, fitter and abler to take care of himself than of any other person." This is true because his own sensations are real, while those of others are only imagined (*TMS*, VI.ii).[20]

Care proceeds from self to family. Family affection depends on "habitual sympathy," so it must be sustained by continued proximity. Smith thus finds a boarding-school education destructive of family ties. He prefers domestic education, which is "the institution of nature," over education that is "the contrivance of man." After the family, our nearest attachments are friends. Smith discusses friendship using the threefold distinction of Aristotle, who distinguishes friendships of utility, of pleasure, and of the good. But unlike Aristotle, Smith believes that friendships based on virtue can be numerous. Friendships of virtue "may safely embrace all the wise and virtuous with whom we have been long and intimately acquainted. . . . They who would confine friendship to two persons, seem to confound the wise security of friendship with the jealousy and folly of love" (*TMS*, VI.ii.1.19). If Aristotle's restrictions on friendship are meant to have political ends, perhaps Smith is also making a political declaration. For Aristotle, virtue is philosophical contemplation; for Smith, virtue is sympathy. The former is solitary; the latter, as we have seen, is social (VI.ii.1).[21]

Almost all our attachments in society have the character of beneficial irregularities. We have strong respect for the great and powerful and compassion for the poor and wretched. The degree of passion corresponds, however, to the needs of society. The place and order of society depend more on the great and powerful and on the sentiments of approbation they elicit than on the poor—or on our admiration, if it exists, for the virtuous and wise. In addition to the ambition to which this preference gives rise, consensus on the identity of the great and powerful is easier to achieve than consensus on the identity of the virtuous and wise. Government rests on more stable foundations, and any confusion or even faction that might arise from disagreement among those supporting the wise is avoided (*TMS*, VI.ii.1).

As we seek to promote our own good over that of others but succeed in promoting their good as well, so benefit is derived from our preference for our own country over humanity in general. This attachment mistakenly makes our passions value our own country's success in war more than another nation's success in commerce, engineering, or the arts—"the real improvements of the world." Once again, however, the result of this misapplied affection turns out to be good: it leads to the stability of nations, without which there could be no progress. Moreover, patriotism is in harmony with the possible extent of an individual's abilities and understanding. If the attachment became too widespread, either the affection or the application of the individual's energy might be lost.[22] Even the factious division of society into groups has a valuable effect. Each person's strong affection for his own group allows all groups to maintain the strength necessary to establish a healthy balance among them. Civil stability depends on such a balance (*TMS*, VI.ii.2).

A final irregularity in the moral sentiments causes us to approve what succeeds and condemn what fails solely on the basis of that success or failure. The benefit of this disorder is to entice the many to submit to the inevitable. Their admiration teaches them "to acquiesce with less reluctance under that government which an irresistible force imposes upon them, and from which no reluctance could deliver them." The good of civil society is derived in large part from the irregularity in the sentiments of humankind (*TMS*, VI.ii.2).

We have proceeded, in considering beneficence and justice, from the individual to the family and society. Smith now introduces the question of universal benevolence. Beneficence is perhaps limited to our own country: our good deeds seldom have the energy to extend beyond its borders. Goodwill, in contrast, can be universal.

> This universal benevolence, how noble and generous soever, can be the source of no solid happiness to any man who is not thoroughly convinced that all the inhabitants of the universe, the meanest as well as the greatest, are under the immediate care and protection of that great, benevolent, and all-wise Being, who directs all the movements of nature, and who is determined, by his own unalterable perfections, to maintain in it at all times the greatest possible quality of happiness. (*TMS*, VI.2.iii)

This belief in a divine, benevolent Being allows people to accept their misfortunes and the troubles of their families or countries as necessary for the universal good. The generosity of spirit that arises from this acceptance leads to universal benevolence, which wishes the happiness of every innocent and sensible being. Furthermore, an individual becomes more useful to others to the extent his faith is strong. The administration and contemplation of "the universal happiness of all rational and sensible beings, is the business of God, and not of man." Notwithstanding his place and his limits, a man can use his energies where they are most beneficial, for he knows that "the most sublime speculation of the contemplative philosopher can scarce compensate the neglect of the smallest active duty." His social, moral, and intellectual aspirations will all be in harmony because his passions will be inclined toward his duty (*TMS*, VI.iii.3).

CONCLUSION

Smith's moral theory is rooted in propriety, or the suitability of the passions to their objects. He thereby allies himself with the theories of Plato, Aristotle, and Zeno—that is, with the ancients. Yet his theory diverges sufficiently from the ancient ones he admires to obviate Smith's characterization as a proponent of the ancient philosophical tradition. He parts company with Plato and Aristotle on the question of the measure of suitability. (He dismisses the modern moral systems of propriety on the grounds that they lack any measure of the proper.) "That precise and distinct measure can be found nowhere but in the sympathetic feelings of the impartial and well-informed spectator." Allowing the utmost latitude for the translocation of the impartial spectator into the Greek explanations, there is still a gap between Smith and the ancients on this standard. If we could grant, for example, that sympathetic feelings were the matrix in which Aristotle's standard of the mean in moral virtues were planted, we would still need some guidance to determine which sympathies were worthy of being followed. Smith gives an example and a resolution of the problem when he discusses civilized people's abhorrence of capital punishment, especially when the culprit has been reduced to impotence and shame by his capture. At that time, says Smith, the observer must think of the need to preserve society. This is a standard to which Smith frequently returns, though it is one of several. Simply stated, one can distinguish Smith's from the ancient morality by the fact that the former uses sentiments and the latter uses philosophy as the polestar of its moral man (*TMS*, VII.ii.1).

The shifting nature of opinion is apparently not a problem for Smith, although it seems to cause difficulties when he describes the relationship among the passions, actions, and sympathy in parts I and II. But we must remember that he later claims to be building his system on "perhaps the strongest of our desires"—the desire to be respected with regard to external fortune. This unusual assertion forces us to consider what caused Smith not only to give prominence to this desire but also to assign it a central place in his moral theory (*TMS*, VI.i).

The sentiment of gratitude arises, Smith explains, because of the esteem associated with the beneficent action. We are glad to be distinguished from the rest of humankind, to know that someone values us as we value ourselves. Gratitude and the acts arising from it are not connected to a desire for future benefits; rather, we want to continue to have the favorable opinion of another person (*TMS*, II.iii.1). The distinction we seek provides a clue to what underlies this desire for the esteem of others: when we are distinguished, the self is at the fore. Self-preservation is the primary force behind the concern with the sentiments and opinions of others.

Yet Smith cannot be considered the standard-bearer of the "classical republican" political lineage of self-interest properly understood without the addition of his social morality. Our primary care, Smith says, is for ourselves: we seek security, for we fear most of all a "fall," whether it be a decline in station or fortune or the cessation of life. The difference between this cardinal passion and Hobbes's, however, is that Smith believes this passion is engendered by an observation of *others*. Death, after all, is not an idea we can acquire from sensory experience—still less the distinction between death and violent death. Likewise, a fall is known by the experience of others and thereby leads to fear (*TMS*, VI.i).[23] But just as this passion depends on others for its origin, so too it depends on others for its assuagement. We attempt to prevent or mitigate a fall by seeking the good opinion or sympathy of others—even their love. In the quest not only to receive but also to merit others' good opinion or admiration, we hope to gain those qualities we imagine they admire. This is the source of the impartial spectator within us.

The desire for self-preservation leads to self-fortification with whatever tends to preserve, or appears to preserve, our physical being. It is for this reason that the desire to be respected with regard to external fortune is "perhaps the strongest of all our desires." Again, in the drive to merit this opinion—wishing to be both praiseworthy and praised (otherwise, our security is precarious)—we are impelled in two directions. We are filled with ambition for rank and wealth—an irregular passion that contributes to the good of many—and we seek to benefit others as a sign of our own power or well-being. It must be emphasized that the desire for the admiration or sympathy of others is not the object of any self-interested consideration: the element of calculative reasoning is absent from the first operations of the passions.

We see that "to feel much for others, and little for ourselves, . . . to restrain our selfish, and to indulge our benevolent affections constitutes the perfection of human nature" (*TMS*, I.i.5). Smith characterizes this feeling as the noble or public prudence that "necessarily supposes the *utmost* perfection of all the intellectual and of all the moral virtues" (VI.i.15). One might characterize this virtue as the perfectly balanced concern for oneself and for others. Because society as a whole profits from this mutual support of individual security, those who do not naturally discover its requirements are subject to the external laws of society, through fear of punishment, or the eternal laws of God, through fear of justice (VI.i, I.i.5).

Although Smith roots the virtues in the passions or in sentiment, and although that sentiment may ultimately be reduced to the desire for self-preservation, it is important to emphasize that for Smith, the virtues *are* virtues. They are not simply names given to actions that are useful to people and their preservation. Although they begin in the passions, the virtues transcend their origins by means of sociality, which is in reciprocal relation to the desire for self-preservation itself. Moreover, the irregularities that arise from the disjunction between virtue and self-preservation remain irregularities in Smith's view, despite the good that comes out of them. They do not become good because they happen to achieve good results, any more than an individual's intentions become moral because of the benefit his immoral actions might happen to bestow (*TMS*, VII.ii.1).[24]

The alliance of Smith's moral system with that of Plato and Aristotle and against that of Hobbes and Rousseau—or Tocqueville—is not a deception on Smith's part: the former systems share with Smith's "a measure of the proper" and "the esteem which seems due virtuous actions." Aristotle articulated the link between the moral virtues and the passions, and Plato implied it by connecting some virtues to the passionate parts of the soul in the *Republic*. Smith's distinction between propriety, which is within the reach of every individual and has the capacity to be approved, and virtue, which is the province of a few and to be admired, echoes the ancient belief that the major ethical and political qualities are those that human beings do not share equally (*TMS*, VII.ii.4, VII.ii.1).

But when Smith speaks of the closeness of the systems of propriety and utility, we see how far he really is from Plato and Aristotle. "The only difference between [the system of utility] and that which I have been endeavoring to establish, is, that it makes utility, and not sympathy, or the correspondent affection of the spectator, the natural and original measure of this proper degree" (*TMS*, VII.ii.3). Smith explains the irregularities in propriety by reference to utility, and there is little doubt that all the irregularities of Smith's system represent the requirements of self-preservation over morality. The "regularities," the natural judgments of the impartial spectator, represent morality as well as a kind of reason (VII.ii.4).[25]

Aristotelian virtue is rooted in the passions, in the sense that the passions are the battleground in the struggle between soul and body, between virtue and vice. Through reason, however, the true order of the passions is discovered, and through habituation, the individual changes the disposition of his own passions—whether their former order was natural or due to chance circumstances—in accordance with their true rank. The passions must move so that the good is stable. For Smith, however, stability must be found in the sentiments: the appropriateness of the passions is determined by the passions themselves. It is apparent that Smith was trying to find room in the modern order for the ancient virtues, without rescinding any of modernity's fundamental presuppositions. What Smith calls the irregularities of his system indicate how uneasy his accommodation was.

As a modern, Smith accepts self-preservation as fundamental. It follows that human beings are not by nature social. Yet human beings live in society, and their morality must be social. Therefore, he develops a morality that makes the individual social within himself: Smith provides another standard for determining and judging morality besides the circular standard of self-interest. Moreover, Smith's standard of sympathy necessitates drawing society into morality and thus overcoming, to a large extent, the isolation of "self-interest properly understood." His insistence that sympathy entails becoming the other person as well as placing the impartial spectator within oneself reinforces the social aspect of his morality. The individual is thus *in himself* a social being.

Smith's thought was fundamental to the way the nineteenth century worked its fashions of economic liberalism, economic determinism, and historicism. For Smith, the possibility of universal human benevolence depended on the belief in a great, benevolent, all-wise Being directing all nature to the greatest possible quantity of happiness. When the warp of Smith's thought was woven with the woof of Rousseau's account of the accidental progress of humankind (the disasters of each era giving rise to a new epoch),[26] the great Being directing the whole was called History. History stood outside of humankind but was nevertheless moved by human passions.

Acting in and on this world, History did not require the worship of God or a belief in the afterworld: this world was sufficient to correct its own defects. The "care of the universal happiness of all rational and sensible beings" was no longer "the business of God, and not of man" (*TMS*, VI.ii.3). It was necessary only to harness the passions that moved History, and humankind might be the author of its own good. Smith harnessed those passions through the capitalism of *The Wealth of Nations* and through the impartial spectator of *The Theory of Moral Sentiments*, each acting as an invisible hand.

NOTES

1. Ralph Lerner, "Commerce and Character: The Anglo-American as New-Model Man," *William and Mary Quarterly* 36, 1 (January 1979): 3–26.

2. Quoted in Lerner, 26.

3. Adam Smith, *An Inquiry into the Nature and Causes of the Wealth of Nations* (1776), ed. Edwin Cannan (Chicago: University of Chicago Press, 1976), I.iv.477.

4. Alexis de Tocqueville, *Democracy in America*, trans. and ed. Harvey C. Mansfield and Delta Winthrop (Chicago: University of Chicago Press, 2000), 201. Here, the phrase is translated "self-interest well understood."

5. Adam Smith, *The Theory of Moral Sentiments* (1759), ed. D. D. Raphael and A. L. Macfie (Indianapolis: Liberty Fund Classics, 1982), VII.iii.1; hereafter cited parenthetically in text as *TMS*. It is important to note that *The Theory of Moral Sentiments* was written before *The Wealth of Nations*.

6. Ryan Patrick Hanley, *Our Great Purpose: Adam Smith on Living a Better Life* (Princeton, NJ: Princeton University Press, 2019), 40–43. Hanley's succinct account provides the clearest and most helpful overview of Smith's *The Theory of Moral Sentiments*.

7. This is probably the most often quoted phrase from *The Theory of Moral Sentiments*.

8. This division into parts reflects the difference between *The Wealth of Nations* and *The Theory of Moral Sentiments* while at the same time indicating their connection.

9. Joseph Cropsey, *Polity and Economy: With Further Thoughts on the Principles of Adam Smith* (South Bend, IN: St. Augustine's Press, 2001), 13–17.

10. Thomas Hobbes, *Leviathan* (New York: Collier Books, 1962), chap. 13, 99, 101; chap. 14, 103; chap. 12, 198, 212–215; chap. 27, 217.

11. This is both the basis for and the fundamental problem of liberalism.

12. Hobbes, too, recognizes intention, but his emphasis is on action or, one might say, on the more traditional combination of intention and the ability to foresee results. *Leviathan*, chap. 27, 216–217.

13. Lerner, "Commerce and Character," 6.

14. See Leo Strauss, *Natural Right and History* (Chicago: University of Chicago Press, 1953), 173–175.

15. Note that in the second judgment, it is not the *actual* effect but the *intended* effect that predominates. The distinction between intention and result is essential to the morality of Smith's system.

16. Conscience is the principle that illuminates the point where Smith most disagrees with Hobbes's moral teaching, for conscience allows us to distinguish between petty prudence and magnanimous prudence—a distinction that Hobbes's axioms of simple preservation do not seem to admit. *TMS*, III.ii, III.iii; Hobbes, *Leviathan*, chap. 8, 62–62; chap. 4, 46; chap. 5, 50–52; *TMS*, VI.i.

17. Smith thus foresees his discussion in *The Wealth of Nations*; he cannot, therefore, see them as incompatible.

18. Cf. *TMS*, III.vi and IV.i. Consider James I of Great Britain, who, according to Smith, was very humane but very ineffective.

19. See Hanley, *Our Great Purpose*, 49ff.

20. Cf. Cropsey, *Polity and Economy*, 12.

21. Cf. Joseph Cropsey, "Justice and Friendship in the *Nicomachean Ethics*," in *Political Philosophy and the Issues of Politics* (Chicago: University of Chicago Press, 1977), 272–273.

22. Lerner states that the commercial republic will erode these patriotic qualities unless they are taught to citizens. "Commerce and Character," 21, 26.

23. That a fall is known by the experience of others is proved by the fear of it. Smith shows that happiness does not depend on station and that people have the same amount of happiness at all levels. If a fall were known by our own experience, we would have obtained this knowledge.

24. Cf. the benefits of commerce.

25. See Joseph Cropsey, "Capitalist Liberalism," in *Political Philosophy and the Issues of Politics* (Chicago: University of Chicago Press, 1977), 62; Hobbes, *Leviathan*, chap. 14.

26. Jean-Jacques Rousseau, *Discourse on the Origins and Foundations of Inequality* (*Second Discourse*), in *The First and Second Discourses*, trans. Roger D. Masters and Judith R. Masters (New York: St. Martin's Press, 1964).

CHAPTER 4

Adam Smith, Alexis de Tocqueville, and American Greatness

Ryan Patrick Hanley

Among America's greatest paradoxes is our love—indeed, our worship—of both equality and greatness. For evidence of our democracy's fascination with human greatness we need look no further than the nation's front lawn. At the middle of the National Mall stands a monument to the father of our country—a monument that, at the time it was built, was the tallest structure in the world. To its west sits a monument to the savior of our democracy, housed in a Doric temple larger than the Parthenon. And to its east, the building in which our representatives assemble is crowned by a pediment adorned with a frieze titled "Apotheosis of Democracy."

How can we make sense of this distinctly American and seemingly paradoxical reverence for both equality and greatness? For guides, we might do well to look back to two of the foremost students of equality and greatness and America. One, Adam Smith, published his masterwork in 1776, while privy to the inner machinations of those in charge of managing the colonial crisis. The other, Alexis de Tocqueville, visited America just over half a century later, in time to witness the new democratic revolution of Jacksonianism.[1] Taken together, they offer a remarkably insightful study of the concept of American greatness.

To grasp this requires us to see both Smith and Tocqueville in new lights, allowing them to speak for themselves. There are, of course, many ways to put the two together. As scholars have long recognized, the latter was indebted to the former's understanding of certain economic phenomena, especially the mechanisms of the division of labor and the consequences of primogeniture and entails.[2] So too they are bound together by a certain shared sensibility, a sobriety that enabled them to assess with clear eyes the many trade-offs made in the course of the development of our society.[3] In his last work, Tocqueville tells us this was his aim all along: to show us both "what we have lost in this immense transformation of everything, and what we have gained."[4] Smith sought to do much the same, painting his vision of commercial society warts and all, insistent that we see its benefits and its costs alike.

Yet there is another tie that binds Smith and Tocqueville. It concerns their understanding of greatness and, in particular, their understanding of how the idea of greatness was transformed by the advent of the democratic age. Specifically, they saw that the traditional love of greatness characteristic of ancient and aristocratic orders was too strong to be extinguished in a moment—even by such powerful forces as commercialization and democratization. Far from extirpating the love of greatness from American hearts, commercialization and democratization redefined it in ways that prompted aspirants to greatness to seek new expressions of it and new paths to its realization. In particular, it is the ways in which the old love of greatness received new expressions in a wholly new world that they invite us to consider, such that we might be better able to determine whether our reverence for both equality and greatness is likely to lead "to servitude or freedom, to enlightenment or barbarism, to prosperity or misery."[5]

ADAM SMITH

Adam Smith is not often thought of today as a champion of human greatness. One influential scholarly treatment set the terms for much of what followed by emphasizing "Smith's rejection of the virtues of the great" and describing his battleground as "the field whereon honor was defeated."[6] In the popular imagination, Smith tends to be regarded as the advocate of the bourgeois, an individual more focused on his income than his excellence. Smith thus remains one of the first and most eloquent articulators of what Tocqueville later and famously calls self-interest rightly understood.

We are surely right to see Smith this way. At the same time, this is only half the story. Smith offers us an important window into the full story in his portrait of the "prudent man." The prudent man is the pinnacle of bourgeois virtue, an individual of quintessential honesty, industry, and frugality. Yet Smith also clearly sees his limits. Although this consummately commercial individual, so resolutely and thoroughly dedicated to the pursuit of his own self-interests, "commands a certain cold esteem," Smith insists that he can never command "very ardent love or admiration." The prudent man necessarily strikes us as limited—even petty—and when we set his virtues next to those "of the great general, of the great statesman, of the great legislator," his "inferior prudence" seems to pale before the "superior prudence" of great men in war and politics.[7]

Elsewhere Smith gives us some examples of the sort of great men he has in mind. In a remarkable paragraph dedicated to enumerating the qualities that lead to "great success in the world" and "great authority over the sentiments and opinions of mankind," he names Alexander, Caesar, and Socrates as exemplars (*TMS*, 6.3.28). To be sure, his study of the greatness of these three men is hardly unqualified (to say the least) and deserves careful attention. But for our purposes, what matters most is that they are all ancient examples. This is in keeping with his general approach in *The Theory of Moral Sentiments*: when Smith presents examples of greatness, he tends to draw from the records of antiquity (see, e.g., *TMS*, 1.3.1.13, 7.2.1.29–30). Smith offers relatively few examples of modern greatness, with his striking encomium to the Duke of Marlborough perhaps the most prominent exception (6.3.28).

From all this it is tempting to conclude that Smith saw greatness as the property of a bygone age. But in fact Smith sees glimmers of greatness even in his own age, and in some of the most unexpected places. Foremost among these is America. That he looked to America rather than Britain for examples of greatness is striking by itself. Even more striking is where in America he found these examples. Smith discovered greatness in each of what Tocqueville would later call, in the title of one of his most striking chapters, "the three races that inhabit the territory of the United States" (*DA*, 302).[8]

In each of these three American races Smith finds a greatness that puts Europeans to shame. Celebrating their "heroic and unconquerable firmness" in the face of danger and death, Smith holds up the Native Americans as the revivification of Sparta in the forests of America, exemplars of a noble "magnanimity and self-command" that lie "almost beyond the conception of Europeans" (*TMS*, 5.2.9–10). So too the Africans brought in shackles to America's shores, who exhibit "the same contempt of death and torture" that distinguishes the Native Americans. They too in their excellence far eclipse the Europeans. Indeed, in one of the most arresting passages in his entire corpus, Smith proclaims:

> There is not a negro from the coast of Africa who does not, in this respect, possess a degree of magnanimity which the soul of his sordid master is too often scarce

capable of conceiving. Fortune never exerted more cruelly her empire over mankind, than when she subjected those nations of heroes to the refuse of the jails of Europe, to wretches who possess the virtues neither of the countries which they come from, nor of those which they go to, and whose levity, brutality, and baseness, expose them to the contempt of the vanquished. (*TMS*, 5.2.9)

The lesson is clear: the true claimants to magnanimity are not the ostensibly civilized Europeans but the cruelly subjected Africans.[9]

As for the third race, Smith finds a greatness more akin to that of the other two American races than to the Europeans. Indeed, at the height of the revolutionary fervor, Smith saw in the leaders of the colonial resistance a greatness not only comparable to the greatness of the other two American races but also reminiscent of the legislators and statesmen celebrated in *The Theory of Moral Sentiments*. Smith shows us this greatness by providing a masterful psychological account of the politician's motives. What drives the politician, we are told, is pride: "Men desire to have some share in the management of public affairs chiefly on account of the importance which it gives them."[10] The colonial leaders' desire to gain and keep their sense of self-importance, Smith claims, in part explains the American Revolution. To assume that the Revolution was merely a war waged by self-interested men who resented taxes on their paper and their tea misses the mark. The truth is that the colonists took their denial of a voice in Parliament as an affront to their pride; thus, Smith explains, it was their "desire to preserve their own importance" that led them to reject the indignity of taxation without representation or consent and ultimately, "like other ambitious and high-spirited men," to "draw the sword in defense of their own importance" (*WN*, 4.7.c.74).

Smith clearly recognized the threat this affronted sense of self-importance posed to the British Empire, and in *The Wealth of Nations* and elsewhere he sought to lay out a route whereby it might be most effectively managed to mitigate its destabilizing effects. One of his key proposals concerned offering the colonists the opportunity to represent themselves in Parliament directly. Doing so, he argued, would give the high-spirited colonists a "new method of acquiring importance" and "a new and more dazzling object of ambition" as they competed directly for the "great prizes" of British politics rather than "piddling for the little prizes" of colonial politics. Needless to say, the government did not act on his suggestion.[11] Meanwhile, Smith sought to call attention to the character of the men working to chart the course of the emerging

American democracy, and in their representative bodies he clearly saw the seeds of a new greatness not yet known in Europe:

> The persons who now govern the resolutions of that they call their continental congress, feel in themselves at this moment a degree of importance, which, perhaps, the greatest subjects in Europe scarce feel. From shopkeepers, tradesmen, and attorneys, they are become statesmen and legislators, and are employed in contriving a new form of government for an extensive empire, which, they flatter themselves, will become, and which, indeed, seems very likely to become, one of the greatest and most formidable that ever was in the world. Five hundred people, perhaps, who in different ways act immediately under the continental congress; and five hundred thousand, perhaps, who act under those five hundred, all feel in the same manner a proportionable rise in their own importance. Almost every individual of the governing party in America, fills, at present in his own fancy, a station superior, not only to what he had ever filled before, but to what he had ever expected to fill; and unless some new object of ambition is presented either to him or to his leaders, if he has the ordinary spirit of a man, he will die in defense of that station. (*WN*, 4.7.c.75)

Smith's presentation of this new greatness of the shopkeeper-cum-statesman is striking in itself. But perhaps even more striking in his account of the likely effects of this greatness on others. In his portrait of the Continental Congress, Smith invites us to imagine a trickle-down of virtue, with the noble examples of half a thousand legislator-shopkeepers filtering down to inspire half a million citizens beneath them.

This is, of course, a portrait tinged with more than a little optimism. But elsewhere Smith is less optimistic, especially when he considers the likely moral and political effects of commercialization itself. His claims on this front, though increasingly familiar to specialists today owing to a number of recent studies, deserve the attention of students of American greatness in particular.[12] As we have seen, in pointedly emphasizing that America's leading statesmen began their careers as men of commerce, Smith reminds us of the degree to which America is fundamentally a commercial nation. And in calling our attention to the potential threats to the commercial republic, Smith sets forth a lesson that demands the attention of citizens of such a republic.

Smith's lesson begins with his assessment of the effects of commercialization on the men on its front lines: not the shopkeepers but the makers of the goods in which the shopkeepers deal. It is a story that begins in the first book of *The Wealth of Nations*. There, Smith shows how divided specialized labor—embodied by the famous image of the pin factory—made possible the remarkable increase in productivity that ultimately led to the generation of what Smith calls "universal opulence." In the third book, he shows how divided specialized labor broke the bonds of feudal dependence and generated real freedom in the word's modern sense. But in the fifth book, Smith allows the other shoe to drop. There, he suggests that the same process that created both modern opulence and modern freedom is also to blame for the moral corruption and consequent political instability characteristic of commercial society.

Smith launches this argument with a claim about specialized labor that was of great interest to Tocqueville. "In the progress of the division of labor," he explains, "the employment of the greater part of those who live by labor, that is, of the great body of the people, comes to be confined to a few very simple operations; frequently to one or two." As he continues, he shows that this specialization, which is obviously beneficial for production, is just as obviously detrimental to the human being. Insofar as "the understandings of the greater part of men are necessarily formed by their ordinary employments," one engaged in repetitive acts that leave him "no occasion to exert his understanding, or to exercise his invention," must necessarily lose "the habit of such exertion." As a result, he "generally becomes as stupid and ignorant as it is possible for a human creature to become" (*WN*, 5.1.f.50; cf. *DA*, 387).[13]

This is tragic for a number of reasons. Not least among them, and most important for this study, is that this stupidity renders men unable to fulfill even the most basic duties of citizenship. Among these duties Smith includes military service, noting that the repetitive labor of the worker's ordinary employment typically renders him "incapable of defending his country in war." Smith is clearly worried by this corruption of the capacity to develop the "martial virtues." It not only precludes those who have been corrupted in this way from pursuing one of the traditional paths to greatness but also, by rendering men unfit to defend themselves or their country, leaves the nation precariously susceptible to its foreign enemies. At the same time, foreign enemies and martial virtues are only half the story here. Smith insists that the stultifying repetition that leads to stupidity imperils not only the martial virtues but also, and arguably more importantly, all the "intellectual" and "social" virtues. In this vein, Smith explains that one who has been stripped of the intellectual and social virtues by the process of production is ultimately "incapable of relishing or bearing a part in any rational conversation" or "conceiving any generous, noble, or tender sentiment." And perhaps most tragic of all, "of the great and extensive interests of his country, he is altogether incapable of judging" (*WN*, 5.1.f.50).

When Smith refers to the corruption of the intellectual virtues, his concern is not a lack of capacity for philosophy. His concern is more immediate and more political: corruption of the intellectual virtues is primarily a corruption of the capacity for political judgment, in two senses. First and foremost, Smith sees that stupidity renders men incapable of both rational discussion and sensible deliberation about the national interest, an untenable prospect in an electoral democracy. Second and more worrisome, he shows that stupidity not only incapacitates citizens' ability to judge political arguments but also corrupts their capacity to judge political characters, especially the characters of those who seek to claim the mantle of greatness.

In this respect, commercialization exacerbates certain destabilizing tendencies that Smith takes to be part of human nature. Indeed, one of the core claims of *The Theory of Moral Sentiments* is that human beings have always and everywhere been susceptible to worship of "the rich and the great," often at the expense of the more proper admiration of the wise and the virtuous (*TMS*, 1.3.3.7). In noting this basic fact, Smith takes pains to emphasize its benefits, showing that admiration of the wealthy is a useful stimulant to men's natural desire to better their conditions by pursuing the objects of self-interest. But he also regards "this disposition to admire, and almost to worship, the rich and the powerful" as the "great and most universal cause of the corruption of our moral sentiments" (1.3.3.1). Men dazzled by wealth and celebrity, he explains, are often seduced into giving "some degree of favorable regard" even to "the greatest criminals" (6.3.6). Further, the eyes of men seem to be drawn to those most ready and willing to trample accepted norms of propriety; even as their ambitions are pursued in ways "contrary to every principle of justice, and carried on without any regard to humanity," such figures often elicit "a certain sort of esteem," despite being "very worthless characters" (6.3.8).

In *The Theory of Moral Sentiments*, Smith states as a simple fact that "the great mob of mankind" tends to act in its natural capacity as the "admirers and worshippers" of wealth and greatness (*TMS*, 1.3.3.2). *The Wealth of Nations* adds an account of the implications of this worship in an age shaped by the dual forces of commercialization and democratization. For now, Smith presents us with the possible fate of a society in which the aspirants to greatness appear before a people who are not merely naturally prone to admire greatness (as Smith thinks all people are) but also suffer from "the gross ignorance and stupidity which, in a civilized society, seem so frequently to benumb the understandings of all the inferior ranks of people"—those deprived of "the proper use of the intellectual faculties of a man" and left "mutilated and deformed." In Smith's view, it is precisely these people who are most susceptible to the "delusions" that "frequently occasion the most dreadful disorders" in "ignorant nations." And here again, it is ignorance that matters. Whereas an educated nation is "more disposed to examine, and more capable of seeing through, the interested complaints of faction and sedition" and, "upon that account, less apt to be misled into any wanton or unnecessary opposition to the measures of government," the opposite is found in a benumbed people (*WN*, 5.1.f.61). Deprived of the capacity to accurately judge those who stand before them, they are uniquely susceptible to individuals whose "excessive presumption, founded upon their own excessive self-admiration, dazzles the multitude, and often imposes even upon those who are much superior to the multitude." Smith himself marvels at "the frequent, and often wonderful success" of men he does not hesitate to label "ignorant quacks and imposters," and he is struck by "how easily the multitude are imposed upon by the most extravagant and groundless pretensions" (*TMS*, 6.3.27). Ultimately, what most worries him is the penchant of the imposter, long accustomed to feeling the eyes of the people upon him and emboldened by the prospect of success, to transgress accepted limits in pursuit of his objectives:

> The ambitious man flatters himself that, in the splendid situation to which he advances, he will still have so many means of commanding the respect and admiration of mankind, and will be enabled to act with such superior propriety and grace, that the lustre of his future conduct will entirely cover, or efface, the foulness of the steps by which he arrived at that elevation. In many governments the candidates for the highest office are above the law; and, if they can attain the object of their ambition, they have no fear of being called to account for the means by which they acquired it. They often endeavor, therefore, not only by fraud and falsehood, the ordinary and vulgar arts of intrigue and cabal; but sometimes by the perpetration of the most enormous crimes, by murder and assassination, by rebellion and civil war, to supplant and destroy those who oppose or stand in the way of their greatness.[14] (*TMS*, 1.3.3.8)

There is "greatness," and there is greatness. One of Smith's primary aims is to teach us how to distinguish what the "undiscerning eye" too often misses so that we can clearly see the difference between ruthless expediency and genuine nobility.

ALEXIS DE TOCQUEVILLE

Adam Smith deserves to be considered a student of greatness, even if he is not often regarded as such today. Alexis de Tocqueville, in contrast, has long been recognized as a student of greatness. Among the most familiar aspects of his thought is his study of the greatness of the aristocracy, a social order distinguished by "a certain pride of heart, a natural confidence in its strength, a habit of being respected," together constituting a set of "manly mores" (AR, 173). Similarly familiar are his views on how the egalitarianism of the emerging democratic ethos challenges traditional claims to greatness and "tends to elevate the small to the rank of the great," even as the small seek to "draw the strong to their level" (DA, 52).[15] All this is part and parcel of the Tocqueville we have come to know: the Tocqueville of trade-offs, who seeks to both warn us and console us that although our future is likely to hold "less brilliance," it is also likely to hold "less misery" (DA, 9), who recognizes and reminds us that what is best from the perspective of justice is not necessarily best from the perspective of grandeur.[16]

Yet Tocqueville recognized a limit to this trade-off. Its hope for success rested on the belief that men would be satisfied with the trappings of the new well-being offered by democracy and commerce—or at least sufficiently satisfied to believe that the benefits of this new well-being outweighed its costs. But Tocqueville himself recognized that there was more to this process. At the core of the human being is a longing for something more than social equality and material comfort—a longing that humans did not create and that is unlikely to be bought off with anything they could create: "Man did not give himself the taste for the infinite and the love of what is immortal. These sublime instincts are not born of a caprice of his will; they have their immoveable foundations in his nature; they exist despite his efforts. He can hinder them, but not destroy them. The soul has its needs that must be satisfied" (DA, 510).[17] Put simply: "the aspiration to greatness and admiration of it are in human nature."[18] But this raises a challenge, especially for the question on which we are focused. If the soul indeed has tastes and instincts and "needs" for goods beyond those that democracy and commerce can offer, the advent of the age of democracy and commerce seems unlikely to end our longing for the great and the infinite. Instead, if Tocqueville is right about the needs of the soul, we should expect these longings to persist even in the age that precludes all traditional avenues toward their satisfaction. The challenge for the student of democratic greatness is to understand what new expression the ineradicable love of greatness is likely to take amidst these new conditions.

For insight into these new forms, Tocqueville looked to America. In so doing, he saw that even as the Americans distanced themselves from older conceptions of greatness, they hardly abandoned greatness altogether. Put in his own terms, what he found in America was not the abandonment of but an alternative to "the old aristocratic honor of Europe"—"what in our day we would call American honor" (*DA*, 593). And his efforts to define this new American honor led him, like Smith, to consider each of the "three races" (302). Yet unlike Smith, he finds few traces of greatness in the enslaved Africans; "plunged into this abyss of evils," they were so cruelly mistreated that Tocqueville sees only a precious few traces of "the general features of humanity" (304, 328). The Native Americans are a different story, however. Their lives still exhibit "emotion and greatness" (317), and in explicating their greatness, Tocqueville follows Smith in celebrating the fortitude and self-command that enabled them "to live without needs, to suffer without complaining, to die singing" (25). Indeed, if there is any difference at all in Smith's and Tocqueville's studies of the Native Americans, it is that Smith presents them as the reincarnation of the ancient Spartan, while Tocqueville presents them as the reincarnation of the medieval feudal lord: caring only for hunting, war, and his own self-worth, the Indian in his woods "nourishes the same ideas, the same opinions as the noble of the Middle Ages in his fortified castle" (314).

The Native Americans thus have a greatness, yet it is very much the old greatness. For evidence of the new greatness characteristic of "American honor," Tocqueville looks to the third of the three races, where he finds at least two different dispositions. "The American of the South," we learn, "loves greatness, luxury, glory, noise, pleasures, above all, idleness." That idleness was, of course, facilitated by the institution of slavery, which absolved the southerner of having "to make efforts in order to live," even as it encouraged his penchant for "domestic dictatorship" (*DA*, 360). And ultimately, this southerner who scorns work, "has the tastes of idle men," and "passionately loves hunting and war" shares much with both Native Americans and feudal aristocrats—parallels that Tocqueville underscores by telling us the southerner has all "the tastes, prejudices, weaknesses, and greatness of all aristocracies" (333, 361).

As a result, it is not in the southerner but in the northerner that Tocqueville finds an exemplar of the new American greatness. In the northerner, Tocqueville sees not only the opposite of the southerner—always active, never idle—but also the apotheosis of the drive most characteristic of democracy. "The taste for well-being forms the salient and indelible feature of democratic ages," Tocqueville tells us, and in the northerner he finds a sort of perfection of this drive to such a degree that he regards it as a kind of heroism (*DA*, 422). In summing up his argument, he notes that he "cannot express [his] thought better than by saying that the Americans put a sort of heroism into their manner of doing commerce" (387). And in his extended treatment of this phenomenon, he explains why it deserves to be called heroism. The American of the north

> has placed in material well-being the principal goal of his existence; and as the country that he inhabits presents inexhaustible resources to his industry and offers ever renewed enticements to his activity, his ardor for acquiring has surpassed the ordinary bounds of human cupidity: tormented by the desire for wealth, one sees him enter boldly onto all the paths that fortune opens to him: he becomes indiscriminately a sailor, a pioneer, a manufacturer, a farmer, supporting the work or dangers attached to these different professions with equal constancy; there is something marvelous in the resources of his genius and a sort of heroism in his greed for gain. (*DA*, 333)

The northerner turns an ordinary vice into an extraordinary virtue, transforming what is in others petty greed into the stuff of geniuses or heroes.[19] Tocqueville's twice-repeated claim that this constitutes "a sort of heroism" underscores the degree to which he understood this type of heroism to be distinct from conventional forms of heroism, but heroism nonetheless. In so doing he goes even further than Smith. Smith too praised the economic and ethical benefits of the prudent pursuit of self-interest, but at the end of the day, he felt compelled to judge this disposition "inferior" to that which characterizes the genuinely great. In contrast, Tocqueville finds in these commercial men not an inferior but an alternative form of greatness.

Tocqueville appreciates what was at stake in this shift from one sort of greatness to another. Several times he even suggests that these greatnesses cannot coexist; elsewhere in *Democracy in America* we are told that in pursuing material goods, "one loses sight of the more precious goods that make the glory and greatness of the human species" (*DA*, 509), and in *Ancien Régime* we are told that the "kind of passion for material well-being which is the mother of servitude" is one that perhaps "allows honesty" but "forbids heroism" (*AR*, 178). Tocqueville thus cannot be accused of being unaware of the tension in these two visions of greatness. Yet his focus, by and large, is on the new vision, and his aim is to show how it is likely to shape moral and political life in the days to come. And in so doing, he shows that this new form of heroism or greatness, born of the commercial impulse and fostered by democracy, necessarily encourages two other penchants: a heightened love of military greatness, and a heightened concern for national greatness.

In suggesting that democratic greatness leads to military greatness, Tocqueville has a specific idea in mind. But it is not the simple idea that democracies are susceptible to succumbing to military men; among the many things Tocqueville thinks we ought to be wary of in democratic greatness, the tyranny of the strongman does not rank high. In fact, Tocqueville's experience in Jacksonian America led him to see Andrew Jackson himself as more pathetic than fearsome.[20] Further, he thinks the many commentators who portray Jackson as a threat to the republic miss the mark. In America, Tocqueville "heard it said that General Jackson has won battles, that he is an energetic man, brought on by character and habit to the use of force, desirous of power and a despot by taste." All that may be true, he grants, "but the consequences that have been drawn from these truths are great errors." To think that Jackson, or any man, could become an American Napoleon is to misunderstand both the nation and the moment: "In America, the time for undertakings like this and the century of such men have not yet come." It is also to misunderstand Jackson himself; however gigantic he might seem, Jackson is just "the agent of provincial jealousies" who only "prospers by flattering these passions daily." Herein lies the deepest irony: for all his efforts to project strength, "General Jackson is the slave of the majority: he follows it in his wishes, its desires, its half-uncovered instincts, or rather he divines it and runs to place himself at its head" (*DA*, 377). If Jackson has any talent at all, it is an ability to discern and harness the people's unspoken predilections. And armed with them, he rides "roughshod over his personal enemies everywhere he finds them" and "even comes to treat the national representatives with a sort of almost insulting disdain" (378). Still, Jackson could not carry off a coup, and ultimately he is just the latest instantiation of a certain type of man who arises "from time to time in democratic societies": one of those "enterprising and ambitious citizens whose immense desires cannot be satisfied by following the common route," who "love revolutions and call for them" but are incapable of pulling them off "if extraordinary events do not come to their aid" (609–610).[21]

Tocqueville, then, is not Plato; he makes no attempt in *Democracy in America* to recast on American soil the drama of the degeneration of democracy into tyranny. And this hardly comes as a surprise; after all, Tocqueville famously sought to define a new science of politics for a wholly new age, and his analysis of the new heroism and greatness of this new age was shaped by his appreciation of the forces unique to the modern world. Chief among these, of course, is commercialization, and commerce largely explains why democratic greatness tends toward military greatness. In part, this is merely a matter of practical necessity; wealthy nations need to take measures to protect their gains, and "reason indicates and experience proves that there is no lasting commercial greatness if it cannot unite in case of need with military power" (*DA*, 390).

But Tocqueville has another—indeed, counterintuitive—reason for regarding military greatness as a necessary analogue of commercialization. It is counterintuitive because Tocqueville famously and frequently argues that the driving force of commerce is self-interest, and comfortable and efficient satisfaction of this interest is the fundamental aim of commercial man. On the face of things, this ruling passion would seem to lead men away from the battlefield, not toward it. Yet insofar as "men of democracies naturally have a passionate desire to acquire quickly the goods that they covet and enjoy them easily," this desire leads them to rush headlong into crisis and conflict. It is for this reason, we are told, that "there is no greatness that satisfies the imagination of a democratic people more than military greatness—brilliant and sudden greatness obtained without work, by risking only one's life" (*DA*, 629). Thus, like ancient warriors and modern Indians, the new American thinks it is glorious to seek death on the battlefield, albeit for very different reasons. The American welcomes death in war for the same reason he speculates in markets or plays the lottery: the hope of striking it rich with the smallest amount of effort. Thus, it is not a love of the noble or a habit of courage that leads the modern lover of greatness to long for or even to invent crises that allow him to do battle with perceived enemies; rather, it is a shallowness that prefers quick victories to hard-won nobility.

In addition to tending toward military greatness, democratic greatness tends toward national greatness. Here again, the issue seems paradoxical on its face but is deeply rooted in Tocqueville's core principles. At the heart of his inquiry into the animating forces of democratization lies his famous focus on the paradox of individualism: democracy encourages the individual to become increasingly absorbed with his own individual interests at the same time that it highlights his relative unimportance and the relative unimportance of all other individuals qua individuals. "When the man who lives in democratic countries," Tocqueville explains, "compares himself individually to all those who surround him, he feels with pride that he is the equal of each of them; but when he comes to view the sum of those like him and places himself at the side of this great body, he is immediately overwhelmed by his own insignificance and his weakness" (*DA*, 409). In this lies the core of his account of how love of equality compromises genuine individuality. But this concept also has implications for democratic greatness. Put simply, the democrat longs for greatness, but his commitment to equality and his consciousness of the smallness of individuals forbid him from admiring other individuals.

How can this tension be resolved? According to Tocqueville, the democrat does so by turning his eyes from what is small to what is large. "Habitually occupied in contemplating a very small object"—namely, "himself"—a democrat who wishes to "raise his eyes higher" must be "drawn out of himself." To this end, he "always expects that he is going to be offered some enormous object to look at, and it is only at this price that he consents to tear himself away from the small, complicated cares that agitate and charm his life" (*DA*, 464). And, Tocqueville insists, democrats tend to look at one specific enormous object:

> In democratic peoples, individuals are very weak; but the state, which represents all and which holds all in its hand, is very strong. Nowhere do citizens appear smaller than in a democratic nation. Nowhere else does the nation itself seem greater, nor does the mind more readily make a vast picture of it. In democratic societies the imagination of men contracts when they consider themselves; it extends indefinitely when they think of the state. (*DA*, 443)

Thus, in the search for greatness, the democrat looks to the nation rather than to the individual. With the greatness of statesmen or legislators or lawgivers obscured, the democratic search for greatness can culminate only in a reverence for national greatness.

In suggesting that democrats are better able to see the big than the small, Tocqueville takes a page from Plato. He takes another in describing the likely source of their sights. Democrats, he tells us, look not to statesmen or philosophers for their vision and inspiration; instead, they "demand from their poets conceptions so vast and depictions so excessive." For their part, democracy's poets stand ready and willing to give the people everything they want: "they constantly swell the imaginations, and as they extend them beyond measure, they make them reach the gigantic, for which they often forsake the great" (*DA*, 464). This is the tragedy wrought by the poets of national greatness. Led by an imagination with "no limits" that "stretches and enlarges itself beyond measure," democrats aspire to apprehend greatness with a faculty whose reach exceeds its grasp (460). The upshot is that they necessarily mistake the merely gigantic for the genuinely great.

Tocqueville knows that the horizons of the political world shaped by the love of military greatness and national greatness are necessarily different from those shaped by a traditional love of greatness. Indeed, it may well be his consciousness of the need to satisfy these modern penchants that ultimately explains his support of operations in Algeria that he notoriously suggested would stand as "a great monument to our country's glory on the African coast."[22] Similarly, his consciousness of the need to gratify such penchants may be what led him to articulate a new vision of domestic party politics that could realize this new modern greatness without allowing the agonism at its heart to become politically or socially destabilizing.[23] At the very least, Tocqueville, much like Smith, foresaw the potential danger in the new forms of greatness sought by the new men of democracy.

CONCLUSION

Both Smith and Tocqueville, for all their deep appreciation of the past, were future-oriented men. Better than most others in their respective ages, they understood the degree to which society's future was likely to be different from its past, and they aimed to teach the men of the present how best to live in the world of today and tomorrow. This meant helping them develop the concepts they needed to navigate their world, including the concept of greatness. Tocqueville frequently called "all those who are interested in the future of democratic societies" to work together to spread in these societies "a taste for the infinite, a sentiment of greatness, and a love of immaterial pleasures" (*DA*, 519; cf. *DA*, 670). Even today, there are those who hearken to his call.[24] But he also insisted that the greatness needed by the modern world must be both good and fitting. "We ought not to strain to make ourselves like our fathers," Tocqueville counsels, "but strive to attain the kind of greatness and happiness that is proper to us" (675).[25]

The challenge lies in the fact that both Tocqueville and Smith realized that the kind of greatness longed for, admired, and sought by men of the new democratic age was not always good or fitting. Smith worried that the democratic age's love of greatness was likely to lead to demagoguery and found consolation in the hope that these new demagogues would come and go but leave the essential institutions of society relatively intact. Smith thus invites us to imagine a moment after the man of "excessive self-estimation and presumption" has been defeated, a moment when the eyes of the people will be opened again and "things change their colours and their names"—the moment when "what was before heroic magnanimity resumes its proper appellation of extravagant rashness and folly; and the blackness of that avidity and injustice, which was before hid under the splendor of prosperity, comes into full view" (*TMS*, 6.3.30). At this moment, the nation can start to move forward again, leaving the "discarded" politician to ruminate over his "former greatness" and obsess over "some vain project to recover it" (1.3.2.7). Like Plato's tyrant, the discarded demagogue is left largely alone: he "suspects his best friends," he "rewards their services, not only with ingratitude, but with cruelty and injustice," and he is ultimately left with only "flatterers and traitors" for company (6.3.32).

Tocqueville sees a different possible future. In his view, the issue is not demagoguery but a revolution to which the demagogue is merely epiphenomenal. Early in 1848 he asked his fellow members of the Chamber of Deputies to recognize the extent to which "disorder has penetrated far into men's minds":

> Do you not see that their passions have changed from political to social? Do you not see that opinions and ideas are gradually spreading among them that tend not simply to the overthrow of such-and-such laws, such-and-such a minister, or even such-and-such a government, but rather to the overthrow of society, breaking down the bases on which it now rests? Do you not hear what is being said every day among them? Do you not hear them constantly repeating that all the people above them are incapable and unworthy to rule them?[26]

Tocqueville knew, and hoped to convince others, where this might lead: "Do you not realize that when such opinions take root and spread, sinking deeply into the masses, they must sooner or later (I do not know when, I do not know how) bring in their train the most terrifying of revolutions?" (*R*, 13). Not six months later, he would be present at the storming of the Constituent Assembly—an attempt to interrupt the ordinary transition of power by contesting electoral results. It was one of those "riots," he tells us, in which "the ludicrous was mingled with the terrible" (*R*, 120). And in fact, this was a riot plain and simple—a revolution without greatness. Whereas the Revolution of 1789 was one "of generosity, of enthusiasm, of virility, and of greatness" (*AR*, 244), "there was absolutely no grandeur in this one for there was no touch of truth about it" (*R*, 53). Smith and Tocqueville alike remind us there can be no greatness without truth.

NOTES

1. My understanding of Tocqueville's thought has benefited greatly from the salutary reminder by Marvin Meyers that "Tocqueville's classic commentary on American democracy has been consulted by historians for every purpose but the simplest: as a key to the immediate subject of the work, Jacksonian America." Marvin Meyers, *The Jacksonian Persuasion: Politics & Belief* (Stanford, CA: Stanford University Press, 1957), 33.

2. See, e.g., Jimena Hurtado, "Adam Smith and Alexis de Tocqueville on the Division of Labour," *European Journal of the History of Economic Thought* 26 (2019): 1187–1211; Ryan Hanley, "Tocqueville and the Philosophy of the Enlightenment," in *The Cambridge Companion to Democracy in America*, ed. Richard Boyd (Cambridge: Cambridge University Press, 2022), 62–63.

3. See especially Ralph Lerner, "Commerce and Character: The Anglo-American as New-Model Man," *William and Mary Quarterly* 36 (1979): 21f.

4. Alexis de Tocqueville, *The Old Regime and the Revolution*, ed. François Furet and Françoise Mélonio, trans. Alan S. Kahan (Chicago: University of Chicago Press, 1998), 86; hereafter cited in text as *AR* (*Ancien* Régime).

5. Alexis de Tocqueville, *Democracy in America*, ed. and trans. Harvey C. Mansfield and Delba Winthrop (Chicago: University of Chicago Press, 2000), 676; hereafter cited in text as *DA*.

6. Joseph Cropsey, *Polity and Economy* (South Bend, IN: St. Augustine's Press, 2001), 47. Cf. Eric Schliesser, "The Obituary of a Vain Philosopher: Adam Smith's Reflections on Hume's *Life*," *Hume Studies* 29 (2003): 327–362; Andrew Corsa, "Modern Greatness of Soul in Hume and Smith," *Ergo* 2 (2015): 27–58. I address Smith's understanding of the virtue of magnanimity at greater length in *Adam Smith and the Character of Virtue* (Cambridge:

Cambridge University Press, 2009), 132–174, and "Magnanimity and Modernity: Greatness of Soul and Greatness of Mind in the Enlightenment," in *The Measure of Greatness: Philosophers on Magnanimity*, ed. Sophia Vasalou (Oxford: Oxford University Press, 2019).

7. Adam Smith, *The Theory of Moral Sentiments*, ed. D. D. Raphael and A. L. Macfie (Indianapolis: Liberty Fund, 1982), 6.1.14–15; hereafter cited in text as *TMS*.

8. See Ralph Lerner, "The Complexion of Tocqueville's American," in *The Thinking Revolutionary: Principle and Practice in the New Republic* (Ithaca, NY: Cornell University Press, 1987), 174–191.

9. Cf. Eric Schliesser, *Adam Smith: Systematic Philosopher and Public Thinker* (Oxford: Oxford University Press, 2017), 164–169.

10. Adam Smith, *An Inquiry into the Nature and Causes of the Wealth of Nations*, 2 vols., ed. R. H. Campbell and A. S. Skinner (Indianapolis: Liberty Fund, 1981), 4.7.c.74; hereafter cited in text as *WN*.

11. See Lerner, "Commerce and Character," 18–19.

12. Important treatments of Smith's concerns about commercial corruption include Charles L. Griswold Jr., *Adam Smith and the Virtues of Enlightenment* (Cambridge: Cambridge University Press, 1999), 262–266; Lauren Brubaker, "Adam Smith on Natural Liberty and Moral Corruption: The Wisdom of Nature and Folly of Legislators?" in *Enlightening Revolutions: Essays in Honor of Ralph Lerner*, ed. Sveotzar Minkov (Lanham, MD: Lexington Books, 2006), 194–201. I examine this theme more fully in *Adam Smith and the Character of Virtue*, 15–52.

13. See Lerner, "Commerce and Character," 22. On Tocqueville's adoption of Smith's argument here, see Hurtado, "Smith and Tocqueville on the Division of Labour," 1190, 1195–1196.

14. See Lerner, "Commerce and Character," 15–16.

15. For Tocqueville's understanding of the challenges democracy poses to ancient and aristocratic greatness, see Paul Franco, "Tocqueville and Nietzsche on the Problem of Greatness in Democracy," *Review of Politics* 76 (2014): 442–449.

16. See Pierre Manent, "Tocqueville, Political Philosopher," in *The Cambridge Companion to Tocqueville*, ed. Cheryl Welch (Cambridge: Cambridge University Press, 2006), 117–119.

17. On this passage and the centrality of needs of the soul to Tocqueville's political thought more generally, see Jean Yarbrough, "Tocqueville on the Needs of the Soul," *Perspectives on Political Science* 47 (2018): 126f.

18. Harvey Mansfield, *Tocqueville: A Very Short Introduction* (Oxford: Oxford University Press, 2010), 113.

19. See Lerner, "Commerce and Character," 10; Lerner, "Complexion of Tocqueville's American," 184.

20. Tocqueville's largely dismissive portrait of Jackson deserves comparison to his "complex and ambivalent" relationship to Bonaparte and Bonapartism. See Richard Boyd, "Tocqueville and the Napoleonic Legend," in *Tocqueville and the Frontiers of Democracy*, ed. Ewa Atanassow and Richard Boyd (Cambridge: Cambridge University Press, 2013), 264–288; quote at 273.

21. Cf. Peter Lawler: "Maybe we can say that—in *Democracy in America*—Tocqueville underestimated—but didn't completely neglect (2, 3, 19)—the monstrous forms the longing of particular men for greatness would take against a world in which they believed they had no place." Peter Lawler, "Tocqueville on Greatness and Justice," in *Magnanimity and Statesmanship*, ed. Carson Holloway (Lanham, MD: Lexington Books, 2008), 103.

22. Alexis de Tocqueville, *Writings on Empire and Slavery*, ed. and trans. Jennifer Pitts (Baltimore: Johns Hopkins, 2006), 24. This and other statements of Tocqueville's have long been taken as evidence of his support for colonialism. See, e.g., Jennifer Pitts, "Empire and Democracy: Tocqueville and the Algeria Question," *Journal of Political Philosophy* 8 (2000): 295–318. For critical responses, see Delba Winthrop, review of *Writings on Empire and Slavery*, *Society* 40 (2002): 110–113; Eva Atanassow, "Colonization and Democracy: Tocqueville Reconsidered," *American Political Science Review* 111 (2017): 83–96. In this context, see also Boyd, "Tocqueville and the Napoleonic Legend," 275, 280–281; Franco, "Tocqueville and Nietzsche," 452; Mansfield, *Tocqueville*, 111–112.

23. For an impressively well-developed discussion of this point, see Gianna Englert, "Tocqueville's Politics of Grandeur," *Political Theory* 50 (2022): 477–503.

24. See Robert Faulkner, *The Case for Greatness: Honorable Ambition and Its Critics* (New Haven, CT: Yale University Press, 2007), 12f.

25. See Lerner, "Commerce and Character," 26.

26. Alexis de Tocqueville, *Recollections*, ed. J. P. Mayer and A. P. Kerr (New Brunswick, NJ: Transaction, 2009), 13; hereafter cited in text as *R*.

CHAPTER 5

"The Masterpiece of Policy of Our Century": Rousseau's Response to the Enlightenment

Clifford Orwin

My task in the present volume is to respond to Ralph Lerner's seminal essay on the Enlightenment, "Commerce and Character," by expounding Jean-Jacques Rousseau's volcanic critique of the "enlightened" position on the relation between commerce and character.[1] Admittedly, this position must remain something of an abstraction. As Lerner himself stressed in his essay, the Enlightenment was a big tent that covered a wide range of views, some of them inevitably contradictory. On the question of the pacifying tendencies of commerce, for example, no less a figure than Alexander Hamilton would prove an outlier. (Of course, describing him as such implies the existence of a consensus from which he demurred.) In the pages that follow, I simplify the consideration of the Enlightenment by following Lerner in hewing to that consensus.

This first difficulty is one that would dog anyone who writes about the Enlightenment or any similarly diffuse movement. A second difficulty is particular to anyone writing about Rousseau's relationship to the Enlightenment. That relationship proved to be a two-way street. As Rousseau responded to the Enlightenment, it too responded to him. Considered as a global movement, the Enlightenment long predated Rousseau, so its founding thinkers and the generations that followed were his predecessors. Some Enlighteners who were his contemporaries, however, especially his younger contemporaries, were intensely aware of his critique. Some undertook to refute it, but minds of the caliber of Adam Smith and Immanuel Kant, as well as other thinkers of distinction, sought to achieve a synthesis between the Enlightenment and the insights of its most penetrating critic.[2] In so doing they greatly enriched the thought of the movement's later stages.

Lerner does not discuss Kant or the post-Rousseauian German Enlightenment or any thinkers later than the American founders, with the sole but major exception of Alexis de Tocqueville. Nor, in any case, is the Enlightenment's reception of Rousseau his concern. His themes are the Enlightenment consensus that emerged prior to Rousseau and influenced the American founders, and Tocqueville as an interpreter of their achievement. This being the case, his neglect of Rousseau in no way detracts from his accomplishment. In what follows, I too limit myself to Rousseau's response to the Enlightenment, leaving it to others (including the scholars already cited) to track its response to him. My task is to explain why, despite its allure (the power of which he amply acknowledged), the movement left Rousseau not only cold but also extremely heated.

ROUSSEAU'S TARGET: THE ENLIGHTENMENT CONSENSUS

What, then, was the Enlightenment consensus from which Rousseau so conspicuously dissented? Lerner begins by stating it as follows:

> A case [for commerce and commercial man] had to be made, and then won. The advocates—men as diverse as Montesquieu and John Adams, Adam Smith and Benjamin Franklin, David Hume and Benjamin Rush—were united at least in this: they saw in commercial republicanism a more sensible and realizable alternative to earlier notions of civic virtue and a more just alternative to the theological-political regime that had so long ruled Europe and its colonial periphery. However much these advocates differed—in their philosophic insight, in their perception of the implications of their proposal for the organization of economic life, even in the degree of their acceptance of the very commercial republic they were promoting—for all this, they may be considered a band of brethren in arms.

No one would mistake Rousseau for one of these brethren in arms. Yet he may have seen fit if not to exaggerate his differences with the Enlightenment at least to mute the extent of his agreement with it. He too sought a more just alternative to the theological-political regime. He too promoted "a more sensible and realizable alternative to earlier notions of civic virtue," if that meant the notions promoted by the premodern philosophers both pagan and

Christian. Lerner suggests that "in many respects the commercial republic is best defined by what it rejects: restraints and preoccupations based on visions of perfection beyond the reach of all or most; disdain for the common, useful, and mundane; judgments founded more on an individual's inherited status than on acts and demonstrated qualities." Rousseau agreed with the Enlighteners on every one of these counts.

Why, then, did he emerge as such a formidable adversary of theirs? To answer this question, we must begin from a certain ambiguity in Enlightenment thought, to which Lerner's essay again serves as our guide. If the ultimate goal of the Enlightenment was the emancipation of both individuals and societies, there were crucial respects in which it appeared to be at odds with itself. It was on these ambiguities that Rousseau's critique of the movement focused.

Let us begin by viewing the project of Lerner's commercial republicans as he does: critically but sympathetically. So viewed, this project aimed to release humankind from the grievous bonds, both earthly and spiritual or imagined, that had shackled it under the ancien régime. These bonds had gravely restricted human liberty, including liberty of commerce, and therefore hindered the emergence of a culture of commerce, with its greater prosperity and other attendant benefits. We can use the term *culture of commerce* because the Enlighteners intended more than just economic exchange. As Pierre Manent writes, "[commerce] has, in the 18th C., a much broader sense than today: the term includes not only what we today call commerce, but much of what we call 'civilization' or 'culture,' in short everything that lends substance to the social bond independently of the command of the ruler."[3]

Commerce thus includes what we would describe as "civil society." In encouraging its spread, the Enlighteners aspired to promote a way of life free, in this broader sense, of the need to foster autonomous civil activity. Not only were they freeing commerce and all who participated in it from the dead hand of outworn strictures; they were also freeing human desires and thus human nature iself. In theory, the old regime had suppressed the desires of all by bidding them to lead a Christian life or one of austere aristocratic virtue. In practice, insisted the Enlighteners, it had merely restricted the gratification of desire to the small ruling class of the wealthy (including wealthy prelates).

What the old regime had granted to a few, the Enlightenment aspired to extend to all. The market, in its impersonality, catered to desires both small and great. This was the crucial respect in which it enhanced human freedom. Each would be free to satisfy his desires within his means.

But here, as Lerner admits, the Enlighteners acknowledged two asterisks. While arguing for the dismantling of outworn restraints on human freedom, they remained too realistic to suppose that men could live without any restraints at all. Laws would still be required, and the authorities to enforce them. The Enlighteners merely sought to reduce legal restraints to their necessary minimum. Laws so understood would no longer perpetuate entrenched inequalities.

Nor would the new commercial society rely less than previous ones on restraints of a more informal sort: the *moeurs* appropriate to a free and commercial people. This too was a theme common to the Enlighteners. The greatest apostle here was Montesquieu, and this was one of the most important lessons the American founders learned from him. A late flowering of this teaching is evident in Tocqueville's presentation of his Americans and all the social practices that enabled them to combine equality with freedom.

Last but not least, the new society would rely on the discipline imposed by the market itself.[4] The market, as the Enlighteners recognized, was ambiguous with regard to freedom. Yes, it expressed the sum of the voluntary decisions of all who participated in it and was, in principle, amenable to all legal desires. It excelled, moreover, in the efficiency with which it satisfied those desires. Still, it was a condition of their satisfaction that the desires learn to dance to the market's tune. In the new world defined by the supremacy of commerce, there would be no profiting from the desires of others and hence no amassing of the means of satisfying one's own desires except through submission to the market's dictates. Neither the buyer nor the seller, but the market itself, would determine the price at which the one would have to choose whether to buy and the other whether to sell. Thus the market would impose its salutary discipline on both producers and consumers. The inequalities that had defined feudalism would yield to equality before the impersonal state, on the one hand, and the impersonal market, on the other. Both institutions were understood to be emancipatory, as they freed individuals from personal dependence on their fellows. Each would generate, however, its own distinctive set of constraints.

It is in this duality of the political and the social that the ambiguity of the Enlightenment solution appears most clearly. The Enlighteners presented themselves as liberators, with liberty as their central political goal. Though not entirely misleading, this did not qualify as full disclosure. In fact, they aimed simultaneously to relax and tighten the bonds that united human beings. The state would see to the former task by guaranteeing the personal liberty of each. The market would see to the latter, linking humankind both within and among particular societies by a common dependence on commerce. From the point of view of the Enlighteners, these tasks and institutions were both fully complementary and equally indispensable. Thus Lerner characterizes the goal of commercial republicans as liberty, on the one hand, and novel forms of interdependence, on the other.

The Enlighteners, for their part, saw nothing paradoxical in this. Rather, the pacifying effects of commerce and the discipline imposed by the market would join the proposed political and legal reforms in reinforcing the prospects of political freedom. Yet there remained a tension between liberty and commerce that Rousseau proceeded to exploit. The core of liberty is independence, the primary distinction being between a free man and a slave. The silken ties of commerce, by contrast, though conceived as both impersonal and mutually beneficial, imply (and seek to deepen) reciprocal dependency. To this extent, the "economic" or "social" aspect of the Enlightenment was at odds with the "political" one.

Nor was this the only source of tension in the Enlightenment project. There was also the issue of inequality. In the political sphere, equality would prevail; such was the intention of the institution of representative government and the protection of basic rights for all. There was no plan, however, to install equality in the social realm. There, the market would prevail, and it would not banish (and might not even reduce) social inequality as such. At most, it could be expected to redistribute wealth (and therefore inequality) from older forms to newer ones. Under the old regime, disparities of wealth largely accompanied hereditary inequalities of power and status. Now, with the abolition or inanition of these inequalities, wealth would be generated primarily by commerce, with the market as its medium. While dire need would diminish—in this sense, commerce would be a rising tide that lifted all ships—inequality would remain and, given the anticipated vast increase in prosperity, might well increase.

The success of the Enlightenment thus required the two spheres—the political (equal) and the economic or social (unequal)—to exist side by side in a relation of mutual support, with neither compromising the other. Equal citizens must go equally about their unequal business.

Yet the Enlighteners themselves preached the priority of the economic and social, redefining politics as merely its guarantor and, in that sense, subservient to it. Their project thus inevitably raised the question of whether the notional equality of the political realm could withstand the actual inequality of the social one. Although it was the Enlighteners themselves who invented the primacy of the social, it was Rousseau who first grasped its full implications—which included a radical critique of the Enlightenment.

THE MOST ASTONISHING AND CRUELEST TRUTH

One of Rousseau's most trenchant refutations of the Enlightenment—as well as his most concise—occurred in a work that remains relatively obscure: the preface to the first published version of his comedy *Narcisse* (1753). The comedy itself was written much earlier (Rousseau claims he wrote it at age eighteen, in around 1730), but the preface expressed Rousseau's thinking in the year of its publication.[5] It figures in Rousseau's oeuvre between his polemics in defense of his first *Discourse* and his composition of the second one. Since *Narcisse* was a relic of Rousseau's adolescence, he might have had some explaining to do regardless of the circumstances of its publication. Due to his new status as the artist who objected to artists, however, there was much more at stake in the preface. By publishing *Narcisse*, this notorious critic of the arts was continuing to participate in them. He felt compelled to respond to this seeming incongruity, potentially so useful to his enemies.

In the preface to *Narcisse*, Rousseau counters this objection, but that is not our concern here. It is rather that as the work approaches its conclusion the argument takes a surprising turn. Having defended himself against the apparent consequences of the argument prosecuted in the first *Discourse* and the subsequent polemics, he now restates that argument. This would not be his last statement of it—it would also figure prominently in *Discourse on the Origins of Inequality*—but it is both the briefest and the most emphatic. The crucial passage is as follows:

> There is more, and of all the truths I have proposed for the consideration of the wise, this is the most astonishing and the cruelest. All our Writers regard as the masterpiece of the policy of our century the sciences, the arts, luxury, commerce, the laws, and the other bonds which, by tightening among men the ties of society from personal interest, put them all in mutual dependence, give them reciprocal needs and common interests, and oblige each of them to co-operate for the happiness of others in order to be able to attain his own. Doubtless these ideas are fine, and are presented in a favorable light. But in examining them attentively and impartially, one finds much that diminishes the advantages they seem at first to present.

> It is then quite a marvelous thing to have made it impossible for men to live among themselves without anticipating each other, supplanting each other, deceiving each other, betraying each other, mutually destroying each other! From now on we must take care never to let ourselves be seen as we are: since for two men whose interests agree, perhaps a hundred thousand may be opposed to them, and there is no other means to succeed than to deceive or ruin all these people. This is the deadly source of the acts of violence, betrayals, perfidies, and all the horrors necessarily demanded by a state of things in which each, pretending to work for the fortune and reputation of others, seeks only to raise his own above them and at their expense. (*CW*, 193; *OC*, II:968–969)

Also worth citing is a related footnote:

> I notice that there now reigns in the world a multitude of petty maxims that seduce the simple by a false appearance of philosophy and which, besides that, are very convenient for ending all disputes in an important and decisive tone without any need for examining the question. Such is this one: "everywhere men have the same passions, everywhere *amour-propre* and interest lead them, therefore everywhere they are the same." . . . A Savage is a man, and a European is a man. The semi-philosopher concludes immediately that one is not worth more than the other, but the philosopher says: in Europe, the government, the laws, the customs, interest, all put individuals in the necessity of deceiving each other, mutually and incessantly. . . . Among Savages personal interest speaks as loudly as among us, but it does not say the same things: love of society and the care for their common defense are the sole bonds that unite them. . . . Among them they have no discussions of interest to divide them, nothing carries them to deceive one another: public esteem is the only good to which each aspires, and which they all deserve. . . . I believe that one can make a very just estimation of men's morals by the amount of business they have among themselves: the more they engage in commerce together, the more they admire their talents and industry, the more they trick each other decently and adroitly, and the more they are worthy of contempt. I say this with regret; the good man is the one who does not need to deceive anyone, and the Savage is that man. (*CW*, 194n; *OC*, II:969n)

As Manent observes, interest, unlike need or passion, always supposes a particular social context.[6] It is therefore not prior to the circumstances of any given society but always largely its creature. Clearly, this was also the view of

Rousseau. Men act from self-interest, but society shapes that interest. Rousseau did not question the Enlightenment claim that an expansion of commerce would tighten the bonds uniting people by enlisting their private interests to this end. What he denied was that this strategy would be benign. Rather, the effect of harnessing competition as an agent of cooperation would be to debase the latter as mere camouflage for the former: "from now on we must take care never to let ourselves be seen as we are." Where all cooperation is merely tactical, it is shifting at best and downright spurious at worst.

Rousseau thus anticipated the impending leftist critique of the market that would loom so large in the century that followed and in the versions of it we hear today. True, he did not yet conceive those who fared worst in a market society as a proletariat or any other kind of redeeming social class. They were merely the poor, unredeemed and unredeeming, much as they had always been, victims and dependents of the rich and doomed to remain largely helpless before them. He did not romanticize the poor: as he would remark in *Emile*, "the people shows itself as it is, and it is not lovable."[7] Nor did he view commerce as promising the poor the brighter future Karl Marx and other socialists thought would be realized by a later stage of commerce: industrialization.

This critique of the market and of the battle of interests it fostered called into question another promise of the Enlightenment: political equality. By reducing the poor to tradesmen and laborers subject to the demands of the market, the commercialization of society effectively excluded them from active citizenship. Along with the largeness of commercial republics as the heirs of previously existing nation-states, economics dictated some form of representation as the vehicle of nominal political equality. This in turn offered the opportunity to refine the structure of government to prevent the ascendancy of any one faction (including the most popular one) over the others. An active but not encroaching executive, separation of powers, counterbalancing levels of government, and an expanded political role for the judiciary all depended on a republicanism of representation rather than one of direct participation. As the Enlighteners saw it, this new carefully calibrated republic promised to improve mightily on those of antiquity and the Middle Ages, with their tumultuous oscillations between anarchy and tyranny.

Rousseau, however, rejected any representation of the will of the sovereign (conceived as the will of the people as a whole, the principle of equality required no less). It is regarding this aspect of Rousseau's thought that we find the only mention of him in Lerner's essay. After sketching Tocqueville's dystopian vision of a possible democratic future in which the people, driven by their preoccupation with their private affairs, lapse willingly into living not as the masters of the state but as its wards, Lerner casts Rousseau as Tocqueville's predecessor in this worry: "It was in anticipation of this Tocquevillean nightmare that Rousseau inveighed against those who would rather hire a representative than spare the time to govern themselves, who would rather pay taxes than serve the community with their bodies. Absorbed in their ledgers and accounts, they stood to lose all. 'The word "finance,"' Rousseau wrote, 'is slave language; it has no place in the city's lexicon.'" As I find so often in returning to Lerner's writings, he states this better than I could. He deftly sketches Rousseau's critique of representation as appropriate to ersatz citizens only, content to govern themselves in appearance while submitting to others in reality. This is yet another reason for Rousseau's dismissal of the Enlightenment project of combining a market society with political equality as futile.

In *Discourse on Political Economy*, another work of his early maturity, Rousseau describes the sort of economy that he sees as consistent with a society ruled by the general will and governed by officials loyal to it. (Here, as elsewhere, Rousseau distinguishes sovereignty, whose sole legitimate expression is the general will emanating from the people as a whole, from government, the necessary functioning of an executive bound by that will.) *Discourse on Political Economy* is a fascinating work that contains, among other treasures, Rousseau's primary discussions of the crucial political topics of leadership and civic education. Its economic scheme, however, his alternative to the hegemony of the market, has found few admirers.[8] Agrarian rather than commercial or industrial, it eschews the continuous increase of wealth for which the Enlighteners had looked to commerce. It promotes a moderate prosperity appropriate to the life of citizens, one that satisfies their true needs but demands a salutary austerity. Rousseau was aware that, as with his other practical proposals, he was swimming upstream against a mighty torrent.

UNE CHOSE BIEN MERVEILLEUSE

Rousseau does not offer his critique of commerce in the preface of *Narcisse* as entirely novel. When he states that "of all the truths I have proposed for the consideration of the wise, this is the most astonishing and the cruelest," he clearly implies that he has presented it previously. In fact, his critique of the schemes of "our Writers" began two years earlier with *Discourse on the Sciences and the Arts* and continued in the polemical works that proliferated in its wake. It remained front and center in *Discourse on the Origins of Inequality*, which extended his critique of commerce to the earliest epoch of human society, declaiming against the division of labor and the reliance on the exchange of necessities with others. All these critiques, both prior and subsequent to the preface, stress the link between commerce, on the one hand, and personal dependency, inflamed *amour-propre*, and growing inequality, on the other. Each of these latter pathologies contributes to that favorite theme of Rousseau—the gulf between reality and appearance: the "strange and fatal disposition of things (*constitution*) in which wealth always facilitates the means of accumulating more, and in which it is impossible for those who have nothing to acquire something, in which the good man has no means of escaping from poverty, in which the greatest rogues are the most honored, and in which one must necessarily renounce virtue to become an honest man!" (*CW*, 194; *OC*, II:969). If the elements of Rousseau's critique of the projects of the philosophes (including commerce) are familiar to readers of the preface, his declaration that the truth of this critique is the most astonishing and cruelest truth is new. Characterizing it as such distinguishes this from his earlier declamations, dire as they were.

How can we account for this extraordinary emphasis on the philosophes? The answer is that their activity is, in a crucial sense, unique, which is to say uniquely harmful. Up to this point in the preface, Rousseau's argument has largely resumed that of *Discourse on the Sciences and the Arts*. He has described a phenomenon allegedly as old as recorded history: the ineluctable decline of any society that has taken up the arts and sciences. Only now does he turn to an evil that, unlike the preceding ones, is novel. This evil is not an aspect of the social situation per se but rather of the view that "all our Writers" take of it. The issue is no longer the unintended effects of cultivating the arts and sciences for their own sake or for the sake of the practitioner's vanity. Rather, it is the consequences of cultivating them precisely for their ulterior effects. The problem of the arts and sciences thus appears in a different light—as part of the novel and urgent problem posed by the Enlightenment.

What is this novel problem? It is that indicated by Rousseau's characterization of the litany of particular evils inflicted by the philosophes as *une chose bien merveilleuse*. Why *merveilleuse*? Why is Rousseau not satisfied with calling it *horrible* or the like? What is it about the Enlightenment, as Rousseau presents it, that partakes of the marvelous?

Note again that Rousseau's exposition of the Enlightenment focuses on the second major thread of the commercial republican project as Lerner presents it: not the liberation of humanity from the political bonds previously besetting it but the forging of new social and economic bonds to replace them. Also important is Rousseau's concession that these ideas of the Enlighteners are without a doubt (*sans doute*) fine or beautiful (*belles*), and the writers have succeeded in presenting them in a favorable light.

Rousseau thus admits that the case for commercial republicanism is a seductive one seductively presented. Is this tantamount to an implicit confession that he himself had formerly found it persuasive? (It was only at age thirty-eight that he experienced the "illumination of Vincennes," his sudden insight into both the injustices of society and the fundamental error of all previous analyses of these injustices.[9] At the time of this epiphany, he was a trusted collaborator of the Enlightenment, a close friend of Denis Diderot and a contributor to his *Encyclopédie*.)

It should not be surprising that Rousseau goes on to confirm that freeing oneself from the spell of these opinions is no easy matter. As he states in the preface, only by "examining them attentively and impartially [does one find much] that diminishes the advantages they seem at first to present." In exposing these arguments for the snares they are, Rousseau alleges, as he does so often elsewhere, a vast gap between appearance and reality. And he insists that he is the only man of his time who is capable of explaining it.

It is this gap that qualifies the Enlightenment as *une chose bien merveilleuse*. Marvelous is not the extent of the damage—here, Rousseau could have settled for *horrible*—but the obtuseness of those inflicting it. Rousseau portrays the agents of this sinister plot as themselves deceived by it; they are, as we would say today, in denial about it. In their expectations of Enlightenment, they genuinely mistake black for white and white for black. The first victims of this gulf between appearance and reality are therefore the Enlighteners themselves. Never before has any group of men done so much harm under the illusion that they were doing so much good. Rousseau, who is otherwise prone to present his adversaries in general and the philosophes in particular as actuated by malignant *amour-propre*, here seems willing to concede that their intentions are pure. Although applying their theories to society unleashes the *amour-propre* of others, he indicts the philosophes themselves for nothing but a misguided will to do good. They genuinely believe their scheme to be "the masterpiece of policy of our century."

The preface to *Narcisse* vividly expounds Rousseau's most trenchant critique of the Enlightenment. In precisely those respects in which it most confidently claimed to have liberated humankind it unwittingly deepened its servitude. The Enlightenment proved most repressive in the area in which it deemed itself most emancipatory: in teaching the peoples of Europe that their proper business was business. This was simultaneously the most difficult thing to grasp about the Enlightenment and the most necessary one. It was the fundamental paradox of the project of commercial republicanism because it was what qualified that project as *une chose bien merveilleuse*. Not the least stunning of Rousseau's innovations, and not the least prophetic of the rhetoric of the modern Left, was his casting of the entire project of the commercial republic as an exercise in false consciousness.

NOTES

It is both an honor and a pleasure to contribute to this volume of responses to Ralph Lerner's seminal essay "Commerce and Character." My acquaintance with Ralph goes back a long way, to the fall of 1965. The late Allan Bloom had invited him to teach for a year at Cornell University, where I was a sophomore. At Allan's urging I enrolled in Ralph's undergraduate seminar on *Democracy in America*, which has remained my model of how such a seminar should be led. Ralph displayed an uncanny ability to nudge us to see (and therefore to say) what a lesser teacher would have had to say himself. Rather than place his insights before us, he contrived for us to discover them for ourselves. This capacity was not only unique (none of us had witnessed it before) but inspiring. It encouraged us to think that someday we would be able to interpret masterpieces like *Democracy* on our own. In the decades since I have learned much both from Ralph's writings on the Enlightenment and the founding and from his lifelong engagement with medieval Jewish and Islamic thought. (Among his works, my own particular favorite is *Maimonides' Empire of Light: Popular Enlightenment in an Age of Belief* [Chicago: University of Chicago Press, 2000]). I have lived to see my son Alexander study with Ralph as a graduate student nearly fifty years after I did so as an undergraduate. Still, Ralph made his deepest impression on me during those long-ago days of the young Lerner and the still younger Orwin. As with all great teachers, there is no substitute for studying with him in person.

In the original French, the phrase quoted in the chapter title is "*le chef d'oeuvre de la politique du notre siècle.*" The expression *la politique* is ambiguous; it could be rendered as either "the politics" or "policy" (the definite article having gotten lost in translation). I have adopted the reading of Nannerl O. Keohane, "The Masterpiece of Policy in Our Century: Rousseau on the Morality of the Enlightenment," *Political Theory* 6, 4 (1978): 457–484.

1. All quotations from Lerner's essay are from Ralph Lerner, "Commerce and Character,"

in *The Thinking Revolutionary: Principle and Practice in the New Republic* (Ithaca, NY: Cornell University Press, 1987), 195–221.

2. On Smith and Rousseau, see Charles L. Griswold, *Jean-Jacques Rousseau and Adam Smith: A Philosophical Encounter* (London: Taylor & Francis, 2017); Ryan P. Hanley, "Commerce and Corruption: Rousseau's Diagnosis and Adam Smith's Cure," *European Journal of Political Theory* 7 (2008): 137–158; Ryan P. Hanley, *Adam Smith and the Character of Virtue* (Cambridge: Cambridge University Press, 2009), chap. 1. On Rousseau and Kant, see Susan Meld Shell, "Rousseau, Kant, and the Beginning of History," in *The Legacy of Rousseau*, ed. Clifford Orwin and Nathan Tarcov (Chicago: University of Chicago Press, 1997), 45–64; Richard L. Velkley, *Freedom and the End of Reason: On the Moral Foundations of Kant's Critical Philosophy* (Chicago: University of Chicago Press, 1989). For a treatment of all three thinkers, see Ryan P. Hanley, "Rousseau, Smith, and Kant on Becoming Just," in *Justice*, ed. Mark Le Bar (Oxford: Oxford University Press, 2018), 39–66. On Rousseau's most celebrated quarrel with one of Lerner's "band of brethren," see Robert Zaretsky and John T. Scott, *The Philosophers' Quarrel: Rousseau, Hume, and the Limits of Human Understanding* (New Haven, CT: Yale University Press, 2009). On Rousseau's critique of the Enlightenment, see Terence Marshall, "Rousseau and Enlightenment," *Political Theory* 6, 4 (1978): 421–455; Keohane, "Masterpiece of Policy in Our Century"; Mark Hulliung, *The Autocritique of Enlightenment: Rousseau and the Philosophes* (Cambridge, MA: Harvard University Press, 1994); Arthur M. Melzer, "The Origin of the Counter-Enlightenment: Rousseau and the New Religion of Sincerity," *American Political Science Review* 90, 2 (1996): 344–360; Sally Howard Campbell and John T. Scott, "Rousseau's Politic Argument in the *Discourse on the Sciences and Arts*," *American Journal of Political Science* 49, 4 (2005): 818–828; David Lay Williams, *Rousseau's Platonic Enlightenment* (University Park: Penn State University Press, 2007). There is a vast critical literature on these subjects. The listed works are only initial suggestions for further reading.

3. Pierre Manent, ed., preface to *Les Libéraux* (Paris: Hachette Pluriel, 1986), 15; translation by the author.

4. See Lerner, "Commerce and Character," 201–202.

5. I have used (with slight emendations) the translation of Judith R. Bush in Jean-Jacques Rousseau, *Discourse on the Sciences and Arts and Polemics*, in *The Collected Works of Rousseau*, vol. 2, ed. Roger D. Masters and Christopher Kelly (Hanover, NH: Dartmouth College/University Press of New England, 1992), 186–198; hereafter I cite the *Collected Works* as CW. In addition, I refer to the Pléiade edition of Rousseau's *Oeuvres Complètes*, 5 vols. (Paris: Editions de la Pléiade, 1959–); hereafter cited as OC.

6. Manent, *Les Libéraux*, 21–22.

7. Jean-Jacques Rousseau, *Emile, or On Education*, trans. Allan Bloom (New York: Basic Books, 1979), 225; OC, IV:509.

8. Consider, e.g., Yoav Peled, "Rousseau's Inhibited Radicalism: An Analysis of His Political Thought in Light of His Economic Ideas," *American Political Science Review* 74, 4 (1980): 1034–1045. For a ringing defense of this economic scheme as appropriate to Rousseau's broader argument, see Ryan P. Hanley, "Political Economy and Individual Liberty," in *The Challenge of Rousseau*, ed. Eve Grace and Christopher Kelly (Cambridge: Cambridge University Press, 2012), 34–57.

9. Rousseau describes the illumination in book 8 of *Confessions* (*CW*, 5:294; *OC*, I:351) and at greater length in his second letter to Malesherbes (*CW*, 5:575; *OC*, I:1135–1136).

CHAPTER 6

Thomas Jefferson: Commercial Republican, Creole Nationalist

Peter S. Onuf

The young Thomas Jefferson was an Anglo-American Creole, cultivating a sense of self—and of his place in the world—on the provincial periphery of the British Empire. Displaced from the distant metropole, he constructed his identity within complementary "imagined communities": the "world" that a dynamic, expansive transatlantic market brought to mind; the "republic of letters," a natural aristocracy linking enlightened minds from far-flung places; and a greater British people extending their "empire of liberty" across a vast, unmapped continent.[1] On the eve of American independence, as the old imperial regime verged on collapse, the Virginia planter-patriot deployed these familiar templates to fashion a new narrative for an embryonic nation. Britons and Americans—metropolitans and provincials—"might have been a free & a great people together": this is what Jefferson would have had the latter declare as they disavowed allegiance to the king. King George's war against his former subjects transformed "friends" into "enemies," giving "the last stab to agonizing affection" and forcing Americans to "forget" their "former love" for their "unfeeling" British "brethren."[2]

For Jefferson, the break with Britain was an epochal moment of worldwide historical significance. Yet it also precipitated a profoundly personal crisis that his congressional editors prudently suppressed. Forty-five years later, when he drafted his autobiography, Jefferson was still bitter about the editorial changes to his original version of the Declaration of Independence. Gripped by "the pusillanimous idea that ... friends in England" would be offended, overly cautious and conciliatory congressmen jettisoned Jefferson's strong language, thus compromising the new nation's commitment to fundamental republican principles. The injured author was particularly perplexed by the elimination of his powerful, heartfelt indictment of George III for promoting the slave trade. In this case, he suspected, Congress feared alienating its "northern brethren," who owned "very few slaves themselves" but were "pretty considerable carriers of them to others." But when sensitive slave owners blamed slave traders for slavery, Congress prudently concluded, the less said the better. Showing "a decent respect for the opinions of mankind" meant appealing to universal principles and suppressing local interests and prejudices.[3]

In an oft-cited late-life letter to Henry Lee, Jefferson insisted that when he drafted the Declaration he was "neither aiming at originality of principle or sentiment." It was merely "intended to be an expression of the American mind," a faithful transcription of the people's voice as they declared themselves—in famously circular fashion—into recognizable existence. Much has been made of the false modesty (bordering on megalomania) of this self-serving formulation. But just as Jefferson could blame his editors for the Declaration's nearly fatal flaws, he could distinguish his voice—and his sense of himself—from the voice of the people. He implicitly acknowledged the discrepancy and distinction when he disclosed his original aim and intention to Lee. Did he fall short when he sought to give the people their voice? Or, as he much more likely thought, were the people not quite ready to say the things that were already on the patriot-draftsman's enlightened mind?[4]

At the critical moment when Jefferson imagined and embraced a new collective identity—as a Virginian or an American in a postimperial continental union—he reconfigured his sense of himself. Identification with the people was the great self-defining personal and political commitment of his life and career.[5] Yet that commitment was never perfect, for Jefferson became most acutely aware of self-defining differences at precisely those moments when the world and his place in it seemed to change most radically. As the Declaration's author, he cataloged the grievances of a continent, forging sentimental attachments that drew him closer to former strangers who were now countrymen: his fellow Americans. But even and especially then, continental aspirations illuminated postprovincial particularities; new attachments spawned new enmities. In the heat of the revolutionary moment, Jefferson was hard-pressed to distinguish between principle and prejudice. Nearly half a century later the conflation was complete, and he could believe that he had been absolutely right all along. If Congress had only followed his prophetic lead in 1776 and committed the new nation to end slavery, the controversy over the peculiar institution's future in the new state of Missouri—the "fire bell in the night" that threatened the "knell of the Union"—would have been averted.[6] When that crisis passed and his faith in the union's survival was restored, he could again call himself, as it would state on his tombstone, "Author of the Declaration of American Independence."[7] At the same time Jefferson declared himself to be an American, he defined himself as the Declaration's author, thus securing the unique and everlasting fame of a founding father.[8]

CREOLE IDENTITY AND NATIONAL CHARACTER

Jefferson's self-fashioning was hardly unusual, though few of his countrymen devoted more time, energy, and resources to the project. My goal in this chapter is to build on Ralph Lerner's seminal essay "Commerce and Character: The Anglo-American as New-Model Man" by taking a fresh look at the Declaration's author both as a commercial republican and as a Creole nationalist. When Jefferson and his fellow patriots declared themselves an independent people, they embraced a new national *identity* that was compatible with the *character* of the Anglo-American settler societies Lerner reconstructs in his brilliant account of the "universal type" of "commercial republican" and "its American democratic exemplar."[9] For self-styled Americans, character was enduring, antedating their bid for independence, yet their identity as a people was contingent, the result of the conscious choices of frustrated Creoles who identified with, and sought recognition from, their metropolitan counterparts. Every initiative by state-building, tax-obsessed imperial reformers over the course of the protracted constitutional crisis leading up to independence called into question the rights—and therefore the identity—of these overseas Britons. It was precisely the discrepancy between the character Americans assumed and the identity they imagined that sparked resistance and revolution. As Montesquieu and other enlightened writers asserted, the character of a people was more or less fixed, determined by their country's climate, resources, and capacity to sustain a growing and prosperous population. Environmental circumstances determined and explained differences among peoples who nonetheless shared a universal human nature and could claim the original, natural rights of all humankind.[10]

Enlightenment writers conjectured that history unfolded progressively through successive stages, but the pace of development differed radically from country to country, continent to continent. The "world," they discovered (or imagined), was an elaborate spatial and temporal matrix subject to universal laws and therefore legible to enlightened eyes. But if every nation displayed a distinctive character, the incorporation or constitution of its people as a body politic was the unpredictable result of a unique history punctuated by war, regime change, and dynastic failure. Adam Smith and his fellow economists might postulate universal laws for market societies and for their world as a market, but they understood that politics was a realm of unpredictable contingency: "political science" was aspirational; in the meantime, political economists must accommodate their maxims to the vagaries of the world as they found it.[11]

The emergence of Anglo-American settler societies raised novel problems for policymakers and enlightened "social scientists." Jefferson and his fellow Creoles were displaced Britons with "countries" of their own—the king's distant overseas dominions.[12] Despite their loud professions of loyalty to George III, their provincial identities were—as Jefferson lamented in his draft of the Declaration—necessarily contingent and ultimately consensual.[13] The character of a people, Enlightenment writers asserted, was the product of many generations, time out of mind; it was deeply rooted in their customs (for Britons, the ancient constitution and common law) and evident in their manners. But colonizing Creoles carried the common law and their constitutional rights with them (or so they controversially claimed), imagining themselves "at home" in the metropolis even as they constructed legal regimes and civil societies at the empire's far peripheries.[14]

What sort of character would such recently planted peoples display? Love of country, English philosopher and friend of America Richard Price suggested, is a function of propinquity, with attachments progressively attenuating across space; in stark contrast, the king's metropolitan subjects, however unruly, were thickly embedded in local communities, with their proper place in the social order—their identities—fixed.[15] British commentators were inclined to dismiss Americans' constitutional claims and cultural aspirations with contempt: provincial reliance on the institution of racial slavery called their civility into question, underscoring their degradation and dependence; provincial resistance to imperial taxation and administrative reform betrayed the tenuousness of their allegiance and their long-standing determination to declare independence.[16]

Displaced from the metropolis and lacking a fixed or stable character, Anglo-American Creoles constituted themselves as independent peoples, following the pathways of least resistance by refashioning and upgrading their provincial "constitutions" and substituting a transprovincial Continental Congress and an American identity for the king and empire that had spurned and betrayed them. Independence was thus the result of a protracted constitutional crisis: controversy pivoted on the empire's constitution—if it had one—and the identity of anglicizing provincial peoples who aspired to fuller integration into the empire's political economy on more equal terms. As the unfolding crisis demonstrated, the empire could not survive *without* a constitution, however much—and precisely because—frustrated Creoles cherished a greater British identity. Patriots instead turned inward and looked downward for support, cultivating local attachments and inspiring their countrymen to fight for their liberties as they drafted new constitutions that would guarantee their ongoing participation in and support for revolutionary republican regimes. This democratizing project depended on mobilizing and channeling popular patriotic sentiments—or what Jefferson would call the "spirit of 1776"—by forging powerful national links between a newly self-conscious American people and their continental country.[17] As they did so, they would fulfill the logic of Enlightenment conceptions of national character, but in novel ways that reflected a highly mobile, calculating, and enterprising population's capacity to associate, combine, and identify with one another in the dynamic and unpredictable circumstances of a postimperial federal republic. This required the kind of people who were already being produced by the great transformation in modern Western society driven by the expansive imperatives of commerce and capital. What was needed was a new sort of character that was fixed *not* to particular places but to the emergent ethos of commercial republicanism that Ralph Lerner so brilliantly reconstructs.

COMMERCIAL REPUBLICANS

When the author of the Declaration of Independence articulated the sentiments that inspired Americans and the grievances that enraged them, he "invented" a new people, making provincial Anglo-Americans—whose character was fixed in its long-established transatlantic settings—conscious of their collective identity. To analyze and explicate that character, Lerner enlists the testimony of moral philosopher and economist Adam Smith and aristocratic French visitor and student of political culture Alexis de Tocqueville. Smith limned the framework of an expanding market economy within which Lerner's "new man of commerce" emerged; half a century later, Tocqueville offered a brilliant and influential group portrait of "democracy" in action, charting the often baffling ways these new-model men (and women) assumed and played their roles. Equality was predicate, problem, and prophecy for both of Lerner's witnesses and the central theme of his own essay: Smith's *Homo economicus*, a highly abstract, idealized actor, was defined by reciprocal relations with other putatively equal market participants; Tocqueville focused on the sociology and group psychology of a democratic people fundamentally committed to the principle of equality.

Lerner's only references to Jefferson occur in two footnotes. In the first, he notes Jefferson's concurrence with Smith's commentary on the deracinated character of merchants who are "not necessarily attached to any particular country" in what he calls "the great mercantile republic."[18] Jefferson indicted the whalemen of Nantucket on similar grounds: their loyalties were shaped by the market for whale oil. He also accused his British creditors of reducing indebted Virginia planters to a form of slavery, wistfully imagining disentanglement from the commercial world behind an American equivalent of Chinese isolation.[19] Yet Jefferson was no utopian pastoralist, as Lerner persuasively argues in the second note: "with these commercial republicans we ought to include even Jefferson while he was extolling the chosen people of God who labor in the earth. . . . For all his urging of household self-sufficiency, cottage industry, and the like, Jefferson thought of American agriculture clearly as a business and as a part of a world economy."[20] When Jefferson questioned the unequal terms of trade, he echoed Smith's critique of mercantilism and his warnings about traders who would rig markets.

Significantly, Lerner writes that "we ought to include" Jefferson in his cast of characters, thus acknowledging that the prevailing tendency was to cast him in an oppositional role as the democratic defender of the "people" against the "interests." To consign Jefferson to footnote status suggests that Smith expressed himself much more clearly and consequentially than his too easily misunderstood American avatar. At the time Lerner wrote his essay, most political theorists agreed that pragmatic Americans generated very little worthwhile theorizing (recall Jefferson's acknowledged lack of "originality"). Intellectual historians concurred, positing an "ideological" tradition derived from English commonwealth thinkers—or Machiavelli's neoclassical Florence—that transformed provincial Anglo-American political culture and set the stage for revolution. "The Revolution was in the Minds of the People," John Adams instructed Jefferson, long before his old friend arrived on the revolutionary scene.[21]

Lerner's great contribution is to challenge conventional approaches to the history of ideas, whether in tracing "philosophic reasoning" through the genealogy of canonical (European) thinkers or in reconstructing the linguistic or ideological limits of what contemporaries could say or think at any given moment. Philosophers supposedly transcended their own immediate contexts, contributing to a tradition that spanned generations, but their ideological counterparts could not escape linguistic imprisonment. Lerner rejects both approaches, embracing instead a commonsensical conception of context that foregrounds the responsiveness of thinkers and actors to changing times. He presciently anticipates the inglorious demise of the great debate between "classical republican" ideologists and market-oriented "liberals" over the origins of American politics and culture.[22] Lerner's intention is not simply to collapse two ultimately untenable and indistinguishable worldviews into an amorphous exceptionalism but rather to delineate the ways in which Americans thoughtfully responded to the contexts that defined their changing world. Lerner's "thinking revolutionary," John Adams, helped shape that world, as did Thomas Jefferson and their many allies and adversaries.[23]

Jefferson attributed the authority of the Declaration to "the harmonizing sentiments of the day, whether expressed in conversation, in letters, printed essays, or in the elementary books of public right, as Aristotle, Cicero, Locke, Sidney &c."[24] The great writers in the republican canon came last, and only in their most "elementary" and accessible formulations, as if to confirm the timeless, "self-evident" truths that now animated Jefferson and his fellow patriots. The familiar sentiments that commercial republicans embraced were the commonsense vernacular of an enterprising people, not the legacy of ancient wisdom or sacred texts. Lerner follows Jefferson, disclaiming any intention "to trace the philosophic reasoning" that prepared the way for independence, focusing instead on how patriot leaders succeeded in persuading "their contemporaries to adopt maxims, conclusions, and rules of action so much at odds with the certitudes of the day before yesterday."[25] Rejecting the antiquated, hierarchical order of the old regime, revolutionaries looked to the future, appealing to broadly shared understandings of the way the contemporary world actually worked.

"The advocates of the commercial republic," Lerner argues, were "exceptionally clear- and sharp-sighted moderns," "uncommon men" who recognized what they had in common with their fellow citizens.[26] What they could see so clearly was the immanent orderliness of a world without orders. For Smith, liberating trade from mercantilist restraints would give rise to a "natural system of liberty and justice," channeling the aggressive and destructive energies that characterized Hobbes's anarchic state of nature into reciprocally beneficial and socially productive transactions.[27] The market mediated and sublimated conflict, teaching participants to calculate the immediate consequences of transactions while making them progressively more aware of their situation in the world at large. Smith's "market" may have been an abstraction, a notional "system" displaced from particular communities where local custom ruled and neighbors knew exactly where they stood. But mobile Anglo-American freeholders responded to the demands of distant markets as they cultivated new lands and formed new communities. The progress of settlement thus made colonists "commercial"; at the same time, the need to preserve the peace, define and enforce property claims, and manage labor relations made them "republican."[28]

Lerner's new-model men could take nothing for granted. Colonists' survival and success depended on their capacity to calculate outcomes in highly contingent, often unpredictable circumstances. This practical, ad hoc reasoning was broadly distributed among the settler population, a democratic, commonsense vernacular not to be confused with the elite philosopher's rarefied reasoning. "Far from seconding the proud aspirations of Reason to grasp the whole of society and to direct its complex workings in detail," Lerner writes, "the commercial republicans counseled humility."[29] Imagining they could fully understand and therefore govern the world (or teach monarchs how to do so), proud philosophers could only lead the world astray. By aggregating the expanding domain of knowledge generated and circulated by myriad citizens in their ongoing engagement with the natural world and one another, the "people" collectively could know much more and govern themselves much more effectively than their supposed superiors in the distant metropolis.

The emergence of such a people in Britain's North American provinces came as something of a surprise to Jefferson and like-minded patriots who originally resisted imperial reform efforts in defense of corporate privileges and their own aristocratic aspirations.[30] Patriot leaders encountered (or discovered) the "people" in the process of mobilizing them politically and militarily as they stumbled toward independence.[31] Political and military mobilization accelerated and punctuated commerce's corrosive effects, exposing the artificiality and unnaturalness of an ascriptive, hierarchical status order. The imperial despot stood naked, bereft of authority over his suddenly disillusioned American subjects.

The trope of revolution suggests that this was a world "turned upside down." Yet the colonists' world still turned in familiar ways as they broke with Britain and forged a new collective identity. A later generation of European romantic nationalists would invoke or invent a legitimating genealogy that traced modern nations to ancient progenitors, virtuous common folk who had cultivated their countries for generations.[32] Americans may have "invented the people" (or, more accurately, the modern concept of popular sovereignty), but patriots appealed to their contemporary countrymen.[33] Recognizing and identifying with one another as equals, Americans met on the same level and were oriented toward the same horizon. No longer subjects of a distant monarch or subject to the pretentious claims of would-be aristocrats, ordinary folk now claimed the rights and privileges of citizens. This was not a reversal of fortunes, with the lower sort exalted and the mighty degraded, but a convergence on common ground.

"State a moral case to a ploughman and a professor," Jefferson famously told his nephew Peter Carr. "The former will decide it as well, and often better than the latter, because he has not been led astray by artificial rules."[34] The three participants in this imagined scenario were equally endowed with what the Scottish philosophers called "moral sense," the natural, inborn capacity to distinguish right from wrong (though the proud professor might be more easily misled by irrelevant and useless knowledge). If the process of mobilization was educative and enlightening for the ploughman (Jefferson's idealized yeoman farmer), the professor (representing the "better sort") also had important lessons to learn, and the interlocutor (Jefferson ventriloquizing Carr) played the key role, stating the case, eliciting responses, and discovering the right path to pursue.[35]

In the American revolutionary context, the men Lerner calls "advocates of the commercial republic" were patriot interlocutors and educators like Jefferson who taught the people to trust themselves and listen to their own voices, spurring them into action in defense of their liberties.[36] Jefferson was acutely aware of the compelling need to model the character of the new republic's citizens to guarantee the revolution's ultimate success. Hierarchical regimes and social orders were—or aspired to be—static and unchanging, claiming a timeless legitimacy; the modern commercial republic embraced, rationalized, and channeled change, its authority grounded in and constantly renewed by an engaged citizenry.

Lerner does not need Jefferson to portray "the new man of commerce" and his world. But Jefferson, rising up from the footnotes, becomes a more fully realized and illuminating character within the interpretative framework of Lerner's seminal essay. That reframing of Jefferson in turn suggests important ways that Lerner's insights can be extended, building on a subsequent generation of scholarship on commerce and colonization, nation making, and state formation.

A NEW WORLD

The global expansion of trade in the early modern era led to the emergence of Smith's "great mercantile republic." Lerner persuasively argues that this notional community provided "a model both for a national polity and for the entire trading world." "Producers and traders of movables—the owners and employers of capital stock"—were "citizens" of a world that ignored or transcended "the conventional divisions within nations and among them."[37] If, as Shakespeare put it, "all the world's a stage," market actors performed the leading roles, improvising the scripts that shaped the modern world.[38] Transactions in the commercial world dissolved old solidarities and status distinctions, emphasizing the calculations and expectations of autonomous individuals. The circulation of information accompanied and enabled the movement of people and the exchange of goods; mobility fostered new conceptions of time and space. Citizens of this new world looked to the stars, orienting themselves to wider and more distant horizons. In the absence of thick social relations and enforcement capacities of a well-established social order, men of commerce cultivated character to generate trust: legibility and predictability depended on speaking the same language and dealing in a common currency.

Lerner illuminates the paradoxical logic of market society. Enlightenment conceptions of a universal human nature and natural sociability depended on extricating and abstracting the "individual" from familiar social and cultural settings and relocating him or her in a larger, largely unfamiliar world. Disaggregated, atomized, and stripped of traditional status attributes, these individuals could be redescribed by pioneering political economists as equal and interchangeable. They were men "*of* commerce" who demonstrated by their very adaptation (or subjection) to market imperatives that they were "created equal." On the market's horizontal plane, actors appeared equal to one another, no longer ordered on the old regime's vertical, hierarchical axis. But if the market made individuals autonomous, market transactions drew them back together again. Market participants saw much of themselves in one another, recognizing the "similitude" of their "passions" as well their "common neediness and vulnerability." Reminding "men of their common needs," Lerner writes, commerce "made them more like one another and more aware of that likeness."[39] Smith's "natural system of perfect liberty and justice" thus emerged out of an ongoing history of increasingly predictable transactions, beginning with the "simple recognition of our separate and common needs" and culminating "in a complex, ever-changing interdependence." For Smith, the struggle for subsistence and security naturally led men out of a Hobbesian state of nature and through successive stages of social and economic development. "As each labored intently to satisfy his own wants," Lerner concludes, "men would become commercial cousins, cool fellow-citizens of a universal republic."[40] Discovering himself, the commercial republican discovered the world.

If moral philosophers and political economists abstracted an idealized conception of the self-conscious individual from the complicated contexts of the real world, their abstractions offered a new analytical framework for cataloging and analyzing "natural" differences among nations and within their populations. Smith thus provided a rich empirical foundation for universal laws that governed market relations in his *Wealth of Nations*, even as he explained why *particular* nations—most notably Britain, the most advanced nation—surpassed others in population, wealth, and power in the ongoing regional and global competition for relative advantage. "The spirit of commerce unites nations," Montesquieu asserted, but his prediction that it would "cure destructive prejudices" would be massively disproved in the nation-making age of democratic revolutions.[41] For enlightened advocates of "sweet commerce," the "universal republic" was aspirational, beyond the history that nation-states would continue to make.[42] In the meantime, commercial republicans focused on the enlightened policies and administrative reforms that would generate revenue and enhance states' capacity to make and win wars. Far from disappearing in the new era of global commerce, nation-states emerged in recognizably modern form, mobilizing men and resources on an unprecedented, unimaginable scale—all in the name of the peoples they claimed to represent or embody. It is no coincidence that the "universal histories" of the Enlightenment emerged in tandem with the national histories that shaped conceptions of international order in the modern world.[43] Sovereignty was the key concept, as nation-states proclaimed and enforced exclusive authority over their territorial domains, bringing a new world into view.

Freed from the shackles of tradition and hierarchy, Lerner's commercial republicans modeled a new form of citizenship that was mobile and mobilizable, functionally adaptable to the emerging requirements of modernizing states. But the loyalty and allegiance of such characters could not be taken for granted, as the American revolutionary crisis so clearly demonstrated. When Anglo-American patriots challenged the legitimacy of the imperial state's supposedly unconstitutional revenue demands, their extraconstitutional mobilization raised equivalent questions about the legitimacy of resistance. Resistance to Parliament's novel claim to sovereignty thus led a plurality of reluctant Creoles to declare themselves their own sovereigns, a highly contestable claim that would only be retroactively affirmed when the "powers of earth" finally recognized American independence. Before then, the revolution was a civil war, with Anglo-American loyalties depending on its unpredictably shifting fortunes. Patriots and loyalists, Whigs and Tories, were all more or less commercial republicans. The great question for the founders of independent states and a new federal union was whether their "experiments" in republican self-government would ultimately succeed.

Despite the claims of patriots, American independence did not constitute a clear or decisive break between the old monarchical regime and the new republican one. Adapting to contingencies and calculating their chances, Anglo-Americans either supported or opposed the "common cause" and sometimes changed their minds. Ambivalence was the keynote for a people at war with itself, torn between old attachments and new identities. The tension was latent in contemporary conceptions of republicanism, as some patriots extolled the republic's "classical" form, with its intimate scale and virtuous citizens, and others embraced the emergent form of the modern republic constituted by cosmopolitan, enterprising, and self-interested citizens. Whatever their hopes or fears, Anglo-Americans had to make a choice: seeking to resolve anxieties and ambivalence, patriots chose consent, assuming an equal status with their fellow citizens and struggling to suppress old attachments and lingering misgivings. But consent was always circumstantial, setting the stage for an endless succession of momentous future choices. In the modern republic, as in its market analogue, the citizen's identity was protean, a work in progress, the result of ongoing encounters with other citizens (or market actors) on the same plane, equal "under the law" they collectively authorized. Like everything else in this new world, equality was not a fixed status but rather an abstract and idealized conception of the circumstances in which citizens were supposedly free to act. At the same time, equality functioned as a standard or metric, enabling citizens to locate and distinguish themselves from one another, a goad (or threat) to an anxious and ambitious people in their varied pursuits of happiness.

The distinctive characteristic of the commercial republican world was its leveling effect. "Like the plain teachings of the Gospels, like useful knowledge," commerce would "assimilate all men everywhere to one another." It was, as Lerner glosses physician-founder Benjamin Rush, "an engine that would assault and level the remaining outposts of pride," including "family pride, aristocratic pride ... [and] pride in whatever led men to believe that they could rise above the workaday world."[44] Yet if, as Rush implied, commerce cleared the way toward republican redemption, subverting the artificial distinctions that sustained the old hierarchical regime, it was not clear what forces would sustain attachments among atomized individuals in this brave new world. Perhaps, Rush feared, the commercial world did *not* give rise to new-model men capable of governing themselves, for "when pursued closely," commerce "sinks the man into a machine," making him incapable of thinking (or calculating) beyond his own evanescent needs.[45] Character formation would therefore have to take place in public schools, tax-supported sites for the fabrication of good citizens—or, as Rush famously put it, "to convert men into republican machines."[46] The need for conversion resonated in both a Christian world, where "natural" (sinful) man could not save himself without divine intervention, and a revolutionary world, where anxious subjects embraced—or rejected—the new republican dispensation. If Rush's social engineering betrayed the mechanistic and dehumanizing tendencies of Enlightenment thought, it is also eloquent testimony to the exhilarating (and frightening) sense of the potential power of autonomous individuals—and of the people collectively—in the midst of revolutionary regime change.

Lerner is surely right in arguing for the emergence of a broadly recognizable commercial republican character in the Anglo-American world long before the onset of the imperial crisis and the Revolutionary War. But notwithstanding paeans to a liberty-loving people's common sense and their supposed genius for self-government, this commercial republican character cannot explain the British Empire's collapse or republicanism's triumph. The very idea that Americans constituted a distinct people depended on forging new attachments and embracing a new national identity in radical tension with the cosmopolitan logic of commercial expansion and integration. Indeed, national independence—the unintended consequence of provincial Anglo-American mobilization against metropolitan reform efforts that inadvertently destroyed the empire—initiated a new democratic epoch of state formation that would transform a world of orders into a more or less orderly world.

A NEW NATION

How would Lerner's commercial republican be incorporated in the world Americans encountered when they declared their independence in 1776? In more optimistic moments, revolutionaries might imagine that national distinctions were fading away with the enlightening progress of commerce: the United States would model a new world order and help usher in the commercial millennium. Montesquieu believed commerce would disarm belligerent states in an emerging regime of reciprocally beneficial exchange; they would become increasingly interdependent, blending into "a single state, of which all the [particular] societies are members."[47] This was the progressive spirit of John Adams's model treaty of 1776, offering liberal commercial relations to prospective allies and anticipating peace in the midst of war; it was also the fundamental premise of a more perfect, free-trading union among the American state republics.[48] The American Revolution was the inadvertent outcome of a massive mobilization of provincial Anglo-Americans in defense of their liberties, a war to end the war that George III and his minions were systematically waging against them. Since these commercial republicans sought "gain not conquest," they were "pacific from principle."[49]

Anglo-American patriots did not intend to make war against their metropolitan countrymen and break the British Empire into "wretched fragments"—Washington's description of the disunited states on the eve of the federal Constitution's ratification.[50] To the contrary, fulfillment of their commercial republican vision depended on a "more perfect" incorporation in an ever-expanding British "empire of liberty." Creole constitutionalists thus envisioned the empire as a collective security organization, or "peace pact," that would secure the rights of overseas Britons, guarantee provincial autonomy, and facilitate free trade to its distant limits.[51] This idealized vision of empire provided a template for reluctant revolutionaries as they sought to construct a postimperial regime. If, in its successively more perfect iterations, the new federal union reconstituted the familiar broad distribution of authority in the old decentralized empire, it also required independent Americans to create a new central government with an enhanced capacity to make war and enforce the peace on a continental scale.[52]

Expanding commerce did not eliminate the causes of war; it substituted the "interests" of an emerging republican era for the dynastic "passions" of the old regime.[53] Far from fading away, states took on new importance as they promoted economic development and exploited expanding revenue sources; by mobilizing patriotic sentiments and claiming a mandate from the nation, they gained legitimacy and enhanced their capacity to project power in a highly competitive, war-prone system of sovereign states. Unlike its predatory, monarchical counterparts, a republican government would not prey on its own subjects. At peace with itself, the modern republic could mobilize the extraordinary power of a fully mobilized people. The United States could therefore claim to have "the strongest government on earth," as newly inaugurated president Jefferson told his fellow Americans in 1801. Its apparent weakness—the absence of powerful and privileged military and naval establishments—was the new nation's greatest strength, for "every man, at the call of the law, would fly to the standard of the law, and would meet invasions of the public order as his own personal concern."[54]

Jefferson was well situated to experience and articulate the conceptual changes—and confusion—of the revolutionary age. With his predilection for exaggerated, even hyperbolic juxtapositions—between New World and Old, republic and empire, Whig friend and Tory foe—the author of the Declaration of Independence had a keen eye for what was "new under the sun" on the American horizon, "for this whole chapter in the history of man is new."[55] By the same token, he was prone to overlook or take for granted the social, political, and constitutional continuities *across* the regime change that so impressed Tocqueville and other commentators—including the institution of slavery. Jefferson's bifocal vision was a function of the peculiar situation of Creole Anglo-Americans appalled (and attracted) by the corrupt metropolis and convinced that wicked ministers were conspiring against their liberties.

The imperial crisis precipitated an identity crisis for this scion of the Virginia plantocracy. No longer imagining the mother country as his spiritual home, Jefferson instead identified with the rustic virtues of his countrymen, for "those who labour in the earth are the chosen people of God, if ever he had a chosen people."[56] The revolutionary patriot found himself at home among his neighbors, recognizing them as a people and Virginia as their common country and thus resolving the Creole dilemma of distance and displacement.[57] This was not a social revolution, for Jefferson and his fellow Virginians remained firmly planted on home ground; rather, it was a revolution of political consciousness and collective identity that set the stage for regime change, nation making, and state formation. It was the revolutionary moment in which Jefferson, the Creole nationalist and commercial republican, channeled the principles and sentiments of an independent, self-governing people, blending his voice with theirs and fashioning a new sense of his own personal and political identity.

Following Thomas Paine's lead, Jefferson and his fellow patriots activated and exploited a commonsense constitutional vernacular that came naturally to provincial Anglo-Americans on the empire's provincial periphery. They could declare themselves "Americans" because they identified so closely with their distant British home, drawing on metropolitan sources to defend themselves against metropolitan efforts to reform the empire. As Lerner rightly emphasizes, the commercial republican ethos reflected a new conception of individual character that emerged in the wake of expanding market relations across and beyond the British Atlantic. Yet if the market subverted traditional social and political hierarchies, the ultimate shape of the "modern" commercial republican world remained radically indeterminate. If commerce brought distant actors together in reciprocally beneficial exchanges, enabling them to transcend space and imagine one another as equals, long distances challenged traditional, place-bound conceptions of governance and rule. Britain's disintegrating North American empire would be a laboratory for novel experiments in "political science" as Americans sought to constitute republican regimes that would channel and exploit the expansive energies of an enterprising people in their many "pursuits of happiness."[58]

Commercial republicanism—or what we now call democracy—was a protean force, threatening to spin out of control into anarchic disorder and despotism. On the edge of empire and in the midst of rebellion against (what they had only recently acknowledged was) legitimate authority, patriot leaders were forced to declare independence, write new constitutions, and create a new institutional infrastructure to mobilize men and resources to sustain war and negotiate peace. Under these circumstances, the imperatives of commercial republicanism and Creole nationalism converged in the logic of modern nation-making political economy.[59] Smith and his fellow economists sought to promote the state's prosperity and power by liberating the flow of commerce from onerous regulation and by enhancing tax revenue. The key to rational and efficient administration was information: the more rulers knew about their subjects, the less they would need to deploy their limited coercive resources against them. In the words of Smith's friend David Hume, the sovereign's "best policy" was "to comply with the common bent of mankind, and give it all the improvements of which it is susceptible." By following (or enabling) "the most natural course of things," the philosopher concluded, "industry, and arts, and trade, [will] increase the power of the sovereign, as well as the happiness of the subjects."[60]

This was Thomas Jefferson's moment. As provincial Anglo-Americans became more anglicized, pursuing refinement, enlightenment, and commercial advantage within the empire, misguided metropolitan reformers embraced unnatural, unconstitutional policies against "the common bent." Unhappy, alienated American subjects mobilized to vindicate their rights and pursue happiness as an independent, self-governing people in an empire of their own. Independence revolutionized the world in which these commercial republicans found themselves as they made war against their former fellow subjects and sovereign and sought alliances with old enemies. The character they had cultivated as provincial Britons would stand them in good stead, making it possible to recognize themselves as a united people embarked on a "common cause." But given the volatility of loyalties and the accidents of war, there were many good reasons to fear that the revolution would fail. Nor did the enlightened exponents and exemplars of commercial republicanism offer useful guidance to reluctant nation makers in the emerging age of democratic revolutions.[61] The challenge for Creole nationalists was to construct and justify a modern republican regime that could mobilize, constitutionalize, and institutionalize the power of the people, transforming the fiction of popular sovereignty into facts on the ground.

Jefferson may not have been—and did not claim to be—an original thinker, but he was a gifted improviser who grasped the extraordinary challenges of inventing a new nation. His great contribution was to conceive of the American future in geopolitical terms as an "empire of liberty" and a dominant power in the new Western world.[62] The commercial republican's horizons were unobstructed by the unnatural hierarchy and artificial privilege that consigned the unenlightened world to perpetual darkness. But if the Virginian could see farther, across time and space, he could also bring his immediate neighbors and their world into sharper focus, recognizing them as fellow citizens, the constituents of a new body politic and the source of its legitimate authority. Of course, the enlightened Creole overlooked much in his radically reductive view of a postimperial new nation that remained inextricably tied to, and dependent on, an old world that was itself the site and source of epochal changes. Nor were New World societies suddenly purged of all traces of their Old World origins: one notably conspicuous example was the institution of racial slavery, which became more deeply and widely entrenched in the independent United States. But all visionaries are necessarily limited, and what Jefferson could envision—about the new nation's scale and scope and popular participation in its political life (again, despite its now conspicuous limits)—would be lastingly significant.[63]

The break with Britain forced Anglo-American patriots to constitute new republics in their rebellious provinces and to establish a federal and republican union among them. Before the imperial crisis, Lerner's commercial republicans focused more on markets than on politics. In the new era of Parliamentary sovereignty and domesticated monarchy, they could think of the United Kingdom as immanently or essentially republican, a "royal republic"; overseas Britons imagined themselves as part of a greater Britain, secure in their rights under provincial constitutions in an effectively federal and republican empire. After the break, the republican character of the Anglo-American world could no longer be assumed but had to be formally declared, defined, and constituted; it was no longer the shared transatlantic culture of enterprising traders and enlightened commentators (new-model commercial republican characters) that reinforced and, to a significant extent, constituted the provinces' attachment to metropolis in the imperial union. In declaring their independence, the American republics individually and collectively asserted territorial boundaries and sovereign prerogatives that redefined the old empire, their former protector, as the new enemy. Nation making introduced Americans to a "state of nature," the anarchy of independent sovereignties.

The conventional wisdom, most famously articulated by Montesquieu, held that republics had to be small in size to foster virtuous citizens who would defend them to the death. Immersed in their classical sources, students of classical republicanism have thus concluded that establishing the "extended republic"—and a federal republic of relatively small state republics—was the fundamental problem for the American revolutionaries and founders. But Lerner's commercial republicans did not think so. To the contrary, the logic of markets was expansive, obliterating boundaries and liberating trade: the genius of the federal Constitution, admiring exponents of national economy would later argue, was to create an expansive customs union and free-trade regime *within* the jurisdiction of a great sovereign power with the capacity to enforce the rule of law domestically and promote and protect the national interest (and nationals' interests) in the larger world.[64] Jefferson did not fully grasp the intricacies of modern public debt and credit, but he *did* understand that the United States could only survive and prosper *as* an empire. Thinking like a commercial republican and overcoming his early infatuation with Montesquieu, he recognized that the expanding union's great size was an asset, not the problem that David Hume, James Madison, and a host of subsequent political theorists imagined it to be.

When Jefferson and his fellow patriots broke with the British Empire, they did not abandon the imperial aspirations that animated their resistance to unconstitutional encroachments on their rights. Political and military mobilization fostered commitment to a transprovincial common cause and the creation of a rudimentary institutional infrastructure for continental governance. Mobilization also brought a modern conception of patriotic citizenship to the fore, underscoring the importance of broad popular participation to the revolution's success. Jefferson's Declaration of Independence provided the script for consenting patriots who identified with one another as they pledged allegiance to the new nation they collectively created. This was not the classical ideal of virtuous self-sacrifice and self-negation to the republic but rather the apotheosis of an exalted and enlightened sense of self that would be most fully realized in the happiness of future generations. As they made their fateful choice for independence, newborn citizens shared a heartfelt conversion experience with their countrymen. As Jefferson later explained in his famous love letter to Maria Cosway, "if our country, when pressed with wrongs at the point of the bayonet, had been governed by its heads instead of its hearts, where should we have been now?"[65] Jefferson and his fellow Americans found themselves in this dire situation *because* they followed their heads, but George III would not listen to the reasonable claims a "candid world" would surely endorse.[66] The commercial republican ethos certainly prepared the way for independence, teaching future Americans to see others—as well as trading partners beyond their shores—as equals and to focus on removing obstacles to free exchange. But when the protracted imperial crisis came to a head, the heart assumed its sovereign prerogative, and "we threw up a few pulsations of our warmest blood."[67] This was Jefferson's way of articulating the first and most fundamental law of nature (and of nations): self-preservation. In the moment of truth, he appealed to the highest law, simultaneously imagining a profoundly personal crisis for himself, imputing a collective identity (or selfhood) to the American people, and seeking recognition and support from the "powers of the earth."[68]

Calculating commercial republicans would be reluctant (as deeply divided Anglo-Americans surely were) to risk everything on revolutionary battlefields. Independence came at a steep price, compounding the loss of life, the destruction of property, and the high level of indebtedness and taxation that crippled state governments and nearly destroyed the perilously imperfect union. Only modern-day patriots, animated by identification with one another and a commitment to defend their common country, would willingly make the sacrifices that, as Jefferson told Cosway, secured the new nation's independence. An exasperated Adam Smith thought it was all an absurd waste of blood and treasure. The great commercial republican was convinced, with his transatlantic counterparts, that a bloodless peace could still be negotiated, thus perpetuating a prosperous and expanding transatlantic empire; if it was too late to heal the widening rift, Britain should let its former transatlantic provinces find their own independent way in the world.[69]

Not surprisingly, commercial republicans in America had mixed feelings about the new republican regime, its place in the postimperial trading world, and their countrymen's capacity for self-government. The mobilization—and potential unleashing—of popular power threatened to turn postprovincial Anglo-American societies upside down, subverting the pretensions and ambitions of the would-be "better sort"; for their part, ordinary folk feared antidemocratic conspiracies against their liberties. John Adams feared everybody: "to save 'our bedollared country' from 'the universal gangrene of avarice,'" he sought to make "republican use of the rivals of ambition and pride of birth, thereby employing 'one prejudice to counteract another.'"[70] James Madison thought in similarly mechanistic terms, promising that "ambition" would "be made to counteract ambition" under his proposed federal Constitution.[71]

The American Revolution could not have succeeded without mobilizing "ordinary farmers, mechanics, and tradesmen," Lerner notes, thus giving them a stake in the polity as active citizens and voters. Yet even the "modestly elevated multitude on whom the shapers of the commercial republic placed their hopes" threatened to wield their power in unpredictable (or perhaps all-too-predictable) ways. In a prudent, functional division of labor, the multitude's energies would be directed to the "economic side of life."[72] But this was not to be, for the revolution initiated an ongoing succession of crises and mobilizations that democratized American politics—for better *and* for worse. Politics and economics could not be kept separate under the new dispensation. The ambit of state activity and capacity expanded remarkably in the post-revolutionary decades, most conspicuously in the no-longer-sovereign states, more controversially but nonetheless significantly on the federal level. This expansion could take place only under a regime that plausibly claimed the democratic sanction of the sovereign people.

Jefferson grasped the crucial role of popular political participation in the ongoing process of American nation making and state formation. The imperial crisis revealed the protean character of Ralph Lerner's Anglo-American commercial republicans at the decisive moment they became conscious of themselves as a separate people. The progress of mobilization modeled a dynamic new conception of individual and collective identity, valorizing patriotic sacrifices for a higher cause of incalculable value. The spirit of 1776 was something new under Jefferson's sun, an outburst of popular enthusiasm that in normal times repelled well-bred, cool and calculating provincial elites—like Jefferson—with their exalted social and cultural aspirations. Regime change signaled the destruction of Jefferson's old provincial world, alienating him from the "unfeeling brethren" of an increasingly distant metropolis, obliterating the distances that he and his kind had so assiduously cultivated with their Creole countrymen in Virginia and across the continent.

Commercial republicanism prepared the way for the break with Britain, teaching enterprising provincials that all men (or market actors) were (or should be) "created equal" while illuminating the ways onerous regulation and unconstitutional interference made them effectively unequal—and even threatened to enslave them. Yet if the commercial republicans Lerner invokes could envision a progressively more peaceful and prosperous commercial world emerging from the old regime's hierarchies and privileges that it had helped subvert, the age of democratic revolution initiated by provincial Americans gave rise instead to a highly competitive, war-prone system of modern nation-states with an unprecedented capacity to mobilize men and resources in the name of their peoples and in pursuit of their conflicting interests.

The commercial republican ethos did not disappear, as Tocqueville demonstrated in *Democracy in America*, for free enterprise and flourishing domestic markets guarantee the creation of wealth that enriches states, sustains their public credit, and enables them to fight endless wars. The genius of the commercial republican character, as Lerner shows, was its responsiveness and adaptability to the dynamic circumstances made and constantly remade by commerce. His commercial republicans dreamed of a prosperous and predictable peace that would allow them to pursue happiness and harvest the fruits of their enterprise. Self-declared Americans dreamed such dreams in the midst of a revolution that inaugurated the bloody and protracted process of reconfiguring the political geography of a new world order of nation-states. The career of Thomas Jefferson—commercial republican and Creole nationalist—illuminates that complicated history. The dreams of his enlightened age still survive, casting a critical light on the world he and fellow republicans on the periphery of Britain's expanding "empire of liberty" helped bring to life.

NOTES

1. Benedict Anderson, *Imagined Communities: Reflections on the Origin and Spread of Nationalism*, rev. ed. (London: Verso, 2006).

2. Jefferson's "original Rough draught" of the Declaration of Independence, in *The Papers of Thomas Jefferson Digital Edition*, ed. James P. McClure and J. Jefferson Looney (Charlottesville: University of Virginia Press, Rotunda, 2008–22), https://rotunda-upress-virginia-edu.proxy01.its.virginia.edu/founders/TSJN-01-01-02-0176-0004; hereafter cited as *PTJDE*.

3. Thomas Jefferson (hereafter TJ), Autobiography, January 6, 1821, in *Thomas Jefferson Writings*, ed. Merrill Peterson (New York: Library of America, 1984), 18.

4. TJ to Henry Lee, May 8, 1825, in Peterson, *Jefferson Writings*, 1501.

5. Annette Gordon-Reed and Peter S. Onuf, *"Most Blessed of the Patriarchs": Thomas Jefferson and the Empire of the Imagination* (New York: Liveright, 2016).

6. TJ to John Holmes, April 22, 1820, in *PTJDE*, https://rotunda-upress-virginia-edu.proxy01.its.virginia.edu/founders/TSJN-03-15-02-0518; Peter Onuf, *Jefferson's Empire: The Language of American Nationhood* (Charlottesville: University of Virginia Press, 2000), 109–117.

7. TJ's epitaph, in Peterson, *Jefferson Writings*, 706. TJ's understanding of what "authorship" meant enabled him to distinguish his original text from the text adopted by Congress.

Jay Fliegelman, *Declaring Independence: Jefferson, Natural Language & the Culture of Performance* (Stanford, CA: Stanford University Press, 1993).

8. Robert M. S. McDonald, *Confounding Father: Thomas Jefferson's Image in His Own Time* (Charlottesville: University of Virginia Press, 2016); Francis D. Cogliano, *Thomas Jefferson: Reputation and Legacy* (Charlottesville: University of Virginia Press, 2006). On fame, see Douglass Adair, *Fame and the Founding Fathers*, ed. Trevor Colbourn (New York: Norton for the Institute of Early American History and Culture, 1974).

9. Ralph Lerner, "Commerce and Character: The Anglo-American as New-Model Man," *William and Mary Quarterly* 36, 1 (January 1979): 3.

10. Nicholas Onuf and Peter Onuf, *Nations, Markets, and War: Modern History and the American Civil War* (Charlottesville: University of Virginia Press, 2006), 48–54; Ronald L. Meek, *Social Science and the Ignoble Savage* (New York: Cambridge University Press, 1976).

11. Onuf and Onuf, *Nations, Markets, and War*, 187–218; Donald Winch, *Riches and Poverty: An Intellectual History of Political Economy in Britain, 1750–1834* (Cambridge: Cambridge University Press, 1996).

12. Peter S. Onuf, *Jefferson and the Virginians: Democracy, Constitutions, and Empire* (Baton Rouge: Louisiana State University Press, 2018).

13. On provincial identity formation, see Jack P. Greene, *Imperatives, Behaviors, and Identities: Essays in Early American Cultural History* (Charlottesville: University of Virginia Press, 1992).

14. Onuf, *Jefferson's Empire*, 61–65; John Phillip Reid, *Constitutional History of the American Revolution: The Authority of Rights* (Madison: University of Wisconsin Press, 1986), 118–120.

15. Richard Price, *A Discourse on the Love of Our Country, Delivered on November 4, 1789* (Boston, 1790), 12–13.

16. Jack P. Greene, *Peripheries and Center: Constitutional Development in the Extended Polities of the British Empire and the United States, 1607–1788* (Athens: University of Georgia Press, 1986); Jack P. Greene, *The Constitutional Origins of the American Revolution* (New York: Cambridge University Press, 2011); J. M. Bumsted, "'Things in the Womb of Time': Ideas of American Independence, 1633 to 1763," *William and Mary Quarterly* 31 (1974): 534–564.

17. TJ to James Monroe, May 5, 1793, in *PTJDE*, https://rotunda-upress-virginia-edu.proxy01.its.virginia.edu/founders/TSJN-01-25-02-0603.

18. Lerner, "Commerce and Character," 11n19.

19. Documents concerning the whale fishery, editorial note, *PTJDE*, https://rotunda-upress-virginia-edu.proxy01.its.virginia.edu/founders/TSJN-01-14-02-0064-0001; TJ to G. K. van Hogendorp, October 13, 1785, in *PTJDE*, https://rotunda-upress-virginia-edu.proxy01.its.virginia.edu/founders/TSJN-01-08-02-0497.

20. Lerner, "Commerce and Character," 19n46, referring to TJ, *Notes on the State of Virginia*, ed. William Peden (Chapel Hill: University of North Carolina Press, 1954), query XVIII (Manners).

21. John Adams to TJ, August 24, 1815, in *PTJDE*, https://rotunda-upress-virginia-edu.proxy01.its.virginia.edu/founders/TSJN-03-08-02-0560; epigraph to Bernard Bailyn, *The*

Ideological Origins of the American Revolution (Cambridge, MA: Harvard University Press, 1967).

22. Robert E. Shalhope, "Toward a Republican Synthesis: The Emergence of an Understanding of Republicanism in American Historiography," *William and Mary Quarterly* 29 (1972): 49–80; Robert E. Shalhope, "Republicanism and Early American Historiography," *William and Mary Quarterly* 39 (1982): 334–356; Daniel Rodgers, "Republicanism: The Career of a Concept," *Journal of American History* 79 (1992): 11–38.

23. Ralph Lerner, "The Constitution of the Thinking Revolutionary," in *Beyond Confederation: Origins of the Constitution and American National Identity*, ed. Richard Beeman et al. (Chapel Hill: University of North Carolina Press, 1987), 38–68; Ralph Lerner, *The Thinking Revolutionary: Principle and Practice in the New Republic* (Ithaca, NY: Cornell University Press, 1987).

24. TJ to Henry Lee, May 8, 1825, in Peterson, *Jefferson Writings*, 1501.

25. Lerner, "Commerce and Character," 4.

26. Lerner, 5.

27. Lerner, 8. On Smith and mercantilism, see John C. Crowley, *The Privileges of Independence: Neomercantilism and the American Revolution* (Baltimore: Johns Hopkins University Press, 1993).

28. Christopher L. Tomlins, *Freedom Bound: Law, Labor, and Civic Identity in Colonizing English America, 1580–1865* (New York: Cambridge University Press, 2010).

29. Lerner, "Commerce and Character," 8.

30. Robert R. Palmer, *The Age of the Democratic Revolution*, 2 vols. (Princeton, NJ: Princeton University Press, 1959–64), 1:213–263.

31. On mobilization, see John Shy, "The Military Conflict Considered as a Revolutionary War," in *A People Numerous and Armed: Reflections on the Military Struggle for American Independence* (New York: Oxford University Press, 1976), 213–244. The leading state studies are, on Pennsylvania, Richard A. Ryerson, *The Revolution Is Now Begun: The Radical Committees of Philadelphia, 1765–1776* (Philadelphia: University of Pennsylvania Press, 1977); on New York, Edward Countryman, *A People in Revolution: The American Revolution and Political Society in New York, 1760–1790* (Baltimore: Johns Hopkins University Press, 1981).

32. Eric Hobsbawm, *Nations and Nationalism since 1780: Programme, Myth, Reality*, 2nd ed. (Cambridge: Cambridge University Press, 1992).

33. Edmund S. Morgan, *Inventing the People: The Rise of Popular Sovereignty in England and America* (New York: W. W. Norton, 1988).

34. TJ to Peter Carr, August 10, 1787, in *PTJDE*, https://rotunda-upress-virginia-edu.proxy01.its.virginia.edu/founders/TSJN-01-12-02-0021.

35. Jean M. Yarbrough, *American Virtues: Thomas Jefferson on the Character of a Free People* (Lawrence: University Press of Kansas, 1998).

36. Lerner, "Commerce and Character," 4; Lorraine Smith Pangle and Thomas L. Pangle, *The Learning of Liberty: The Educational Ideas of the American Founders* (Lawrence: University Press of Kansas, 1993).

37. Lerner, "Commerce and Character," 11.

38. William Shakespeare, *As You Like It*, act II, scene VII, line 139.

39. Lerner, "Commerce and Character," 8, 13.
40. Lerner, 11.
41. Lerner, 14, quoting Montesquieu, *The Spirit of the Laws*.
42. Albert O. Hirschman, *The Passions and the Interests: Political Arguments for Capitalism before Its Triumph* (Princeton, NJ: Princeton University Press, 1977).
43. Michael D. Hattem, *Past and Prologue: Politics and Memory in the American Revolution* (New Haven, CT: Yale University Press, 2020).
44. Lerner, "Commerce and Character," 21.
45. Lerner, 23.
46. Benjamin Rush, *A Plan for the Establishment of Public Schools and the Diffusion of Knowledge in Pennsylvania* (Philadelphia, 1786), 27.
47. Quoted in Lerner, "Commerce and Character," 11.
48. James Hutson, *John Adams and the Diplomacy of the American Revolution* (Lexington: University Press of Kentucky, 1980); Peter Onuf and Nicholas Onuf, *Federal Union, Modern World: The Law of Nations in an Age of Revolutions, 1776–1814* (Madison, WI: Madison House, 1993), 103–113.
49. Quoted in Lerner, "Commerce and Character," 14; Reginald C. Stewart, *The Half-way Pacifist: Thomas Jefferson's View of War* (Toronto: University of Toronto Press, 1978).
50. George Washington to Henry Lee Jr., September 22, 1788, in *The Papers of George Washington Digital Edition* (Charlottesville: University of Virginia Press, Rotunda, 2008), https://rotunda-upress-virginia-edu.proxy01.its.virginia.edu/founders/GEWN-04-06-02-0469.
51. David Hendrickson, *Peace Pact: The Lost World of the American Founding* (Lawrence: University Press of Kansas, 2003).
52. Max Edling, *A Revolution in Favor of Government: Origins of the U.S. Constitution and the Making of the American State* (New York: Oxford University Press, 2003); Max Edling, *Perfecting the Union: National and State Authority in the US Constitution* (New York: Oxford University Press, 2019).
53. Hirschman, *Passions and the Interests*.
54. TJ, First Inaugural Address, March 4, 1801, in *PTJDE*, https://rotunda-upress-virginia-edu.proxy01.its.virginia.edu/founders/TSJN-01-33-02-0116-0004.
55. TJ to Joseph Priestley, March 21, 1801, in *PTJDE*, https://rotunda-upress-virginia-edu.proxy01.its.virginia.edu/founders/TSJN-01-33-02-0336.
56. TJ, *Notes on the State of Virginia*, query XIX (Manufactures), 164–165.
57. Onuf, *Jefferson and the Virginians*, 3–19.
58. Steve Pincus, *The Heart of the Declaration: The Founders' Case for an Activist Government* (New Haven, CT: Yale University Press, 2016).
59. Onuf and Onuf, *Nations, Markets, and War*.
60. Quoted in Lerner, "Commerce and Character," 12.
61. The commercial republicans of the Scottish Enlightenment—from a province that was *successfully* incorporated into the United Kingdom in 1707—were particularly influential in the American colonies.

62. Francis D. Cogliano, *Emperor of Liberty: Thomas Jefferson's Foreign Policy* (New Haven, CT: Yale University Press, 2014); Onuf, *Jefferson's Empire*; Onuf, *Jefferson and the Virginians*, 117–154.

63. Joyce Appleby, *Capitalism and a New Social Order* (New York: New York University Press, 1984); Joyce Appleby, "What Is New in the Philosophy of Thomas Jefferson," in *Liberalism and Republicanism in the Historical Imagination* (Cambridge, MA: Harvard University Press, 1992), 291–319; Onuf and Onuf, *Nations, Markets, and War*, 219–246.

64. On national economist Friedrich List's admiration for the federal Constitution and his indebtedness to Adam Smith, see Onuf and Onuf, *Nations, Markets, and War*, 163–172.

65. TJ to Maria Cosway, October 12, 1786, in *PTJDE*, https://rotunda-upress-virginia-edu.proxy01.its.virginia.edu/founders/TSJN-01-10-02-0309.

66. The Declaration of Independence as Adopted by Congress, July 4, 1776, in *PTJDE*, https://rotunda-upress-virginia-edu.proxy1.library.virginia.edu/founders/TSJN-01-01-02-0176-0006.

67. TJ to Cosway, October 12, 1786.

68. Declaration of Independence.

69. See the discussion in Onuf and Onuf, *Nations, Markets, and War*, 212–218.

70. Quoted in Lerner, "Commerce and Character," 23.

71. James Madison, *Federalist* 51, February 6, 1788, in *The Papers of James Madison Digital Edition*, ed. J. C. A. Stagg (Charlottesville: University of Virginia Press, Rotunda, 2010), https://rotunda-upress-virginia-edu.proxy1.library.virginia.edu/founders/JSMN-01-10-02-0279.

72. Lerner, "Commerce and Character," 19.

CHAPTER 7

The Good Republican: Madison's Model Citizen

Colleen A. Sheehan

In Jonathan Swift's imaginative tale *The Battle of the Books*, Thomas Hobbes is inadvertently shelved next to Plato in the king's library. An awful row breaks out between books by the two authors and their respective allies, symbolizing the battle between modern and ancient political philosophy. The story is prefaced by a charming vignette about a similar ancient versus modern quarrel taking place on the hill of Parnassus and a dispute over "prospect." Swift's battle stories mark a war of ideas between two conflicting perspectives on the most fundamental political and human questions, including "How should I live my life?"

LERNER'S NEW-MODEL COMMERCIAL MAN

Ralph Lerner takes up the issue of the American founders' vision of political and social life in his erudite and provocative "Commerce and Character: The Anglo-American as New-Model Man."[1] The question of the American character, as it was conceived during the founding era, constitutes the central inquiry. According to Lerner, the character of the new-model Anglo-American man was decisively shaped by the ethos generated by modern commercial society. Montesquieu described the English version of this modern republican man in chapter 19 of *The Spirit of the Laws*. A few decades later another French aristocrat, Alexis de Tocqueville, took up where Montesquieu left off, describing the American version of the modern republican man. Both Frenchmen saw much to be admired in this assiduous, independently spirited, and, for the most part, unpretentious modern man of commerce. However, both issued sharp warnings as well. The advances in modern science that led to the growth of commerce, industrialization, the division of labor, and materialism were already wreaking irreversible effects on the civic and social lives of modern nations. They also influenced the formation and type of human character such regimes were likely to produce, though in and of themselves, these scientific and historical changes were certainly not determinative of the future. Modern republican life might pave the way for freedom and human flourishing, but it might just as easily be ridden with envy, luxurious but spiritually empty, and terrifyingly despotic.

Like everything from Lerner's pen, his analysis of the modern republican is incisive, thoughtful, nuanced, and vibrant. This new-model man is not simply a cross between Hobbesian brute and Lockean mercenary, as some have made him out to be. Following Tocqueville, Lerner stresses that the American version of the modern republican had to choose between two paths forward—one strewn with the love of materialism, individualism, secularism, egalitarian envy, and soft despotism, and the other a harder road requiring the work of self-government, including moderating selfish desires, strengthening civic associations, retaining a substantial place for the spiritual, and preserving federalism and the love of liberty. In Lerner's account, a number of individuals in the American founding generation did not wholeheartedly embrace the modern commercial ethos—some were rather hesitant, in fact—and it was not rare for them to envision a more moderate version than that of Montesquieu or David Hume. Despite their identification with a safer kind of selfishness, a tamer ambition, quieter virtues, and "decent materialism," Lerner ultimately concludes that, in the aggregate, the American founding generation set out on the path Tocqueville warned against.[2] While they may not have been enthusiastic commercialists like Hume or admirers of the political philosophy of Hobbes, in the end they did not reject Hume's or Hobbes's premises. Since its inception, Lerner claims, the US government was designed to take human beings as they are rather than as one might wish them to be. The founders understood that people generally want security and comfort, and they believed that self-interest trumps civic virtue for most individuals. Accordingly, they followed Hobbes and sought "a surer guide to sane behavior . . . in the operation of a nonrational mechanism, the aggregate of small, anonymous calculations of things immediately known and felt by all."[3] Eschewing the principles of classical ethics and republican citizenship and accepting that men are governed by a different set of passions, they sought to "animate them with a spirit of avarice and industry, art and luxury."[4]

In Lerner's view, passion and interest, not reason, constitute the basis of public decisions in the modern commercial republic, just as the mutual exchange of goods and services rather than civic virtue holds the community together. Where the ancients saw heroic virtue and magnanimity, modern writers such as Montesquieu, Adam Smith, and Hume saw extravagance, folly, vainglorious fantasies, and sometimes "grotesque preoccupation."[5] In place of the beautiful and noble, moderns chose utility and economic justice, opting for "a more sensible and realizable alternative to earlier notions of civic virtue."[6] Thus, despite Lerner's praise for the new-model man's practicality, one is struck by his description of the implied "heights" of modernity that "elicited efforts of heroic proportions from unheroic men for unheroic objectives."[7] In view of the modern commercial man's rejection of the grandeur of the ancients for the sake of small, continuous private profits of material mediocrity and cheapness, Lerner encourages us to see that such a man might not be "entitled to any very ardent love or admiration."[8]

In sum, Lerner's conclusion seems to be that the American founding was essentially Hobbesian at its roots and that it never actually had the chance to become the more respectable type of modern republic of liberty described by Tocqueville. To illustrate this, Lerner highlights the views of American writers and statesmen such as Benjamin Franklin, Benjamin Rush, and John Adams, adding their analyses of the world of commerce emerging around them to those of Montesquieu, Hume, Smith, and Tocqueville. Probably the best description of the best attributes of the modern commercial man comes from the pen of Benjamin Franklin. It is not surprising, then, that Lerner has written extensively about Franklin, matching mind with mind, wit with wit, originality and brilliance with the same. Franklin's self-awareness and his grasp of the nature of the project he was engaged in are encapsulated in his autobiography. Besides the traditional virtues of moderation and justice, Franklin adds such practices as thriftiness, industry, cleanliness, order, silence, chastity, and tranquility to the list. When compared to the classical virtues such as courage, generosity, magnificence, magnanimity, friendliness, and wittiness, the contrast between the two versions of human excellence is striking. The distinction is no less marked by the recollection of the civic-spiritedness and generosity, expansive sociability, and extraordinary wit of Franklin himself (not to mention his deficiency in silence, chastity, and humility). Franklin's ideal man might be someone like Mark Twain's Connecticut Yankee, if not exactly Franklin himself. From the classical perspective, Franklin's ideal man looks bourgeois and banal, someone who has a great deal in common with the Walmart shopper of today. In contrast, the classical great-souled man is neither bourgeois nor banal, and he is certainly not a huckster or a bargain hunter.[9]

GEORGE WASHINGTON AND JAMES MADISON

One American not mentioned in Lerner's account of the new-model man is George Washington. When comparing Franklin's virtues in his autobiography with Washington's "Rules of Civility," a study in contrasts emerges. Although the two lists share certain concerns such as the importance of cleanliness and good table manners, with respect to deeper matters such as religious reverence, honor, pride, and humility, the difference in perspective is palpable. If Lerner's description of the new-model American republican is correct, then Washington would certainly be a one-off. However, perhaps Washington should be understood as representative of an earlier era in America, described by Tocqueville as an age of honor and deference, which was soon displaced by the egalitarianism and social mobility of Jacksonian America. Either way, the contrast between Washington's imposing moral stature and unapologetic pride and Franklin's clever schemes and dalliances reveals how differently they conceived of human excellence. It may not be quite so easy to classify the new American man, after all.

The other major figure of the founding conspicuous for his relative absence in Lerner's essay is James Madison (he is cited once in passing). Besides being the most scholarly of the founding generation, Madison is often considered the chief political architect of the modern commercial republic in America. Although Lerner neglects Madison in "Commerce and Character," he does consider Madison's views on the role of virtue in the modern republic elsewhere. Despite Madison's claim in *Federalist* 55 that a certain amount of virtue is necessary to secure the ends of government,[10] Lerner is not persuaded that Madison's "extended republic" fulfills "the preconditions of republican virtue." "It would be hard," Lerner writes,

> to find in this language a concession that there was a political task involved in sustaining the virtue of the people. Is then the people's republican virtue a "given"—enduring, available, sufficient? Not quite. Though in speaking at all to the issue, Madison differed from many Federalists, his discussion remains

incomplete and hence problematic. The Federalists surely were aware of the insufficiency of their response to nagging Antifederalist questions about republican virtue. They may well have avoided a detailed discussion of that theme out of fear that the answer they would be obliged to give could only harm the more urgent cause of ratification.[11]

Ultimately, Lerner concludes, "we are left to wonder" how the Federalists' thought republican virtue could be sustained.[12]

Lerner is correct that Publius's (Madison's) discussion of the role of virtue in *The Federalist* is incomplete. However, in the first years under the new Constitution, Madison took up where he left off in his *Federalist* essays and set out to make a more "thorough investigation" of republicanism, ancient and modern.[13] To this end, he concentrated his studies on a complex, multi-volume work on classical Greece that Jefferson had recently shipped to him from France. This eighteenth-century work, *Voyage of the Young Anacharsis in Greece* by Jean Jacques Barthélemy, takes the reader on a journey through the ancient world, with chapters on politics, philosophy, religion, art, music, mathematics, and culture. Madison studied these volumes to learn from the "great oracles of political wisdom" in both the ancient and the modern world. These included ancients such as Thucydides, Strabo, Plato, and Aristotle and moderns such as Montesquieu, Hume, Edward Gibbon, and William Robertson. Shortly thereafter he began publishing a series of essays in the *National Gazette*, a number of them produced from rough drafts of his 1791 "Notes on Government." A hefty handful of these newspaper articles treat the subject of the character of the republican citizen, as well as various influences on that character, including commerce, materialism, luxury, colonialism, and slavery. One of the articles examines a new type of "republic" in which the forces of the new commercialism are evident and where self-interest takes the place of public duty.

As a conscious continuation of his explication of the principles and processes of republican government in *The Federalist*, these 1791–92 Party Press Essays flesh out Publius's vision of a "new and more noble course" for America. What were the contours of this course? What was Madison's view of commerce and its effects on foreign policy and domestic civic relations? What way of life did he envision for his fellow citizens, and to what extent did it depend or not depend on the cultivation of republican virtue and the formation of civic character? Perhaps we can summarize these questions by returning to

Swift's account of the careless cataloger in the king's library: If *The Federalist* and other writings of Madison were inadvertently placed between Hobbes and Plato in the bookcase, would Plato be aghast by the presence of his new shelfmate? Or would Hobbes be tempted to elbow Madison hard enough to send him to the floor?

MADISON'S REPUBLICAN CITIZEN

One eighteenth-century aspect of commercialism was the idea of free trade across national borders. According to Lerner, "commerce inclined men to consider one another primarily as demanders and suppliers, to consider the world as constituting but a single state, of which all the [particular] societies are members." Dubbed by Adam Smith "the great mercantile republic," this new polity was constituted by "producers and traders" and by "owners and employers." It had more "citizens of the world" than citizens of any particular nation or country; they might be thought of as "commercial cousins, cool fellow-citizens of a universal republic."[14] For Montesquieu, the modern commercial republic was "less of a union of fellow citizens, bound together by ties of friendship, than of an alliance of contracting parties"—of "buyers and sellers" in a "world in which everything had its price."[15]

Thus, although the bonds of citizenship would be substantially weakened in the modern commercial republic, alliances of market utility—among both individuals and nations—would be markedly strengthened. This gave birth to the hope for a more peaceful world. The adherents of *doux commerce* believed that they were entering a time when manners and mores would be softened and destructive prejudices would be cured by the new commercial spirit of the modern age. Navigation, travel, trade, and colonization would take the place of war.[16]

Like Alexander Hamilton, Madison found flaws in the *doux commerce* thesis.[17] In an essay titled "Universal Peace," he argued that there are two classes of war: one resulting from the will of the government, the other from the will of the society. The only way to prevent the first kind of war is by making the will of the government dependent on the will of the society—in other words, by establishing republican governments. Skeptical of the view that, in the modern commercial world, monarchs would choose commerce over conquest, Madison claimed that the same old passions and interests—ambition, avidity, caprice, and revenge—that motivated hereditary monarchs in the past would continue to drive their actions in the age of commerce. He contended:

> Whilst war is to depend on those whose ambition, whose revenge, whose avidity, or whose caprice may contradict the sentiment of the community, and yet be uncontrouled by it; whilst war is to be declared by those who are to spend the public money, not by those who are to pay it; by those who are to direct the public forces, not by those who are to support them; by those whose power is to be raised, not by those whose chains may be riveted, the disease must continue to be *hereditary* like the government of which it is the offspring.[18]

As for the second class of war, Madison thought there was no simple cure. He advocated laws against perpetuating the national debt and in favor of making the generation that incurred the debt responsible for repaying it, so that "avarice would be sure to calculate the expences of ambition." In this argument in the Party Press Essays, reminiscent of the famous passage in *Federalist* 51 that declares, "ambition must be made to counteract ambition," we see the influence of Montesquieuian political science. However, in this same passage, Madison steps beyond Montesquieu, making passion and interest work to create a space for reason: "In the equipoise of . . . passions," Madison writes, "reason would be free to decide for the public good; and an ample reward would accrue to the state, first, from the avoidance of all its wars of folly, secondly, from the vigor of its unwasted resources for wars of necessity and defence."[19] The question that immediately presents itself is what Madison meant by "reason" that decides the public good. Is this reason—or perhaps what he calls elsewhere the "reason of the public"—grounded in moral precept, or is it merely the rational calculation of self-interest?

If Madison was not persuaded by the notion that in modern times conquest is replaced with commerce by way of self-interest—in other words, that economics (and profit) can replace politics (and war)—he nonetheless was an enthusiast for free trade. Agreeing with the French physiocrats that there is a natural course of trade and economic growth, he advocated free enterprise both within the nation and internationally to the extent politically possible and prudent, unrestricted by subsidies or monopolies. This included a rejection of governmental subsidies to jump-start certain kinds of industry and influence men's choice of occupations, even if such governmental action would enable the nation to compete with more industrially advanced nations.[20] This was one of the chief disagreements between Madison and Hamilton in the early 1790s and one of the primary causes of the origin of American political parties. Though not mentioned by name, Hamilton is surely the main target of Madison's 1792 *National Gazette* essay "Property," which asserts: "That is not a just government, nor is property secure under it, where arbitrary restrictions, exemptions, and monopolies deny to part of its citizens that free use of their faculties, and free choice of their occupations, which not only constitute their property in the general sense of the word; but are the means of acquiring property strictly so called."[21] Note that Madison's argument here is based on the oft-quoted—but also oft-misunderstood—passage in *Federalist* 10 regarding the "first object of government." It is not unusual to hear this statement condensed into the maxim that the first object of government is the protection of property. But this is not what Madison actually said. *Federalist* 10 reads: "The diversity in the faculties of men, from which the rights of property originate, is not less an insuperable obstacle to a uniformity of interests. The protection of these faculties is the first object of government. From the protection of different and unequal faculties of acquiring property, the possession of different degrees and kinds of property immediately results."[22]

According to Madison, the most fundamental and important work of politics is the protection of the human faculties. Why? These faculties, or powers of the human mind, separate human beings from the other animals. They are the uniquely human capacities, the loci of human freedom and choice. According to Madison, the "faculties of mind" include "sense, perception, judgment, desire, volition, memory, [and] imagination." The most important right of property that originates from the protection of these faculties is that of conscience. "Conscience is the most sacred of all property," he wrote in "Property"; it is the purest of inalienable rights, all others depending in part on positive right.[23]

For Madison, protecting the freedom of the mind and conscience requires limited government, for no government has the right to dictate an indivdual's spiritual beliefs or to punish him for his religious convictions. Our first duty, he argued in "Memorial and Remonstrance," is to the Creator, and this can be directed only "by reason and conviction, not by force or violence" or by "the opinions or dictates of others." As such, limited government is one condition necessary to protect the free exercise of human faculties; also required is the opportunity to pursue a way of life compatible with independent thought and responsible moral choice. For Madison, this way of life was encapsulated in that of the independent yeoman farmer. In two essays, one included in a set of research notes and the other a published essay titled "Republican Distribution of Citizens," he addressed the character of the republican citizen in the modern era. Madison's model republican citizen stands in contrast to the modern commercial individual depicted by Montesquieu in *Spirit of the Laws*, and it anticipates a response to Tocqueville. This person is not primarily a seller or a buyer; he is not preoccupied with material comforts and luxuries, nor is he neglectful of the spiritual life. He is not acquisitive or envious of others because he possesses what he needs to live a healthy, moderately comfortable, and, for the most part, self-sufficient life. Above all, Madison's republican citizen is an independent human being with a sense of self-assurance, dignity, and pride—a straightforward, unpretentious pride, if that is not a contradiction in terms. He is nobody's slave or servant or fool, and he does not make slaves or dependents or dupes of others.

According to Lerner, if some proponents of the new-model man of commerce found him wanting in some respects when compared with the ancient artistocrat or citizen-soldier—if he was materialistic, mediocre, private, absorbed in business, a bit cheap and vulgar—at least he was practical rather than grotesquely vain and extravagant or fanatically self-abnegating. Madison too saw the vanity and extravagance, not to mention the deceptiveness, of ancient political practice, noting the incredible charade at the Cave of Jupiter (constructed to dupe the people into political submission), where "Minos, Epimenides & Pythagoras pretended to have [received] a divine sanction to their laws." At "Athens death was decreed by the people to the Orator who should propose to apply to the public defence the money destined to pay for the seats of the poor at the Spectacles." And the "money with which Pericles decorated Athens, was raised by Aristides on the confederates of Athens for common defence, and on pretext of danger at Delos." Athens's principal revenue "consisted of tributes from her dependencies."[24]

However, Madison was no more a proponent of the publicly spiritless, materialistic man of commerce than he was of the haughty, garish public exhibitionists of ancient times. For some modern authors, trade, navigation, and colonization were key to moving from conquest and war to commerce and comfort, but Madison saw things through a different lens. For example, while the British colonies of the East and West Indies were a "source of some riches" and provided a lucrative market for the superfluities of British industry, they were nonetheless "Dependent Colonies." The relation between them and Great Britain was not akin to child and mother but rather slave and master. "They cherish pride, luxury, and vanity" and "make the labor of one part tributary to the enjoyment of another."[25]

The manufacturer, mechanic, and artisan ranked higher than the sailor in Madison's list of occupations fit for the republican citizen, but these occupations were not to be promoted while there were still unfilled posts in agriculture. "Whatever is least favorable to vigor of body, to the faculties of the mind, or to the virtues or the utilities of life," Madison argued, should be seen as a regretful choice, not "forced or fostered by public authority" while "occupations more friendly to human happiness lie vacant." At the bottom of the hierarchy of occupations was the sailor, whose contributions to the possibly civilizing effect of commerce were negated by the poor and dissipated existence that accompanies life at sea. "How unfortunate that in the intercourse by which nations are enlightened and refined, and their means of safety extended," Madison bleakly observed, "the immediate agents should be distinguished by the hardest condition of humanity."[26]

Madison's evaluation of the various occupations fit for citizens of a republic was based on the ends of human life, which he explicitly named: "health, virtue, intelligence, and competency." Note that Madison does not prioritize material wealth and luxurious comfort but instead focuses on the well-being of the body, mind, and soul, supported by moderation in the accumulation of wealth and material goods. For Madison, agriculture was the chosen occupation for the republican citizen because it was most conducive to achieving the ends of intellectual and moral virtue and to attaining safety, liberty, moderate comfort, and the "happiness of the individual." Madison called health "an appurtenance" of the agricultural way of life. He looked on this way of life as favorable to the cultivation of learning, quiet reflection, and moral virtue, which he defined as the "health of the soul." Eschewing luxury and fashion and all forms of economic dependence that make some people servilely reliant on others, Madison advocated a condition of economic "competency"—that is, a moderate and comfortable sufficiency of income and goods, without needless superfluity.[27]

The more elevated professions included lawyers, doctors, merchants, statesmen, philosophers, and theologians; the most educated and thoughtful Madison designated "literati." In Madison's republican schema, the literati possessed a deeply significant public responsibility to their neighbors and fellow citizens. Adopting the language associated with material exchange and commodification, he cleverly highlighted the importance of immaterial human goods by juxtaposing them against merely material goods. Madison's literati "are the cultivators of the human mind—the manufacturers of useful knowledge—the agents of the commerce of ideas—the censors of public manners—the teachers of the arts of life and the means of happiness."[28]

According to Madison, his disagreement with Montesquieu's conception of the new republic and the character of its citizens may have been at least partially due to the fact that Montesquieu lived and wrote in the era just prior to the advent of the politics of public opinion, of which he had but a coup d'oeil. In a newspaper article titled "Spirit of Governments," which was essentially a response to Montesquieu's new and provocative political analysis, Madison praised the Frenchman for the political insight he demonstrated at midcentury but claimed that Montesquieu had only a "glimpse" of the important changes that would mark the second half of the eighteenth century.[29] In this context, Madison took aim at Montesquieu's new regime classification and especially his description and praise of the modern republic in which self-interest replaces civic duty:

> A government operating by corrupt influence; *substituting the motive of private interest in place of public duty*; converting its pecuniary dispensations into bounties to favorites, or bribes to opponents; accommodating its measures to the avidity of a part of the nation instead of the benefit of the whole: in a word, enlisting an army of interested partizans, whose tongues, whose pens, whose intrigues, and whose active combinations, by supplying the terror of the sword, may support a real domination of the few, under an apparent liberty of the many. Such a government, wherever to be found, is an imposter. It is happy for the new world that it is not on the west side of the Atlantic. It will be both happy and honorable for the United States, if they never descend to mimic the costly pageantry of its form, nor betray themselves into the venal spirit of its administration.[30]

Madison was alluding to Montesquieu's description and praise of the regime he identified as a new republic hidden under the form of a monarchy, which was generally understood to be Great Britain. According to Montesquieu, although commerce unites nations, it does not unite individuals. Instead, economic competition and party rivalry characterize the domestic politics of modern republics. While this conflict model of politics reveals the *inquietude* at the core of modern commercial life, manifest in the people's fear of losing their liberties, this fear is a false one. The Newtonian-like political system of rival forces actually produces an equilibrium in government, which serves to secure liberty. As a result, Montesquieu argued, it does not matter whether citizens reason well or ill but only that they reason; that is, it matters not whether citizens' opinions or characters are sound, but it is essential that they voice their views and make demands of the government, thereby instigating the clash of interests and powers within government that produces equipoise.

Madison then contrasted this so-called republican model with his vision of the American republican model. The latter derives "its energy from the will of the society, and operat[es] by the reason of its measures, on the understanding and interest of the society." This is a true republic, Madison contended. And it is "the government for which philosophy has been searching, and humanity been sighing, from the most remote ages. Such are the republican governments which it is the glory of America to have invented, and her unrivalled happiness to possess."[31] Madison's republican model was new and modern, in the sense that it was the product of the modern age. Indeed, Madison's model was not an option for the ancients, for it became conceivable only with certain advances in science and technology that opened up the possibility of establishing a republic over a large territory. Nonetheless, Madison's republic was based on the age-old quest of classical republicanism. Ancient political philosophy tried and failed to conceive of a republic capable of achieving internal justice and the common good and, at the same time, able to defend itself against aggressive and powerful external polities. Montesquieu proffered a new solution to this dilemma: "a society of societies" built on the interplay of commercial interests. In Madison's view, Montesquieu's discovery answered neither the quest of classical philosophy nor the lamentations of humanity.

In contrast, Madison's "genuine" republic is grounded wholly in the sovereignty of the people and the authority of public opinion. It utilizes the multiplicity of interests and passions to cancel out narrow wants and prejudices that cannot be accommodated or repurposed toward the common good.[32] Although it employs the separation of powers to create checks and balances and achieve equilibrium in government, it does not substitute economic self-interest and partisan rivalry for the refinement and enlargement of public views. "Auxiliary precautions" sometimes serve as a "substitute for better motives," but that is not always the case: there are times when public duty, not to mention the spur of courage and magnanimity, is no less necessary in the modern republic than in the ancient one.[33] Moreover, auxiliary precautions are, as the term connotes, ancillary; they are not intended to replace the "primary control on government," which always rests with "the people."[34]

In Madison's writings in the late 1780s and early 1790s, the attentive reader will note a constant refrain: in republican government there can be no will independent of the society or the majority; republican government necessarily depends on the will of the society or the majority.[35] This goes hand in hand with his earlier statement in "Notes on Vices of the Political System of the United States," made in preparation for the federal convention, that the majority ultimately determines the law.[36] The problem, of course, is that the majority does not always act justly. The fundamental republican challenge, as Madison defined it, is how to place power on the side of right.[37] Put another way, in popular government the majority is both a party to the case and the ultimate judge in the case.[38] Therefore, it is necessary to attend to the education of public opinion—to shape, refine, enlarge, and modify the public views—so that the opinions and demands of the most powerful segment of society accord with justice and the general good. The extended republic and representation, as well as all the prudential institutional measures set forth in *The Federalist*, are in place to stymie majority faction. But Madison's ultimate goal was not to thwart the people's will in favor of rule by elites. Neither was it to magnify self-interest and minimize the power of opinion, nor to dispense with civic character formation and rely instead on a multiplicity of factions and shrewd institutional arrangements.[39] Rather, Madison's aim was to make government dependent on the will of the society (the majority) and to make the will of the society dependent on the reason of the society.[40] This coalition of a majority is achieved over time through a layered process that not only cancels out unpopular and partial claims but also provides deliberative forums to refine and coalesce reasonable views. As one part of the main Publius duo learned from the other, "the differences of opinion, and the jarring of parties in that [legislative] department of government, though they may sometimes obstruct salutary plans, yet often promote deliberation and circumspection; and serve to check excesses of the majority."[41]

"Public opinion ... is the real sovereign in every free [government]," Madison declared in an essay titled "Public Opinion." The "modification of the sovereignty" is the modification of public opinion from the mere will of the public or majority to the reason of the public. The multilayered and complex political system of the United States was envisioned by Madison with this purpose in mind. The will of society is refined and enlarged, moving through the multifaceted deliberative processes, as it works its influence on the views of citizens. Just as citizens' demands on society are shaped by this process, so too is their understanding of what they owe to one another. The "debt of protection" that republican citizens are obliged to render one another is present in the original social compact, but for it to become part of the people's ethos requires civic engagement, public practice, and the formation of republican habits; ultimately, it requires the embodiment of the spirit of republicanism in the citizens' character.

Accordingly, in contrast to the self-absorbed, avaricious, civically tone-deaf citizen Lerner identifies as the new-model American man, Madison introduced us to an American citizenry formed and educated in the processes and principles of republicanism. Volubly objecting to Montesquieu's model, in which private interest is substituted for public duty, he called for Americans to embody the principles of the revolution and meet the challenge of self-government.[42] Rejecting the type of "community" in which atomistic private men know little to nothing about one another, Madison called on Americans to eradicate narrow local prejudices and needless rivalries and to come together in their mutual public labors, consolidating "the affairs of the states into one harmonious interest." "Let it be the patriotic study of all," he said, "to erect over the whole, one paramount Empire of reason, benevolence and brotherly affection."[43]

Madison's model republican citizen is a man of the modern world, but he is not the man depicted by Montesquieu, Hume, or Lerner. Nor is he the classical slaveholding aristocratic citizen envisioned by Aristotle. With scientific and technological advances that enabled people in the modern era to communicate effectively over a large territory, Madison envisioned a republic in which free, equal, self-sufficient, and civically educated citizens formed the basis of a new order of the ages. This new republic, however, was intended to achieve age-old political ends—namely, the health, competency, intelligence, and virtue of its citizens. In essence, Madison viewed the health of the body, mind, and soul as the ends toward which the good legislator directs his efforts, albeit in ways that protect the human faculties, not dictate to them. The civic bar set by Madison was anything but low or vulgar. His ambitions were hardly tamed, and his aspirations were nothing short of historic. He envisioned a republic in which the citizens genuinely governed themselves, both at the level of society by majority rule and at the level of the individual human soul. In Madison's view, at the core of the American social compact is a civic promise—a promise to treat one another with the respect that is due to human beings qua human beings. This is the foundation for civic trust and civic friendship and for the "benevolence, and brotherly affection" that infuses the spirit of Madison's good republican.

ANCIENTS VERSUS MODERNS

The ancient versus modern dispute recounted by Jonathan Swift was taken up by various authors in the ensuing years, including twentieth-century scholar Leo Strauss and his students. The break with the classical world was initiated by Machiavelli, though it was not until Hobbes and the incorporation of modern science into politics and ethics that the split became complete. The issues at stake were many, but the overarching quarrel concerned the ends of human life (including the summum bonum) and how human beings should live their lives. It is not uncommon to hear the dispute summarized this way: the classics talked much of happiness and virtue; the moderns speak only of security, comfort, wealth, and freedom.

As significant as chronology is to classifying the ancient-modern dichotomy, the divide cannot be comprehended simply by a dateline. As Strauss taught, "ancient" and "modern" connote eras, but even more importantly, these terms refer to modes of political philosophical thought, especially with respect to questions regarding human nature and the good life. Use of the ancient-modern dichotomy to understand the vying alternatives to the most fundamental human and political questions is complicated by certain extraordinarily significant historical phenomena—namely, the advent of Christianity as a universal religion and the rise of modern science and technology. These were game-changing events in the West, rendering ineffective and outdated significant aspects of classical republican politics. Christianity as a universal religion raised the specter of universal monarchy and world despotism. The protection of civil liberty in the Christian West necessarily went hand in hand with the protection of religious liberty and freedom of conscience. Accordingly, the doctrine of limited government became a necessary, but not necessarily sufficient, condition of republican government in the modern world. Like Locke and Montesquieu, Madison enthusiastically endorsed the tenets of limited government and rejected the heavy-handed sumptuary laws, rites, and sacrifices of ancient times.

Taken as a whole, the ends proffered by Madison in "Republican

Distribution of Citizens"—physical health, economic competency, intellectual development, and moral virtue—seem more compatible with the aims of the classics than with those of the modern commercial man. Still, even though Madison calls on both governmental representatives and leading intellectuals to take up the task of civic education in America, the extended republic of individual rights and liberties really does not resemble an ancient polity. No one would mistake it for Athens, Carthage, Sparta, or Rome.

Although the concern with human virtue and human happiness may be shared by ancient and modern philosophers and statesmen, the means of achieving such ends would necessarily be substantially different. The considerable changes that occurred toward the end of the Middle Ages and exerted an influence in the early modern era (e.g., the invention of gunpowder, the compass, the printing press) caused thoughtful authors and lawgivers to think differently about the political task and the means of achieving the desired ends. For some, it meant a calculated change in human ends themselves. For others, it did not.

A new and immensely different scene characterized the political landscape of the eighteenth century; consequently, the means of addressing these new political realities required rethinking as well. Although history does not take the place of natural right, natural right changes in different historical times and circumstances, impacting the choices available to the political philosopher and statesman. "A perfect Theory" on the subject of the best republican character, Madison wrote, cannot simply "be reduced to practice by any plan of legislation." Nonetheless, the philosophical legislator ought to provide "a model to which successive spontaneous improvements might approximate the condition of the Society."[44]

CONCLUSION

The case Lerner presents for the rise of the materialistic, self-immersed, and crass type of human character is one result of the historical and scientific changes that impacted the Western world in the seventeenth and eighteenth centuries. Montesquieu's observations regarding the new type of society he saw developing in Great Britain and the type of man and citizen this society was molding are perceptive and indispensable to comprehending the crossroads between the old world of divine right and deference and the new world of liberty and equality. If Montesquieu, Smith, and Hume show us one model of the new republicanism, Madison shows us quite another. Limited government and individual liberty may be compatible with the type of modern liberalism that could lead to soft despotism, materialism, secularism, and hedonism. But, from Madison's perspective, limited government and individual liberty may be just as compatible with a political model that forms habits of mind and heart worthy of genuine republican citizens. Madison took seriously the challenge of the experiment in self-government, for as he argued in *The Federalist*, no other way of life would be reconcilable with the principles of the Declaration of Independence or the "genius" of the American people. A particularly perspicacious poet of American politics once observed that the commitment to self-government was the thing that motivated James Madison and informed his thoughts and labors.[45] By this he meant not simply majority rule but self-government at the level of the individual soul, which requires each of us to exercise self-restraint and take guidance from the principles of republican right. Such is the "debt of protection" that lies at the core of the American social compact and obliges each of us to defend the rights and liberties of others.[46]

Tom Sawyer, Jo March, George Bailey, Frederick Douglass, Amelia Earhart, Robert Frost—none of these characters are of the old world; none of them were captivated by the ancient longing for wanton grandeur or the pretense of aristocratic aloofness. All were industrious types, to be sure, but their vitality and spiritedness were not products of avarice or materialistic ambitions. Rather, these men and women are prototypical Americans: self-made, courageous, fiercely independent and spirited people with quick wits and true grit and with a keen sense of justice and civic goodwill. Their virtues are not precisely Aristotelian virtues. For one thing, they did not possess the degree of wealth necessary to the virtue of magnificence or the contemptuous pride of the classical magnanimous man. But neither are they models of the commercial acquisitor—greedy, vulgar, hedonistic, politically and socially indifferent to their fellow citizens. It is not that their selfishness is gentler or their ambitions tamer than the modern commercial sort described by Lerner; rather, their souls are markedly different. Generosity, pride, and ambition, not to mention civic friendship and justice, are as much qualities of the republican American model as they were of the model citizen in classical Greece or Rome. Resolution and industry are also deeply embedded American traits that may be directed toward nonmaterial as well as material goods, depending on how one chooses to exercise one's faculties. American republican citizens, as envisioned by James Madison, were men and women whose commitment to the great experiment in self-government offered new hope to the age-old republican quest. This is perhaps what Tocqueville meant when he said that he "saw in America more than America."

NOTES

1. Ralph Lerner, "Commerce and Character: The Anglo-American as New-Model Man," *William and Mary Quarterly* 36, 1 (January 1979): 3–26.
2. Lerner, 10.
3. Lerner, 8–9.
4. Lerner, 13, quoting David Hume's "Of Commerce."
5. Lerner, 5–8.
6. Lerner, 3.
7. Lerner, 10.
8. Compare Lerner's analysis of the character of the American founding and American republic with that of Martin Diamond in "Ethics and Politics: The American Way," in *The Moral Foundation of the American Republic*, ed. Robert H. Horwitz (Charlottesville: University of Virginia Press, 1977), 39–72. Cf. Thomas Pangle, *The Spirit of Modern Republicanism: The Moral Vision of the American Founders and the Philosophy of Locke* (Chicago: University of Chicago Press, 1990). According to Diamond, the United States is a modern commercial society established on a low but solid basis, constituted by a political system that "deliberately risks magnifying and multiplying in American life the selfish, the interested, the narrow, the vulgar, and the crassly economic" (59). Diamond relies heavily on Madison as Publius to make his argument, erroneously claiming that Madison advocated a "multiplicity of factions" (a term never used by Madison) and that, to the extent possible, he wanted to diminish the force of opinion in the formation of public policy.
9. An example of the great-souled man in modern literature is Mr. Darcy of Jane Austen's *Pride and Prejudice*. Mr. Knightley of Donwell Abbey in Austen's *Emma* might be another example, though he lacks the contemptuousness shown by Darcy (and described by Aristotle), perhaps because of the influence of Christianity on his upbringing and character; he does live at an abbey, after all. Real-life examples of the magnanimous man in modern times might include George Washington, Winston Churchill, and Lawrence of Arabia.
10. Alexander Hamilton, John Jay, and James Madison, *The Federalist*, ed. George W. Carey and James McClellan (Indianapolis: Liberty Fund, 2001), *Federalist* 55, 291. All subsequent references to *The Federalist* are to pages in this edition.
11. Ralph Lerner, "The Supreme Court as Republican Schoolmaster," *Supreme Court Review* 1967 (1967): 158–159.
12. Lerner, 160.
13. "Notes on Government," in Colleen A. Sheehan, *The Mind of James Madison: The Legacy of Classical Republicanism* (Cambridge: Cambridge University Press, 2015), 127;

hereafter cited as *MJM*. Cf. *Federalist* 51, where Madison notes that his treatment of the subject is incomplete and should not be considered "a full development" of the subject (267).

14. Lerner, "Commerce and Character," 10–11.

15. Lerner, 21.

16. Lerner, 17.

17. For Hamilton's skepticism concerning the pacific nature of commercial republics, see *Federalist* 6, 23; *Federalist* 11, 54.

18. "Universal Peace," in *MJM*, 253.

19. "Universal Peace," 253.

20. He even imagined a world federation of free republics—one that he vividly outlined in notes for a speech on the floor of the first Congress but never publicly delivered. See *The Papers of James Madison*, ed. William T. Hutchinson et al., 17 vols. (vols 1–10, Chicago: University of Chicago Press, 1962–77; vols. 11–17, Charlottesville: University Press of Virginia, 1977–91), 12:68.

21. "Property," in *MJM*, 263.

22. *Federalist* 10, 43.

23. "Property," 263.

24. "Notes on Government," 143.

25. "Notes on Government," 143; cf. "Dependent Territories," in *MJM*, 237.

26. "Republican Distribution of Citizens," in *MJM*, 258–259.

27. For more on the eighteenth-century notion of "competency," see *Oxford English Dictionary* (1933), II:719. Cf. John Dwyer, *The Age of the Passions: An Interpretation of Adam Smith and Scottish Enlightenment Culture* (Edinburgh: Tuckwell Press, 1998), 69; Daniel Vickers, "Competency and Competition: Economic Culture in Early America," *William and Mary Quarterly* 47, 1 (January 1990): 3–29; Charles L. Griswold Jr., *Adam Smith and the Virtues of Enlightenment* (Cambridge: Cambridge University Press, 1999), 218.

The emphasis on the "distribution" of citizens in a given polity calls to mind Plato's *Republic*, in which 5,040 citizens are assigned classes and occupations, determined by the type of metal—gold, silver, or bronze/iron—that runs through their veins. The purpose of this "myth of the metals" or "noble lie" is to structure the city to produce unity and the common good.

According to Aristotle, the good legislator must understand what types of goods are most desirable and what way of life is most worthy. Of the three types of goods—internal goods of the soul, internal goods of the body, and external goods—Aristotle states that external goods are for the sake of the body and the soul, with the virtue of the soul being the highest human concern. Aristotle, *Politics*, Carnes Lord ed. (Chicago: University of Chicago Press, 1986), VII:1322a15–1323b20. The legislator must also inquire what tasks the city requires and thus what arrangement of citizens is best for each sort of regime. (Madison interlined "arrangement" over "distribution" [as in the title "Best Distribution of People in Republic"] in his "Notes on Government.") First in order of necessity are farmers; next artisans; then those who bear arms. There should also be present those responsible for the superintendence of the divine and those capable of good judgment regarding the advantageous and just. Some of the occupations necessary to a self-sufficient polity, however, are incompatible with a life of virtue, and those performing them should not be citizens. These include sailor, merchant, mechanic, and artisan. The way of life associated with these tasks is "vulgar" and "ignoble" (*Politics* 1328b40).

Aristotle also excludes the farmer from citizenship in the best regime. However, his reasoning is not that the husbandman's life is corrupting but that it requires so much time that there is insufficient leisure to attend and participate in the assembly. Nonetheless, Aristotle notes, farmers are the best kind of common people, and they are the best rulers in a democracy. Finding their work sufficient to meet the needs of their families as well as satisfying, agricultural people tend not to covet their neighbors' goods and prefer laboring in their own vineyards over participating in politics. As a result, Aristotle argues, it is customary for an agricultural people to elect magistrates. Accordingly, men of excellence will fill the positions of magisterial authority with the consent of the common people and therefore without envy. In turn, this arrangement is acceptable to the aristocratic class.

Some scholars have argued that Aristotle's democratic model of farmer-citizen and aristocratic magistracy is akin to the representative republican model recommended by the American founders. Aristotle's best democracy is, for all intents and purposes, a natural aristocracy or even a sort of representative democracy. At the Virginia Ratifying Convention, Madison echoed his thoughts in *Federalist* 55, arguing that the American people possess sufficient "virtue and intelligence to select men of virtue and wisdom." *Papers of James Madison*, 11:63. In *Federalist* 57 he called for the people to elect rulers "who possess most wisdom to discern, and most virtue to pursue, the common good of the society" (295). A year earlier his call for a ruling natural aristocracy was even more explicit, as he acknowledged that his theory of republicanism was intended to "extract from the mass of the Society the purest and noblest characters which it contains." "Notes on Vices of the Political System of the United States," in *MJM*, 204.

In his description of intellectual virtue, moral virtue (the goods of the soul), health (the goods of the body), and competency (sufficiency and moderation in external goods), Madison's stated purpose of the republican way of life sounds a lot like Aristotle's discussion of these qualities in book VII of *Politics*. In addition, Madison's list of worthy occupations in a republic could have been copied from Aristotle's discussion of the best democracy in *Politics*, not to mention their agreement regarding the tasks thought to be harmful to body and soul. Madison's best republic looks a great deal like Aristotle's best democracy, with the significant difference being that in Madison's best republic, there is no slavery. As Madison observed in his "Notes on Government," citing book III of *Politics*, because of the practice of slavery, the ancient polities were republics in name only and were in fact aristocracies. The same could be said of the southern states of America, Madison wrote, which made the United States less than a full republic. One possible inference from Madison's comparison in "Notes on Government" is that the classics were unable to find the leisure required for the life of a citizen without the institution of slavery; in modern times, no such necessity exists, just as there is no reason to promote occupations that create the dependency of one individual on another or one nation on another.

28. "Notes on Government," 165.
29. "Spirit of Governments," in *MJM*, 256.

30. "Spirit of Governments," 256–257; emphasis added.

31. "Spirit of Governments," 257.

32. See "Consolidation," in *MJM*, 235–236.

33. See *Federalist* 57, 397; *Federalist* 73, 371.

34. *Federalist* 51, 269.

35. See and compare *Federalist* 51, 270–271; *Federalist* 49, 264; *Federalist* 50, 266; "Spirit of Governments," 257; "Universal Peace," 252–253.

36. "Notes on Vices," 201.

37. "Notes on Vices," 196.

38. *Federalist* 10, 44. Cf. *Federalist* 51, 271 (the will that is dependent on society is the majority will; in other words, it is also the judge in republican government).

39. This is the argument set forth by Diamond in "Ethics and Politics."

40. See *Federalist* 51, 270–271; *Federalist* 49, 264; *Federalist* 50, 266; "Spirit of Governments," 257; "Universal Peace," 252–253.

41. *Federalist* 70, 365.

42. See *Federalist* 39, 194, where Publius declares that only the republican form of government is "reconcilable with the genius of the people of America; with the fundamental principles of the revolution; . . . [and] with that honourable determination which animates every votary of freedom, to rest all our political experiments on the capacity of mankind for self-government."

43. "Consolidation," 236.

44. "Notes on Government," 164; "Republican Distribution of Citizens," 258.

45. See Robert Frost, "A Talk for Students," commencement address at Sarah Lawrence College, 1956, chrome-extension://efaidnbmnnnibpcajpcglclefindmkaj/https://scholarworks.uni.edu/cgi/viewcontent.cgi?article=1055&context=hearst_documentshttps://scholarworks.uni.edu/cgi/viewcontent.cgi?article=1055&context=hearst_documents.

46. "Property," 263.

CHAPTER 8

On the Significance of *Federalist* 6

Peter McNamara

The Federalist begins with Alexander Hamilton's famous statement on the great question then confronting Americans: whether political societies might be founded by reflection and choice rather than by accident and force. He also provides advice on the spirit that should guide the debate: attend to arguments and do not speculate on the motives of opponents. Hamilton's introduction is followed by four essays by the eminently sober and always diplomatic John Jay, stressing the common values and interests of Americans and emphasizing how union will, by providing a uniform foreign policy, make war less likely. Hamilton announces that he will continue the same line of argument in *Federalist* 6, but what follows is a marked departure in style and to some degree in substance. Admittedly, Hamilton warns that he is about to address "dangers of a different and, perhaps, still more alarming kind," but what comes next is still a shock: "A man must be far gone in Utopian speculations who can seriously doubt that [states or confederacies] would have frequent and violent contests with each other" (27).[1] This opening is hardly a soft sell. Hamilton's argument is jarring for another reason. It seems to fly in the face of the views of leading authorities—the great men of the age. Thinkers such as David Hume and Montesquieu, whom Hamilton repeatedly relies on, embraced the *doux commerce* thesis that Hamilton seems to reject. In what follows I lay out the argument of *Federalist* 6, place it in the context of *The Federalist* as a whole, and conclude with some reflections on the significance of Hamilton's rejection of one of the great hopes of the eighteenth century—a hope that extends, in some quarters and in a somewhat different guise, to our own time.

THE ARGUMENT OF *FEDERALIST* 6

Hamilton remarks that he intends to expand on the themes of Jay's essays by discussing two things: the likelihood of conflict among thirteen independent states or confederacies, and the problem of "domestic factions and convulsions" (27). Having announced his subjects, Hamilton comes out swinging, as noted by his "a man must be far gone" statement. He continues: "To presume a want of motives for such [violent] contests would be to forget that men are ambitious, vindictive, and rapacious." To believe otherwise "would be to disregard the uniform course of human events, and to set at defiance the accumulated experience of ages" (27).

It is not clear whom Hamilton is attacking here. He gives no names. The essay was first published on November 14, 1787. By then, the more important Anti-Federalist writers—Federal Farmer, Brutus (both almost certainly New Yorkers), and Centinel—had begun publishing, but commerce and peace were not their major concerns. James Winthrop (Agrippa) of Massachusetts did make the supposedly peaceful, unifying effects of commerce a major theme, but he did not start publishing until November 23, 1787.[2] Of course, the debate over the proper shape of the national government had been proceeding vigorously for more than a decade, and we are not privy to the behind-the-scenes conversations that took place. As interesting as Hamilton's omission of specific opponents is, it pales in comparison to his failure to mention the leading authority on the subject of peace and commercial republicanism: Montesquieu. Given the reliance on and indeed celebration of the "oracle" Montesquieu in subsequent papers, Hamilton's silence here is striking.[3] It is all the more striking when we consider that Hamilton's fidelity to Montesquieu was deeper than that of many of the founding generation, going so far as to emphasize, like Montesquieu, that the republican form of government might not be universally applicable.[4] Rhetorically, of course, it would have been highly inconvenient and awkward to associate Montesquieu with the "visionary or designing men, who stand ready to advocate the paradox of perpetual peace between the States, though dismembered and alienated from each other" (29–30).

Hamilton's approach appears to be something of a puzzle. Did he really mean what he said? Was Hamilton conjuring a straw man to scare readers into embracing a stronger union? Or was he saving Montesquieu's authority for later papers, when so many arguments (federalism, size of the republic, separation of powers, the judiciary) make vital use of the Frenchman? Or did Hamilton simply believe what he wrote?

Next, Hamilton turns to the private motives that sometimes lead to war (and not to commerce or republicanism or commercial republicanism). These private motives, he argues, act with force and effect in *all* forms of society. He illustrates the point with a number of colorful examples, starting with Pericles's famous mistress Aspasia: "The celebrated Pericles, in compliance with the resentment of a prostitute, at the expense of much of the blood and treasure of his countrymen, attacked, vanquished, and destroyed the city of the *Samnians*" (28). Then he provides a number of modern European examples. Ambitious prelates and resentful and ambitious women are mentioned to illustrate the general point that, independent of regime type, "personal considerations" play a role "in the production of great national events, either foreign or domestic" (29). Hamilton closes with an example that is much closer in time: Shays's Rebellion. "If Shays had not been a *desperate debtor*, it is much to be doubted that Massachusetts would have been plunged into a civil war" (29). Hamilton's point is not that the problems created by personal ambition leave us helpless. The rest of *The Federalist* aspires to show that constitutional design might check and channel the passions, even the irregular and dangerous ones. His point is that these personal considerations are always present, and their effects will be felt to a greater or lesser extent. A "tolerable knowledge of human nature" is sufficient to recognize that commercial progress will not solve the problem (29).

Hamilton then moves to the issues of commerce and republicanism. Again, his language is memorable: "But notwithstanding the concurring testimony of experience, in this particular, there are still to be found visionary or designing men, who stand ready to advocate the paradox of perpetual peace between the States, though dismembered and alienated from each other" (29–30). It is of note that there are at least two sorts of advocates: those motivated by a vison or theory, and those motivated by some sort of design (or plan). The latter may be moved by the kind of personal and private ambition Hamilton just discussed. He proceeds to explain the precise arguments of his unnamed opponents: "The genius of republics (say they) is pacific; the spirit of commerce has a tendency to soften the manners of men, and to extinguish those inflammable humors which have so often kindled into wars. Commercial republics, like ours, will never be disposed to waste themselves in ruinous contentions with each other. They will be governed by mutual interest, and will cultivate a spirit of mutual amity and concord" (30).

This is the precise set of arguments made by many of Hamilton's contemporaries. He responds with a dozen history-based interrogatories, and his conclusions are as follows: Republics and monarchies are almost equally susceptible to the passions that lead to war. Commercial societies generate new, sometimes alternative causes for war, and commercial republics have no better track record. Athens and Carthage, two ancient commercial republics, were continually at war. In modern times, Venice, Holland, and (partly republican) Great Britain were constantly at war. Hamilton includes a reference to what was later known as the War of Jenkins' Ear (1739–48) between Britain and Spain. This was surely a case where passions were "kindled" into war. British ships and merchants were consistently violating a commercial agreement between Spain and Britain. In one clash in 1731, Captain Robert Jenkins's ear was somehow severed. Some seven years later he appeared before Parliament and, according to some accounts, exhibited said ear. Hamilton writes: "The complaints of the merchants *kindled* a violent flame throughout the nation which soon after broke out in the House of Commons and was communicated from that body to the ministry" (32, emphasis added).

Hamilton concludes with more vigorous language: "Have we not already seen enough of the fallacy and extravagance of those idle theories which have amused us with promises of an exemption from the imperfections, weaknesses, and evils incident to society in every shape?" (33). Here, he rejects one iteration of what is sometimes called "American exceptionalism." This rejection of American exceptionalism runs through Hamilton's thinking more generally, such as in his views on political economy.

The ideas and insights of *Federalist* 6 do not disappear in Hamilton's later contributions to *The Federalist*. In *Federalist* 7 he turns to the potential causes of war among the thirteen independent states or several confederacies in North America. He lists territorial disputes, competition between different systems of commercial policy, taxation policies designed to shift the burden to different states and regions, allocation of the existing public debt, violation of contracts by certain states, and the interference of foreign powers. In fact, the first four had been conspicuous features of American political life under the Articles of Confederation.

Hamilton was very aware of the revolutionary changes wrought by the spread of commerce. As he points out in *Federalist* 8, it changed the nature of warfare. Modern nations, including the United States, were not and could not be nations of soldiers along the lines of Sparta and the Roman Republic.

"The industrious habits of the people of the present day, absorbed in the pursuit of gain, and devoted to the improvement of agriculture and commerce are incompatible with the condition of a nation of soldiers." For the most part, modern armies must be professional. Furthermore, commerce and, more specifically, the financial revolutions it gives rise to have "produced an [e]ntire revolution in the system of war" (44). On this latter point, Hamilton does not agree with Thomas Jefferson and James Madison that public borrowing encourages war. Hamilton grants that it might make wars longer in duration, but it would not make them more frequent. The causes of war lie elsewhere.[5]

Federalist 9 revisits the problem of domestic faction. Here, Hamilton cites Montesquieu copiously on the benefits of a federal republic that combines the strength of a monarchy with the advantages of small republics. He adds another advantage, again citing Montesquieu: a federal republic's ability to "suppress" or "repress" domestic faction or insurrection in a particular part of the confederacy (49, 51). Thus, Hamilton does not think the necessity for such actions on the part of governments, including federal commercial republics, will disappear. Two related observations on Hamilton's contributions to the first part of *The Federalist*, both of which concern war, deserve mention. *Federalist* 23 addresses whether there should be limitations on the national government's power to raise taxes and to make military preparations. With respect to the latter, Hamilton observes, "The circumstances that endanger the safety of nations are *infinite*, and for this reason no constitutional shackles can be wisely imposed on the power to which the care of it is committed" (140, emphasis added). Hamilton follows up on this thought in *Federalist* 34. After commenting on signs of a "storm" in Europe, he remarks that even if the storm does not touch the United States this time, there is no guarantee it will not affect the nation some other time. Hamilton concludes: "To judge from the general history of mankind, we shall be compelled to conclude that the fiery and destructive passions of war reign in the human breast with much more powerful sway than the mild and beneficent sentiments of peace" (203). Again, the point is that there is no "exemption" from the challenges nations must always confront.

THE SPIRIT OF THE AGE

Hamilton does not name names in *Federalist* 6, but it is not difficult to find many examples of the kind of thinking he describes. Thomas Paine stands out as someone who fits the bill. Commerce, he says,

> is a pacific system, operating to cordialize mankind, by rendering nations, as well as individuals, useful to each other. As to the mere theoretical reformation, I have never preached it up. The most effectual process is that of improving the condition of man by means of his interest; and it is on this ground that I take my stand.
>
> *If commerce were permitted to act to the universal extent it is capable, it would extirpate the system of war, and produce a revolution in the uncivilized state of governments.* The invention of commerce has arisen since those governments began, and is the greatest approach towards universal civilization that has yet been made by any means not immediately flowing from moral principles.[6]

Paine's statement is almost a paraphrase of Hamilton! Paine promises the golden age that Hamilton describes as a "deceitful dream" in *Federalist* 6.

There are much more sober and qualified statements by other luminaries of the age. Adam Smith, for example, argues for the civilizing, liberating, and pacific effects of the spread of commerce in the modern era, but his generalizations are usually more restrained and judiciously hedged. Jefferson and Madison both had great hope for a commerce-based peace once the international trading system was radically transformed and put on a free and rational basis. They, of course, underestimated the feasibility of "commercial warfare" against the great powers.

The key thinker to consider, however, is Montesquieu and his *Spirit of the Laws*. To evaluate the significance of *Federalist* 6, we must consider Hamilton's silence on and implicit rejection of one of Montesquieu's most radical yet quietly stated claims. Montesquieu believed that commerce dulls or eliminates our most noble sentiments but strengthens the virtues associated with commerce such as industry, punctuality, and so on. Furthermore, commerce creates communication among nations and peoples, leading to more peaceful relations between nations and a lessening of national differences. Montesquieu's most dramatic claim is that commerce in the modern era has emerged as a powerful and independent aspect of human life. In a striking chapter, he describes how finance has escaped the power of governments. The invention of bills of exchange allowed money to move between nations without government supervision. This development liberated the Jews, to some degree, from centuries of persecution. Montesquieu concludes: "One has come to be cured of Machiavellianism, and *one will continue to be cured of it*. There must be more moderation in councils. What were formerly called *coups d'état* would at present, apart from their horror, be only imprudences."[7] Hamilton was no Machiavellian, and he accepted many of Montesquieu's claims regarding commerce and character, but he did not see a future in which commerce would revolutionize the world in the way Montesquieu anticipated.

CONCLUSION

Why did Hamilton argue as he did in *Federalist* 6? The simplest answer is that he believed what he was saying. Looking to history and to experience (including his own) rather than theory, Hamilton thought the matter was clear. In fact, looking to experience by itself might be enough to gain "a tolerable knowledge of human nature." Hamilton's favoring of history and experience over the mere suggestions of theory is a constant in his thinking about politics and human nature. He had the examples of Britain, France, and Holland in front of him when he considered politics and political economy. History and experience led him to reject the idea that the United States might somehow exempt itself from the necessities confronted by all other nations.

In conclusion, it might be worthwhile to place Hamilton's thinking in *Federalist* 6 in an even broader context. In an unpublished fragment on the French Revolution (maybe from 1794), Hamilton writes: "Facts, numerous and unequivocal, demonstrate that the present era is among the most extraordinary, which have occurred in the history of human affairs." He goes on to describe what seems to be his understanding of the Enlightenment (before the French Revolution): "Wise and good men took a lead in delineating the odious character of Despotism; in exhibiting the advantages of a moderate and well-balanced government, in inviting nations to contend for the enjoyment of rational liberty." But, he continues, "Fanatics in political science have since exaggerated and perverted their doctrines. Theories of Government unsuited to the nature of man, miscalculating the force of his passions, disregarding the lessons of experimental wisdom, have been projected and recommended."[8]

Hume, Montesquieu, and Smith could hardly be characterized as "fanatics," but they did have great hope regarding the promises of commercial progress—hope Hamilton did not share. In a conversation with Chancellor James Kent of New York, Hamilton outlined a plan for a book that would be a more philosophical sequel to *The Federalist*.[9] Alas, he never got to write that book, so we do not know how he would have treated Montesquieu and the *doux commerce* thesis in a more extended manner. But we can say with certainty that he had grave reservations about it, and he believed it had the potential to mislead citizens and statesmen about the nature of political life.

NOTES

1. Throughout, page numbers refer to Robert Scigliano's edition of *The Federalist* (New York: Modern Library, 2001), which includes corrections and additions to the original newspaper printings.

2. For the relevant Agrippa essays (Letters VI–IX), see Herbert Storing, ed., *The Anti-Federalist: Writings by the Opponents of the Constitution* (Chicago: University of Chicago Press, 1985).

3. Madison characterizes Montesquieu as an "oracle" in *Federalist* 47, 308. Hamilton, of course, would have agreed.

4. See Hamilton to the Marquis de Lafayette, January 6, 1799 in *The Papers of Alexander Hamilton*, 27 vols., ed. Harold Syrett and Jacob Cooke (New York: Columbia University Press, 1961–87), 23:404–405.

5. See Alexander Hamilton, "The Defence of the Funding System," July 1795, in *Papers*, 19:56–57. This long unpublished piece is of great interest because Hamilton reprises the language and arguments of *Federalist* 6; see 24–25, 55–57.

6. Thomas Paine, *The Rights of Man* (1792), in *Thomas Paine: Collected Writings*, ed. Eric Foner (New York: Library of America, 1995), 598–599.

7. Charles-Louis de Secondat, baron de La Brède et de Montesquieu, *The Spirit of the Laws*, trans. Anne Cohler, Basia Miller, and Harold Stone (Cambridge: Cambridge University Press, 1989), 389; emphasis added.

8. Alexander Hamilton, Fragment on the French Revolution (1794), in *Papers*, 26:739.

9. See Ron Chernow, *Alexander Hamilton* (New York: Penguin, 2004), 666.

CHAPTER 9

Tocqueville on Democracy and the Commercial Republic

John C. Koritansky

In his article "Commerce and Character: The Anglo-American as New-Model Man," Ralph Lerner writes a qualified endorsement of the characteristics of citizens of a commercial republic. Such citizens are prosaic, industrious, responsible, calculative, and sober—traits that are at a premium in the pedestrian pursuit of material gain. Lerner's spokespersons are Montesquieu, David Hume, and Adam Smith and, among the founders of America, James Madison, Alexander Hamilton, Benjamin Franklin, John Adams, and Benjamin Rush. For all their differences, these men shared the conviction that such characteristics were the stuff of an emerging kind of civic virtue and that a society of such citizens would be stabler, freer, and more just than what preceded it.

Also among these luminaries and deserving of special mention is Alexis de Tocqueville. As Lerner reads him, Tocqueville is especially important because, as a witness to the Jacksonian period in America, he was able to see and describe a commercial republic that the others largely imagined.[1] Tocqueville is also important because he most squarely faced the problem resulting from the incompleteness of those pedestrian virtues, and he alone among Lerner's champions offered something of a solution. The problem is this: why should people dominated by a passion for private gain be expected to provide support for public order, even the necessity of law-abidingness? Just how reliable is the derivation of public virtue from private vice, as the saying goes? Lerner argues that Tocqueville's response to this problem is contained in the doctrine of self-interest well understood, as the Americans understand and live it. Lerner concludes, in words chosen carefully to indicate his own trepidation, "And oddly enough, a system that frees men to try to satisfy their physical wants is more likely than any alternative to lead them to see their need for liberty.

More apt, that is, if their egoism were enlightened." And he quotes Tocqueville directly in saying that each American "'has the sense to sacrifice some of his private interest to save the rest.'"[2] But is this satisfactory? Did Tocqueville think so? Lerner has misgivings, although he despairs of any alternative. Why does the whole American system not dissolve into the mud of selfish venality? Why would people continue to endure the myriad small, and occasionally not so small, sacrifices for the greater good, even if they hoped for a share of that greater good? To be sure, people might recognize that they could effectively serve their own interests through voluntary cooperation and even public service. They might develop a habit of seeing things that way. Lerner thinks that Tocqueville believes such habits are enlightened by practical experience. But would such habits avail indefinitely, or for very long, against the ever-present temptation to exploit their fellows for the sake of some immediate satisfaction? Might not the formula "self-interest well understood" be taken as a mantra for a shrewd and selfish knave?

There is no completely satisfactory solution to this problem within the framework of the dispensation of the liberal Enlightenment. If we are constrained by the abandonment of more traditional virtues that, in one way or another, honor self-sacrifice, we seem to be left with only partial solutions, which we fear are no solutions at all. However, if Tocqueville is a "liberal," he is a liberal of a new type. In fact, what he says about self-interest well understood indicates how his overall understanding differs from that of the classical liberal brethren. Tocqueville's assertion is that Americans combat the sentiment of individualism through the *doctrine* of self-interest well understood. In other words, in pursuing their self-interest, they are acting out a public teaching regarding right and wrong. Whatever the cogency of their doctrine—and Tocqueville has his doubts—the important point is that it is a moral dogma. And as moral dogma, it must be connected with a public religious faith. In the chapter that follows his description of self-interest well understood, Tocqueville goes on to show how religion is involved—that is, how self-interest both informs the content of religion and is informed by its sentiment. The importance Tocqueville ascribes to religion in general is one aspect of the distinctive richness of his description of American democracy. Religion is not merely an "auxiliary precaution," as that term might be used to describe Madison's or Hamilton's thought; for Tocqueville, it is a vital ingredient of the overall project of his political science.

To understand how this works—in fact, to fully comprehend Tocqueville's observations and recommendations in his great work *Democracy in America*—we must recognize the debt Tocqueville owes to Jean-Jacques Rousseau and to the powerful critique Rousseau launched against the legion of earlier modern political philosophers, beginning with Thomas Hobbes. We scarcely need to be reminded that Rousseau repudiated the earlier notion of legitimate authority derived from a social contract in which each natural individual grants authority in return for the protection of unalienable natural rights. Rousseau showed that such authority can be legitimate only if each individual gives up "every last one" of his or her natural rights to attain membership in civil society on equal terms or equal standing with all the rest. For each and all, it is in for a penny and in for a pound, we might say. In that way, and in that way alone, we are *as free* as we were outside civil society—*as free*, but not in the same way. Freedom *in* civil society is moral freedom—that is, the freedom of adhering to a law in whose making we were equal participants. With this, Rousseau opened up a new perspective, a new set of considerations for the philosophy of politics. One might say that Rousseau intensifies the neutralism of previous liberal thought to yield an endorsement for what would emerge as "democracy," in a distinctively modern sense of the term. Tocqueville's "new science of politics" follows in that train. Tocqueville thus exhibits his new understanding of what is fundamentally at stake in political life—in a word, freedom. But for him, freedom means the active participation in self-government and common life. Because freedom in that sense was realized in the towns of Puritan New England well before the founding of the American nation, Tocqueville asserts in the early part of his work that those towns contain "the seed of what is to follow."[3]

Freedom is at stake; the evil that threatens it is despotism. To be sure, in the first volume of *Democracy in America* Tocqueville also writes of "tyranny" and even of majoritarian tyranny. His use of this term may cause some readers to obscure the difference between Tocqueville's thought and that of Publius, for example. However, a careful reading reveals that democracy is almost always a majoritarian tyranny, in the sense that only an expression of the popular majority can exercise any significant influence in a democratic polity (235–241). The democratic majority becomes pernicious when it becomes despotic because freedom, in Tocqueville's sense, is lost. Much of the first part of his first volume is a description of how this might happen. A decrepit, "debased" form of the democratic passion for equality can manifest as jealous hostility toward all instances of provincial independence. A centralized authority would be despotic insofar as it deprived common citizens of the opportunity and the necessity of voluntarily cooperating with one another to handle their own local affairs. To guarantee equal treatment among localities, the heavy hand of central authority would deprive citizens of their freedom within those localities. To this reader, there is no more powerfully chilling statement about the sort of despotism democratic nations have to fear than the one Tocqueville delivers in the context of his assault on the political consequences of centralization:

> What does it matter to me, after all, that there should be an authority always on its feet, keeping watch that my pleasures are tranquil, flying ahead of my steps to turn away every danger without my even needing to think about it, if this authority, at the same time that it removes the least thorns on my path, is the absolute master of my freedom and my life, if it monopolizes movement and existence to such a point that everything around it must languish when it languishes, that everything must sleep when it sleeps, that everything must perish if it dies? (88)

In volume 2 Tocqueville drops the term "tyranny," but this is not because he has reached a different assessment of the problem of democracy. That problem remains; his concluding statement in the fourth part of volume 2 regarding the sort of despotism democratic nations need to fear is fully congruent with his warnings in the first volume (661). However, he is now dealing with a different aspect of that problem. Volume 1 depicts the proclivities of the ruling majority, which he treats as a sort of collective entity, telling us how *it* rules. The concentration in volume 2 is on the individual citizen or the subject of democracy: the democratic individual's opinions, sentiments, and mores. From this perspective, the primary problem, the pathology that besets democratic individuals, is what Toqueville terms "individualism." He defines this term carefully and explicitly. "Individualism" is not "egoism" or selfishness; it is a sentiment consequent to a considered judgment that who and what one is does not derive from one's association with other human beings, whether natural and familial or voluntary. Individuals are psychologically isolated from one another. They are prevented from strengthening themselves through all sorts of associations and cooperative endeavors insofar as they internalize a sort of despotic hostility toward every sort of partial society as a source of resistance or an insult to equality. "As each class comes closer to the others and mixes with them its members become indifferent and almost like strangers among themselves. Aristocracy has made of all citizens a long chain that went from the peasant up to the king; democracy breaks the chain and sets each link apart" (483).

Rich as Toqueville's description is, it is in the service of his "new political science," which is diagnostic and ultimately recommendatory (7). The diagnosis is clear enough, once one cracks the code. Is it the same, though, for the recommendations? Here we are confronted with the most puzzling feature of the work. Tocqueville's Americans resist despotism, even if they remain vulnerable to it. Tocqueville does not explicate with full clarity and candor what he might recommend to preserve freedom in the European democracies. We are left to draw inferences from the American example, and yet a variety of circumstances specific to America preclude it from serving as a model for straightforward imitation.

> I am, for the rest, very far from believing that we ought to follow the example that American democracy has given . . . ; for I am not ignorant of the influence exerted by the nature of the country and antecedent facts on political constitutions and I would regard it as a great misfortune for the human race if freedom had to be produced with the same features in all places. (302)

With this, it is understandable that we might experience a sense of frustration. Tocqueville guides us through a painstaking, detailed description of the structural features of American democracy, both formal and informal, whereby Americans exhibit vigor and vitality. Yet we are never far from mindfulness of the accidents, unique to America, that allow those features to exist. We see the problem, but for there to be a solution elsewhere, we have to think for ourselves. How so?

Up to a point, it is not difficult to see *how* Americans resist despotism. The watchwords are "administrative decentralization" and "voluntary association." Much of the first part of volume 1 of *Democracy in America* is devoted to describing the complex constitutional structures whereby Americans actively participate in administering their own public affairs at the local level. But how do they resist centralization? The answer lies in the complex structure of American federalism There are several important details, but the gist of it is that in the America of the 1830s, with its dispersed population, the danger from centralization comes from the state governments. This danger, however, is mitigated by two factors. First, Americans have grown accustomed to the relative independence of towns and townships, whose existence predates the larger governmental structures. Second, the states are not fully sovereign. Their authority is constitutionally subordinate to the limited but superior authority of the national government. As for the national government, it has little occasion to employ the most important dimension of its authority: foreign policy and war. In sum, the provincial freedom Tocqueville admires about America depends on a complex of historical and physical circumstances that do not obtain elsewhere. The legislators of Europe that Tocqueville hopes to inspire and educate will need to find substitutes.

A similar point must be made with respect to voluntary association. Such associations are a nonformal version of vital local governmental units, and their "political" advantages are the same. Indeed, one might conclude that Americans' appreciation of the benefits of local freedom is a reflection of the broader habit of cooperating among themselves in a variety of ways, whether under governmental authority or not. As such, voluntary association is clearly vital to Tocqueville's recommendations—so much so that he calls knowing how to combine "the mother science." "In order that men remain civilized or become so, the art of associating must be developed and perfected among them in the same ratio as equality of conditions increases" (492). Through voluntary association, Americans exhibit the antithesis of the pernicious tendency among democratic citizens to trust a central authority to administer all of life's details.

> The inhabitant of the United States learns from birth that he must rely on himself to struggle against the evils and obstacles of life; he has only a defiant and restless regard for social authority and he appeals to its power only when he cannot do without it.... The same spirit is found in all the acts of social life ... the ills and trials of life; he is restless and defiant in his outlook toward the authority of society and appeals to its power only when he cannot do without it.... The same attitude turns up again in all the acts of social life.... In the United States, they associate for the goals of public security, of commerce and industry, of morality and religion. There is nothing the human will despairs of attaining by the free action of the collective power of individuals. (180–181)

The benefits derived from voluntary association are frequently attested among Tocqueville's readers. Perhaps less frequently they acknowledge and consider the significant attending problem. As was true for provincial governmental freedoms, Tocqueville observes how remarkable it is that the frequent recourse to voluntary association is carried further in America than elsewhere—moreover, further than it could safely be carried elsewhere. To recognize this, one needs to see how Tocqueville understands the relationship between civil associations and political ones—that is, associations that aim to influence or perhaps even to exercise public policy. The distinctive terms are his. On the one hand, Tocqueville argues that the habit of association may tend to develop when individuals have a common interest in something, perhaps a trading enterprise or an industrial undertaking. In this way, "civil associations therefore facilitate political ones," yet it is also and more importantly the case that political associations are necessary to sustain the habit of engaging in associations of various sorts. "When a people has a public life, the idea of associations and the desire to associate with each other are therefore presented daily to the minds of all citizens: Whatever natural repugnance men have for acting in common, they will always be ready to do it in the interest of a party" (496). Political associations are the sine qua non. Indeed, they are the "great schools, free of charge, where all citizens come to learn the general theory of association" (497).

Political associations, though, are dangerous. They exist to challenge governmental authority, sometimes by legitimate means, but sometimes they try to threaten it by illegitimate ones. There have to be limits, then; this requires a delicate balance between competing considerations. Freedom to associate for political purposes is indispensable to the vitality of the all-important voluntary associations, but it has to be curtailed. Tocqueville contrasts freedom of association with freedom of the press: "*unlimited* freedom of association in political matters cannot be entirely confused with the freedom to write. The former is at once less necessary and more dangerous. A nation can set bounds for it without ceasing to be master of itself; it sometimes must do that to continue to be such" (182).

The warning is both dire and perfectly sensible. What is so amazing is that in America there are no restrictions on political association! "In America the freedom to associate for political ends is unlimited" (182). So how do the Americans achieve this miracle? Do they exhibit such a high level of prudence or moral virtue that they can moderate their own political passions without the need for legal restriction? Hardly. This clearly cannot be Tocqueville's answer. The answer he does give, though, involves an irony that cannot be stated except at the risk of apparent contradiction. Everywhere but in America, the danger of political associations is clear. They may be formed for purposes of discussion, "but the thought of acting next preoccupies all minds . . . legal resources appear to be means, but they are never the sole means of succeeding" (184). Such associations do not always seek only to appeal to the ruling authority; they often want to *become* the ruling authority. However, in America the rule of the majority is *so* powerful that there is no thought of displacing it. The concession to majority rule is to a moral authority, and it is fulsome. Americans form political associations knowing that they are not the actual majority but conceding the rightful omnipotence of the majority. Therefore, they seek only to persuade the majority to their view. "When they say they wish to triumph only through laws they are generally telling the truth" (185). This makes sense as far as it goes, but this all but unquestioned authority of the majority in America is also what Tocqueville designates the "tyranny of the majority": "In our time, freedom of association has become a necessary guarantee against the tyranny of the majority" (183). But it is also the case that the effect of that tyranny narrows the possibilities, rendering political differences small and safe, and freedom of association can be tolerated without limit. "In a country like the United States, where in which opinions differ only by nuances, the right of association can remain so to speak without limits" (185). Americans do not escape the necessary limits on political association, nor do they violate them; rather, they live *as if* they did not exist. Thus, at least in this one important respect, the tyranny of the majority entails a mitigating corrective for the problem it poses. Tocqueville concludes this remarkable argument with a sentence that should compel extended reflection: "Thus it sometimes happens that in the immense complication of human laws that extreme freedom corrects the abuses of freedom and that extreme democracy prevents the dangers of democracy" (186).

Amazing! The American tyrant is not despotic; it can afford to tolerate and even enjoy, so to speak, the self-reliance and vitality and freedom of association of its citizens. It is friendly to freedom. To be sure, Europe will become increasingly democratic as well, but it will not exhibit America's ignorant innocence of nondemocratic charms—not for a very long time, and perhaps never. This means that for the democracies of Europe, there will be a persistent need for enforced limits to political association. More broadly, it means that the benefits America enjoys largely as a gift of fortune will have to be provided elsewhere, or substituted for, through self-conscious political art. This is the great challenge for understanding Tocqueville's *Democracy in America* and his "new science of politics." He shows us the aim and the stakes, but we must determine for ourselves much of what is required in connection with "the immense complication of human laws."

When Tocqueville returns to the subject of voluntary association in the second volume, he elaborates on his previous discussion by concentrating on how individuals *feel* about their associations. It is in this context that he develops his thesis regarding "self-interest well understood." To judge by appearances, the cause of voluntary association in America seems to be self-interest. While this is certainly true, it is not simply true. That is, it misses a certain irony about how Americans understand their "selves" and their "interests" and how they tend to misunderstand their own fundamental motivations. Tocqueville discusses this matter directly in the eighth chapter of part 2, volume 2. Earlier in this part, Tocqueville describes the baleful effects of democracy on the "sentiments" of individuals as "individualism." That is, by breaking the traditional and natural bonds that link persons together, democracy isolates them as atoms of an unstructured mass. Too weak to do anything for themselves, they are prepared to be the objects of the despot. So why do Americans *not* exhibit this pathology? The answer *they* give is that they are fully capable of seeing the material advantages attainable through cooperation, and so they cooperate. The wonderful thing about this, of course, is that such a motivation puts no premium on any distinctive, distinguishing virtue. It does not involve pride in noble self-sacrifice. Nor does it insist on a saintly (and rare) self-sacrifice. Calculative self-interest is more modest, more commonplace—in a word, more democratic.

Can it really be true that Americans are animated by something as pedestrian as self-interest? The answer is yes, to a considerable extent, but not as far as one might guess. Americans are not quite as venal as they believe themselves to be. What is important is that Americans *enjoy* explaining their behavior, even their small sacrifices, with reference to the *doctrine* of self-interest well understood. Tocqueville explicitly refrains from endorsing this doctrine in his own name or even discussing it in any detail (501). Rather, he treats it sociologically, with a certain mixture of contempt and concession that we might find amusing: "I think . . . it often happens that they do not do themselves justice; for one sometimes sees citizens in the United States as elsewhere abandoning themselves to the disinterested and unreflective sparks that are natural to man; but the Americans scarcely avow that they yield to movements of this kind; they would rather do honor to their philosophy than to themselves" (502).

The doctrine of self-interest well understood is a moral doctrine. It is the only one compatible with democratic conditions, and as such, it is practically indispensable:

> I shall not fear to say that the doctrine of self-interest well understood seems to me of all philosophic theories the most appropriate to the needs of men in our time, and that I see in it the most powerful guarantee against themselves that remains to them. The minds of the moralists of our day ought to turn, therefore, principally toward it. Even should they judge it imperfect, they would still have to adopt it as necessary. (502–503)

The doctrine is "necessary" but "imperfect," which is to say that Americans are conscious of the benefits of cooperating to serve their self-interest, but their self-interest operates within the limits of moral constraint. They have a sort of common decency that they take for granted without full awareness, and it is deeper than their "philosophy." This—their common virtue—still needs to be explained.

One might presume, at this point, that Tocqueville is guiding us toward religion as the subtly operative factor that compensates for the incompleteness of the doctrine of self-interest well understood in America. One would be correct. However, this subject is replete with an irony of its own. Americans are by no means unmindful of the importance of religion to their ability to sustain their freedom. Here too, though, and here especially, they probably understand themselves imperfectly. Tocqueville follows his chapter on how Americans combat individualism with the doctrine of self-interest with one titled "How the Americans Apply the Doctrine of Self-interest Well Understood in the Matter of Religion." The two chapters obviously need to be read together; the second one in particular requires careful attention.

Just as Americans tend to do themselves an injustice by insisting on explaining even their self-sacrifice as "self-interest well understood," they are loath to confess that their obedient adherence to the tenets of religious faith is based on anything more sublime than their "interest," albeit an interest in obtaining happiness in the afterlife. They seem like perfect disciples of Pascal, for whom faith is the conclusion of a wager concerning the fate of one's soul. Their faith is accommodated to self-interest, but this involves a question—or, rather, it extends the subject of religion to our previous question. If Americans apply their doctrine of self-interest to religion, how can religion be the independent variable that sustains the habit of cooperative association, strengthens their spirit, and prevents them from becoming fodder for the democratic despot?

To be sure, one might hold that it is reasonable to sacrifice some worldly goods for the sake of an otherworldly reward. That is Pascal, as Tocqueville reads him. For his part, though, Tocqueville appears to think that self-restraint and self-sacrifice cannot become part of human beings' second nature if it is based on a self-interested calculation, even of an elevated sort. He refuses "to believe that all those who practice virtue out of a spirit of religion act only in view of recompense."

> It is true that Christianity tells us that one must prefer others to oneself to gain Heaven; but Christianity tells us as well that one ought to do good to those like oneself out of love of God. That is a magnificent expression; man penetrates Divine thought by his intelligence; he sees that the goal of God is order; he freely associates himself with that great design; and all the while sacrificing his particular interests to the admirable order of all things, he expects no other recompense than the pleasure of contemplating it. (504–505)

Tocqueville is certain that Americans feel this sublime sentiment. They do not readily acknowledge it, but in applying their doctrine of self-interest well understood to their religion, they do themselves an injustice Their religious sentiment is belied by the terms they employ to express it. We might be tempted to call this hypocrisy, but that would not accord with Tocqueville's judgment. Rather, Americans' sense of self-interest mixes with their more sublime religious impulses to give them a certain color and weight. Tocqueville commends the Americans insofar as they do not "affect a coarse indifference to the other life; they do not put on a puerile pride by scorning the perils from which they hope to escape" (505). Theirs is a sober religion. It involves an uncanny mixture of sober concern about a heavenly reward for virtue and a longing for the possibility of genuine self-sacrifice and self-transcendence that lies deep in the human heart.

If we understand the ironic half-truth in the way Americans explain their motivations to themselves and how that irony extends to their religion, it comes as no surprise that they tend to abstract concern for the hereafter. Although they are not indifferent to their future state, they "often place in this world the interest that one can have in following it . . . to touch their hearers better (American preachers) make them see daily how religious beliefs favor freedom and public order, and it is often difficult to know when listening to them if the principal object of religion is to produce eternal felicity in the other world or well-being in this one" (505–506). Thus Tocqueville concludes the chapter with a terse remark that reminds us of the more elaborate description of religion in America toward the end of volume 1 under the heading "On the Principal Causes Tending to Maintain a Democratic Republic in the United States" (257–288). It turns out that religion *is* the principal cause. Tocqueville's statements at the end of the first volume provide his fullest account of religion in America and of religion itself.

In America, all religious sects tend to support republican democracy rather than any sort of antidemocratic order or a despotic form of democracy. This is true because almost all religious sects are Christian, and they fall into two broad categories: Protestant and Roman Catholic. Protestants were present in America from the time of the earliest European settlements. Being Christians, they all embrace the idea of the equal worth of every human being in the eyes of God, but beyond that, "Protestantism . . . generally brings men much less to equality than to independence" (276). On the direct effect of this, Tocqueville says no more. About Catholicism, a more elaborate statement is required. Catholicism is like an absolute monarchy. "The priest alone is raised above the faithful; everything is equal below him" (276). From this, one might be tempted to think that Catholicism inclines men to despotism. "Yet this is not the case in America and the reason is that the Catholics are a distinct minority. As such, they have their own special interest in religious freedom, which they might adopt with less zeal were they rich and predominant." Catholics especially have to divide the world of thought and belief into two parts, one of which is governed by religious authority and the other by political truth. "They think that God has abandoned it to the free inquiries of men" (276–277). The upshot is that both Protestants and Catholics support republican freedom: one as a matter of instinctive disposition, the other by a sort of calculative instinct.

So much for religion's direct support. Religion's indirect influence on republican democracy is both stronger and more interesting. Tocqueville asserts in the most uncompromising terms that religion provides an indispensable support for morality. To his contemporaries (or ours) who would challenge him and ask, "Why do men need God to be good?" Tocqueville responds by stating only that it is a fact that men do. It is a fact he claims to perceive, and the Americans share his perception.

> Such are the opinions of the Americans; but their error is clear: for, it is proven to me daily in a very learned manner that all is well in America except precisely the religious spirit which I admire; and I learn that on the other side of the ocean the freedom and happiness of the human species lack nothing but to believe with Spinoza in the eternity of the world and to assert with Cabanis that the brain secrets thought. To that I have truly nothing to respond if not that those who hold to this language have not been in America, and have no more seen religious peoples than free peoples. I therefore await them on their return from America. (281)

Perhaps part of the reason that atheists and agnostics are wont to deny the moral utility of religion is that they oppose a straw man. That is, they think the defenders of religion believe that in religion's absence, men would be governed by a wholly self-centered venality. But according to Tocqueville, that is not the problem. He does not think atheists would cease to defend their actions with reference to a standard of what is good or right. There would likely still be some notion of society's interest, or a common good, whereby men would "explain" what they aimed to do. The real problem is that if the common good were simply *the good*, men would pursue it without the restraints of moral scruple. Tocqueville is sure that religion, and religion alone, explains why, "up to now, no one has been encountered in the United States who has dared to advance the maxim that everything is permitted in the interests of society. An impious maxim—one that seems to have been invented in a century of freedom to legitimate all the tyrants to come" (280). Thus, those who think that freedom from religion is kindred with political freedom have it backward. "Despotism can do without faith, but freedom cannot. . . . And what makes a people master of itself if it has not submitted to God?" (282).

Of all the distinctive features of American life that Tocqueville observes and describes, this compresence of religion and political freedom, and the necessity of it, is the one that he most hopes to impress on the minds of readers outside America. What is amazing and also arresting is that Americans tend to see the relationship between religion and political freedom just as Tocqueville does. For them, nothing could be more obvious. "If you interrogate these missionaries of Christian civilization, you will be altogether surprised to hear them speak so often of the goods of this world, and to find the political where you believe you will see only the religious" (281). We encounter this thought throughout the work; it is never far removed from any of Tocqueville's discussions of religion. In this chapter near the end of volume 1, however, the puzzle surrounding this thought is especially obvious. If Americans, seeing that religion has political benefits, value it in that way, *is* religion the cause they take it to be? Or is their love of freedom and their prudence primary, and their religion a consequence of their prudence? In other words, is religion among Americans *genuine*, or is it a sort of prudent pretense almost universally shared—something both subtle and common?

The question is, are Americans *genuinely* religious? This has been the question all along. The more Tocqueville stresses the fact that Americans perceive the value and utility of religion, the more we are inclined to ask whether they genuinely hold their faith to be *true*. Or is their religion only a kind of pretext, dictated by their prudence? The question never comes more fully to the surface than in the context of the passages discussed here, for Tocqueville admits, "I do not know if all Americans have faith in their religion—for who can read to the bottom of their hearts—but I am sure that they believe it necessary to the maintenance of republican institutions" (280).

Who can read the secrets of the heart? And where does the difficulty lie, exactly? Is it merely that, with regard to their religious convictions or lack thereof, men hide their truest thoughts and sentiments? Or is it that those thoughts and sentiments are beset with an ambiguity that precludes articulation with one's intimates and even with oneself? What, in other words, *is* religion? Tocqueville is not completely silent in response, although what he says is constrained by considerable caution. He approaches these questions: How is it possible that in America there is a wide distance between secular and sectarian authority and a nearly complete social tolerance of sectarian diversity, yet there is near universal agreement about the social and political importance of religion? Why do the Americans think they need God?

Tocqueville reflects on these questions by focusing internally and then generalizes from his own situation and sentiments to those of humankind at large:

> The short space of sixty years will never confine the whole imagination of man; the incomplete joys of this world will never suffice for his heart. Alone among all the beings, man shows a natural disgust for existence and an immense desire to exist; he scorns life and fears nothingness. These different instincts constantly

drive his soul toward contemplation of another world, and it is religion that guides it there. Religion is therefore only a particular form of hope, and it is as natural to the human heart as hope itself. Only by a kind of aberration of the intellect and with the aid of a sort of moral violence exercised on their own nature do men stray from religious beliefs; an invincible inclination leads them back to them. Disbelief is an accident; faith alone is the permanent state of humanity.

In considering religions from a purely human point of view, one can therefore say that all religions draw from man himself an element of strength that can never fail them, because it depends on one of the constituent principles of human nature. (284)

Tocqueville's understanding of the natural, psychological core or root of religion explains how Americans are both sincere in their devotion to one sect or another and at the same time highly tolerant—in fact piously tolerant— of sectarian diversity. Their tolerance is not merely something that each sect grants to others to ensure being tolerated in turn. It is something deeper, more strongly connected to the sentiment of hope that each of the faithful feels at the core of his own faith and senses among others. This is the key to the meaning of Tocqueville's observation that "all agree on the duties of men toward one another. Each sect therefore adores God in its manner, but all sects preach the same morality *in the name of God*" (278; emphasis added). That describes their common faith. It is as if all Americans believe in a God who enjoys the various ways he is worshipped, at least up to a point. Americans are religious in two senses: there is the sect, and there is the civil religion they share in common.[4] If this analysis involves a certain incoherence, Tocqueville would claim that the fault is not his but lies in the nature of the phenomenon itself.

The caution that governs Tocqueville's discussion of the whole subject of religion prevents us from clearly discerning his own personal religious beliefs. However, his statements about religion "from a human point of view," regarding the importance of religion to the mind and soul, are very clear and rich. This is enough to make sense of what he says about how religion functions in America and his prescriptions for democracy in general. Why do people need religion? The answer is that they live poetically. That is, for all human beings, the duration of their mortal, mundane existence cannot help but be seen as merely a wink under the aspect of eternity. We wonder about our ultimate origin and our ultimate destiny, and with that wonder comes hope. Reflecting this wonder and hope, religion causes people to imagine their own little lives as part of a great drama, and their lives are meaningful because that drama is witnessed by God. This helps us understand another aspect of what Tocqueville says about the way Americans exhibit and understand self-interest. In the final chapter of volume 1, he discusses matters more specifically American than democratic. The chapter is devoted largely to describing the current and likely future condition of the three races in the United States, a discussion that has become justly famous in our own day. Of the whites, Tocqueville observes:

> The American navigator leaves Boston to go to buy tea in China. He arrives at Canton, remains there a few days and comes back. In less than two years he has run over the entire circumference of the globe, and he has seen land only a single time. During a crossing of eight to ten months, he has drunk brackish water and lived on salted meat; he has struggled constantly against the sea, against illness, against boredom; but on his return he can sell the pound of tea for one penny less than the English merchant: the goal is attained.
>
> I cannot express my thought better than by saying that the Americans put a sort of heroism into their manner of doing commerce. (387)

This passage is astounding, even thrilling, and not a little amusing. At least as it operates in America, self-interest and "self-interest well understood" are not merely gray, pedestrian relics of a more glorious morality. Americans live in a Technicolor world.

Recognizing the fundamentality of religion in the success story of Tocqueville's *Democracy in America*, seeing it as the prescriptive centerpiece of his "new science of politics," we are left with an obvious question: What, exactly, is the task for democratic statesmanship? In other words, if religion is all-important and all but inextinguishable from the human heart, what could stand in the way of its dominion? Tocqueville asks precisely this question. His answer involves an accidental and particular cause that prevented the human spirit from following its natural inclination. The accident in question was the church's alliance with antidemocratic political powers, aristocracy and monarchy, as defenders of the faith. Thus the partisans of democracy viewed faith as their enemy. Even though those powers were defeated, the old partisan hostility remained. For his part, Tocqueville is certain that this alliance of partisans is not only unfortunate but also perverse. How can partisans of human freedom insist on denying the special kinship between human being and divinity?

In the introduction to his great work, Tocqueville notes that it could only be as a result of a "strange concurrence of events (that) religion finds itself enlisted for the moment among the powers democracy is overturning, and it is often brought to reject the equality it loves and to curse freedom as its adversary" (11). So the discussion of religion at the end of volume 1 returns to a thought Tocqueville expressed in his introduction. Religion is "a living [thing] that someone wanted to attach to the dead: cut the bonds that hold it back and it will rise again" (288). In a way, then, the task for democratic statesmanship seems simple: do nothing to get in the way of religion. But this is not as easy as it might initially appear, for the task also involves not allowing anything to "tie" religion—that is, to politicize it and thus impede its salutary effects. This is no small task, and Tocqueville knows it. Americans have it relatively easy, since they established their democratic system without enduring a revolutionary struggle against the ancien régime that ruled in Europe. Still, European legislators and leaders might find *some* things about America that are feasible and worth imitating. The institutional separation of church and state is clearly one principle that Tocqueville commends to his European readers. Another, merely implicated but also important, is for those in a position to influence the opinions, sentiments, and mores of Europeans to speak and act as persons of religious faith without apology or embarrassment. This is both the deepest and the subtlest task for those Tocqueville calls "legislators," to whom his prescriptive "new science" is ultimately addressed.

NOTES

1. Ralph Lerner, "Commerce and Character: The Anglo-American as New-Model Man," *William and Mary Quarterly* 36, 1 (January 1979): 10.
2. Lerner, 26.
3. Alexis de Tocqueville, *Democracy in America*, ed. and trans. Harvey C. Mansfield and Delba Winthrop (Chicago: University of Chicago Press, 2000), 29. The parenthetical page references that follow are to this work.
4. The term "civil religion" is not Tocqueville's, but I think it is apt. The term is Rousseau's and derives from chapter 8 of the fourth book of *The Social Contract*. Obviously, my interpretation of Tocqueville's account of religion in America tracks Rousseau's argument, and I find it impossible to believe that Tocqueville did not have Rousseau in mind when he included this feature in his account and indeed in his entire "new science of politics."

EPILOGUE

Commerce and Character Revisited

Ralph Lerner

Back in 1979, I was an unlikely contributor to the esteemed *William and Mary Quarterly*. Much of my earlier work had focused on twelfth-century Muslim Spain, not on the eighteenth-century North Atlantic world, let alone tidewater Virginia. So it was fortunate that when I tossed my manuscript over the transom of that journal it landed on the desk of an editor who was not risk averse. Thanks to Michael McGiffert and the referees he enlisted to judge and improve my submission, the work of an author who was not a member of their guild found its way to the front of an issue.

In this chapter, I address three questions: What did my 1979 essay "Commerce and Character" claim to show? What did it not claim to show? And finally, how well has this argument held up in the light of subsequent scholarly research?

When I started some five decades ago to collect my thoughts about the relation of the newly evolving commerce and the human characteristics it fostered, I did not presume to be opening a hitherto unknown or neglected line of inquiry. The example of the seventeenth-century Dutch republic's astonishing emergence as the greatest and richest mercantile empire of the age was not lost on contemporaries. It offered much material for reflection on the power of commerce to dissolve or undermine old prejudices and to destabilize seemingly impregnable economies and polities. Nor did historians and political scientists, long immersed in studying the major figures and thinkers of the seventeenth- and eighteenth-century North Atlantic world, need any introduction to the likes of John Locke, Montesquieu, David Hume, and Adam Smith. The value added by my essay was its proposed change in perspective on those diverse, heterogeneous thinkers. I chose to attribute to them a *common intention* (a proposition neither demonstrable nor falsifiable). In that view, they could appear to be a band of brothers, each in his own way intent on overcoming the earlier social order whereby a few, wrapped in the authority of throne and altar, could lord it over the many.

That is as far as the argument of my essay claimed to go. It did not presume that all those thinkers took the same political stance on the issues of their day. Some were monarchists, others republicans. Some were cautious, others impatient. Some cherished a few of the inanities of the old order for their grandeur. Others wanted to make a clean sweep of the old and start fresh. But all recognized in the commercial way of thinking a powerful solvent of existing habits of mind. If my characterization of those thinkers as sharing a common intention is plausible, so too is this corollary: they were aware that their promotion of the commercial way of thinking would give rise to new, ever-expanding expectations. Expectations previously barely dreamt of now seemed within ordinary people's grasp. The façade of unchanging, immovable stability, like the fabled emperor's new clothes, need only be called what it was—an illusion—for it to fade away. As Edmund Burke put it in one of his elegiac flights: "the age of chivalry is gone.—That of sophisters, œconomists, and calculators has succeeded; and the glory of Europe is extinguished for ever." It was precisely that mixed system of opinion and sentiment that the promoters of commercial republicanism hoped to replace with a new system of opinion and sentiment. At the end of that road stood the Anglo-American as new-model man.

The essays collected by the editors of this volume all touch to a greater or lesser degree on themes raised in my 1979 *WMQ* contribution. The sheer number of the contributors' interpretations and arguments precludes my responding to all of them in detail. Rather, I focus on passages that challenged me to think afresh and reconsider old thinkers and old texts from a different vantage point. Implicit in my responses, readers may detect the extent to which my original argument holds up or needs revision.

MICHAEL ZUCKERT

Michael Zuckert would draw a sharp line between John Locke and David Hume. At first, they seem to be perspicacious observers of the commercial society emerging at the time. But soon enough it becomes clear that they were also determined promoters of the practices and habits of mind we associate with the triumphant capitalism of the nineteenth and twentieth centuries, notwithstanding their different points of departure. For Locke, natural rights shaped his understanding of the origins and use of property. He ventured into territory that Hume's conventionalism and utilitarianism rejected out of hand. Zuckert's account of Hume makes him, in effect, a prefiguration of the hardheaded, hard-hearted William Graham Sumner. That sociologist's famous answer to the question What do social classes owe one another? was (beyond the opportunity to run the race of life as best they could) "Nothing." Locke, in contrast, afforded the unfortunate at least a slim basis for claiming a right to charity.

If Locke made such a stipulation on behalf of the desperate losers in society's scramble for more, it would indeed mark a significant difference. But if I am not mistaken, nowhere in the *Two Treatises on Civil Government* did Locke speak of a "right to charity." He purported to know that God had given the "needy Brother a Right to the Surplusage of his [wealthy brother's] Goods." In view of that divine injunction, "'twould always be a Sin in any Man of Estate, to let his Brother perish for want of affording him Relief out of his Plenty." Corresponding to Justice giving every man a "Title" to have and to hold is Charity giving "every Man a Title to so much out of another's Plenty, as will keep him from extream want, where he has no means to subsist otherwise."[1] This, it should be noted, is between man and God: for the rich man to turn a deaf ear to this desperate cry for help and (worse yet) to use this desperation as an opportunity to enslave the pauper would be a clear violation of God's command—a sin. But what of Locke's civil government? What is its stance toward the needy?

True to form, Locke's carefully worded and repeated restatements gradually shifted the ground on which a claim for social support could rest.[2] All said, the poor man's claim is a weak reed on which to lean if the rich man is left to decide for himself what surplusage, if any, he can spare. Compare this situation to the scriptural stipulations on behalf of gleaners, the vulnerable, and the poor more generally. A genuine believer such as the judicious Richard Hooker (whom Locke delighted to quote) would have had no trouble recognizing and acting on the duty imposed by God on all.[3] But a latter-day Ruth and Naomi, hoping to find unharvested corners in a Lockean farmer's field to allay their pangs of hunger, would likely find cold comfort instead.

I am led to conclude that for both Locke and Hume, the determination of whether society ought to intervene to mitigate the great inequalities engendered by market forces is left, in the last analysis, to the haves. Locke and Hume understood the limited efficacy of a reliance on charity and compassion. But they expected the emancipation of acquisitiveness to result in a vast improvement in everyone's standard of living. Already one could see that the comforts enjoyed by even a common day laborer in England far exceeded those available to "a King of a large and fruitful Territory" in the American wilderness.[4]

In promoting the kind of thinking that would sustain a commercial republic, both Locke and Hume were issuing a promise and a challenge. Their new way of thinking, if adopted, would begin by freeing individuals and entire societies from the economic strictures and constraints embodied in earlier religious and philosophical teachings. All would now be confronted with barely imagined opportunities. But this new world was, at the same time, filled with risk and uncertainty; individuals and families might rise or fall in the great scramble for place and advantage. The gap between the top and bottom strata of society, far from being reduced or eliminated, would most likely be widened.

PAUL A. RAHE

Montesquieu is rightly famous for investigating with penetrating insight the psychic profile of a nation and its constitutive individuals devoted to commerce. Yet it cannot be said that he made it easy for readers to plumb the depths of his thoughts. Here, Paul A. Rahe comes to our rescue.

His masterly essay is at once a bibliographic exploration of how *The Spirit of the Laws* came to be the book we presently have and a patient guide through Montesquieu's convoluted manner of presentation. Montesquieu cannot be faulted for failing to warn those who pick up his book that passive reading will not unlock its full teachings; the philosophe made that clear from the outset in his brief preface. It is a virtual forest of "I"s, putting the author front and center. It began with an appeal to readers, asking them not to rush to judge a work that took him twenty years to produce. It then offered instructions for uncovering "the design of the author": first, recover "the design of the work" (a bog into which multitudes of critics have sunk!). Finally, the preface ended with a notable assertion. Daunting as the task Montesquieu set for himself was—to cure humankind of the prejudices that hinder individuals from getting to know themselves—he ended with an assertion that he was up to the challenge: "When I have seen what so many great men in France, England, and Germany have written before me, I have been filled with wonder, but I have not lost courage. 'And I too am a painter,' have I said with Correggio."[5] Here, within a mere three pages, Montesquieu gave his potential readers a taste of what was to come. The ultimate challenge emerged with perfect clarity almost two hundred pages later: "One must not always so exhaust a subject that one leaves nothing for the reader to do. It is not a question of making him read but of making him think" (*SL*, 2.11.20, 186). Let the work begin!

Of special interest is the final section of Rahe's essay, titled "The Very Model of a Modern Commercial Republic." It comes to grips with Rahe's central theme as well as that of this entire collection. It turns out that a republic that adopts commerce as its lodestar will exhibit quite distinctive characteristics both in its members (they cannot be called "citizens," for reasons to be explained) and in society as a whole.

The famous chapter in which Montesquieu explained how laws can contribute to the mores, manners, and character of a nation has long been understood as citing England as a model commercial republic (*SL*, 3.19.27, 325–333). Yet the name "England" never appears in that chapter, and the detailed description of that model is always stated in the conditional. There was a studied effort to abstract from the singularities of the real-life England without slighting the importance of that nation's distinctive climate, insularity, and geographic location.

In judging the society that is likely to emerge from a people's wholesale devotion to getting rich and getting ahead, Montesquieu visibly held back from awarding his wholehearted endorsement. Where he found behavior to be praised—for example, promptness in paying debts, choosing to be peaceful on principle—he accompanied such praise with reference to the "necessities" impelling such behavior. The truth is that in such a society the interests of commerce are sovereign. One need not seek any higher.

And what of the individuals who constitute this people? Do their singularities display the effects of commerce? Rahe quotes a line from another part of *The Spirit of the Laws* where Montesquieu spoke explicitly of the spirit of the English people: "This is the people in the world who have best known how to take advantage of each of these three great things at the same time: religion, commerce, and liberty" (*SL*, 4.20.7, 343). How, then, do these savvy individuals take advantage of these great things?

As for liberty, the activity of these residents in a commercial republic would not pass muster with the ancients. Rather, they act more in accord with the motto "Don't fence me in." Their byword is "independence." They keep to themselves and think for themselves. As solitaries who are indifferent to pleasing others, they "abandon themselves to their own humors" (*SL*, 3.19.27, 332). This is fertile soil in which all sorts of eccentrics can develop and flourish, and historically, England has not taken second place to any other country in this respect.

How does this state of mind play out with regard to religious belief? More of the same. With everyone free to follow "his own enlightenment or his fantasies," the result might be either indifference or zealotry. "It would not be impossible for there to be in this nation people who had no religion and who would not for all that want to be obliged to change the one they would have had if they had had one."[6] The clergy, too, now bereft of the force to compel others, resort to persuasion and turn to composing "very fine works ... written to prove the revelation and the providence of the great being" (*SL*, 3.19.27, 330–331).[7]

Individuals whose lives are shaped by the spirit of commerce may enjoy the dazzling luxuries that are now within reach. But that pleasure is not cost free. Everything, so to speak, is now available—but for a price: "there is traffic in all human activities and all moral virtues; the smallest things, those required by humanity, are done or given for money." In place of an open-handed hospitality, one finds an unlovely feeling for "exact justice," a kind of moral bookkeeping preoccupied with counting nickels and dimes, and overhanging all this, a vague sense of unease (*SL*, 4.20.2, 338–339). Anticipating Tocqueville's depiction of Americans' persistent fear that some good is escaping their grasp, like a receding horizon, Montesquieu's Englishman is beset with uneasiness (*SL*, 3.19.27, 326).

What a contrast is Montesquieu's depiction of his native land! Again, France is not named, and the whole account is cast as conditional:

> If there were in the world a nation which had a sociable humor, an openness of heart, a joy in life, a taste, an ease in communicating its thoughts; which was lively, pleasant, playful, sometimes imprudent, often indiscreet; and which had with all that, courage, generosity, frankness, and a certain point of honor, one should avoid disturbing its manners by laws, in order not to disturb its virtues. If the character is generally good, what difference do a few faults make? (*SL*, 3.19.5, 310)

Montesquieu spent lengthy periods abroad, observing not with the casual eye of a tourist but studying men and manners with the keen eye of a Duc de

Saint-Simon. But unlike that sour courtier, Montesquieu was a great-souled man; he settled no private grievances in his publications and wielded his gentle irony to combat gross acts of criminal cruelty.[8] Indeed, I would argue that his characterization of this counter-England—namely, the land of his birth—is no less a self-portrait. Deeply opposed to pedantry and heavy-handed moralizing, Montesquieu followed his natural genius in treating frivolous things seriously and serious things gaily.

D'Alembert captured this side of the great man in a lovely section of the eulogy he delivered and later published as a preface to volume 5 of the *Encyclopédie*. His account of Montesquieu's physical travels is no less an account of the philosophe's intellectual journey and of where he chose to come to rest. "As he had examined nothing either with the prejudice of an enthusiast or with the austerity of a Cynic, he brought back from his travels neither a shocking disdain for foreigners nor a still more uncalled for contempt for his own country. It was the result of his observations that Germany was made for traveling in, Italy for staying in, England for thinking in, and France for living in."[9]

ANN CHARNEY COLMO

Ann Charney Colmo's essay offers readers a thread to help them find their way through and out of the maze that is Adam Smith's *Theory of Moral Sentiments*. This is no small gift. Colmo focuses on Smith's wrestling with the problem of ascertaining the basis of those general rules of morality without which human society could not exist. How much is owed to reason and philosophy? Or is it ultimately religion or God's command or the fear of divine punishment that impels us to try to perform our duties, however demanding and inconvenient we find them?

This is hardly a trivial issue; it has prompted much debate, and we must be grateful for the help provided by Colmo's patient analysis. Furthermore, in addressing this issue, we are obliged to confront the persistent uncertainty about how best to read Smith in general and *The Theory of Moral Sentiments* in particular. Colmo is right to leave aside the sham "Adam Smith problem" of yesteryear that purported to confront the seemingly conflicting stances of this work and his later *Wealth of Nations*. (That alleged problem may have run its course and passed away.) But there is no denying that *The Theory of Moral Sentiments* presents unusual challenges. More than three decades separated the publication of the first edition and the sixth. All were published in Smith's lifetime and with his authorization. In a sense, that work never left his easel. Changes large and small were made over the years. These might be attributed to a meticulous writer's refinement of his diction or to an altered sense of how openly he felt he could express himself or, more fundamentally, to a change of mind.

In studying how Smith addressed the question of the basis of a community's moral rules, some readers might wonder why he did not just settle on "God" or "deity" instead of throwing up such a chaff of alternative terms to becloud who or what he was referring to.[10] Nor is this overabundance of terms the only or even the most significant obstacle to pinning down Smith's views on religion. Consider Colmo's discussion of the role Smith's God plays in getting human beings to do the right thing. In her summary of Smith's argument, she states categorically that general rules of conduct need and receive fortification "from God and nature"; further, the "assurance of God" strengthens the entire moral edifice. And finally, in Smith's famous contrast between the fortunes of "the industrious knave" and "the indolent decent man," the former will prosper and the latter will not (*TMS*, 3.5.9, 168). We might wish that it were otherwise and more in accord with our notion of just desserts, but at least that decent sluggard "will no doubt be succored by his appreciative neighbors." I confess I have been unable to find any text in *The Theory of Moral Sentiments* that expresses this comforting "no doubt" or that even invites such an inference. Nor did Smith hold out an assurance in his own name that God, as a last resort, would set things right, in the hereafter if need be.

In recent years, the underlying issue—whether Smith himself thought that belief in an omnipresent and caring God was both necessary and natural to sustain a decent human society—has generated some impressive scholarly debate. Ryan Patrick Hanley, in a painstaking microdissection of the relevant text, concludes that it is "beyond dispute" that Smith genuinely thought so. Given our all-too-human anger and resentment at the miserable spectacle of the wicked springing up like the grass and all the workers of iniquity flourishing, we console ourselves with the thought, "It is that they may be destroyed for ever."[11] But alas, conclusions in such matters are never "beyond dispute."[12] Here, I raise other considerations pertinent to how we are challenged by Adam Smith in reading and interpreting *The Theory of Moral Sentiments* as a whole.

First, a necessary excursus: let us acknowledge at the outset that Smith's book is a work of art and even of artfulness. We would expect no less from a professor of logic and rhetoric, and Smith does not disappoint. Both of his major writings abound with extended passages in which he presents complicated analyses with admirable clarity and cogency. What, then, are we to make of other passages studded with small, barely noticed but consequential words—"seem," "appear," "imagine," "hope," "suppose," "perhaps"—that can quietly, even unobtrusively, convert a declarative sentence into a hypothetical? These cannot be dismissed as harmless tics of careless speech. Smith's sentences neither stutter nor falter. But these little words convey a kind of hesitancy—verbal speed bumps, as it were—alerting some readers to at least slow down and pay closer attention. In this particular respect, Smith partakes of the prudent man's character (as portrayed in *TMS*, 6.1.8, 214): always sincere, but not always frank; never speaking anything other than the truth, but not bound to tell the whole truth. In short, a man who is cautious in his actions and reserved in his speech.

Taking his bearings based on the capacity and behavior of "the bulk of mankind" (*TMS*, 3.5.1, 162, 163), Smith would not have us think for a moment that we can do without those general rules of morality. Less clear is his account of what sustains their grip on our passionate natures. Consider his examples of reluctant gratitude as displayed by a cool beneficiary, a less than warm wife, and an imposed-on host. They all act "as if" they were propelled by genuine warmth and gratitude, employing a *not* "blamable dissimulation," Smith says, but dissimulation nonetheless. Why do they bother with this charade? "Merely from a regard to what they saw were the established rules of behaviour." This "regard," later called "sacred regard" and still later "reverence," is bolstered by habit and custom.

> This reverence is still further enhanced by an opinion which is first impressed by nature, and afterwards confirmed by reasoning and philosophy, that those important rules of morality are the commands and laws of the Deity, who will finally reward the obedient, and punish the transgressors of their duty.
>
> This opinion or apprehension, I say, seems first to be impressed by nature. Men are naturally led to ascribe to those mysterious beings, whatever they are, which happen, in any country, to be the objects of religious fear, all their own sentiments and passions. They have no other, they can conceive no other to ascribe to them. . . . And thus religion, even in its rudest form, gave a sanction to the rules of morality, long before the age of artificial reasoning and philosophy. That the terrors of religion should thus enforce the natural sense of duty, was

of too much importance to the happiness of mankind, for nature to have it dependent upon the slowness and uncertainty of philosophical researches. (*TMS*, 3.5.3–4, 163–164)

In the end, Smith can say no more about this account of the rules of morality and their provenance than that it is "salutary doctrine" (*TMS*, 3.5.8, 166).

If I have dwelled too long on matters of seemingly small consequence, it is with the aim of supporting an admittedly minority view that the final version of *The Theory of Moral Sentiments* evidences Smith's distance from orthodoxy and that he had good reasons for camouflaging those thoughts and keeping them below the notice of ministers of the Glasgow Presbytery. Those clerics of the Scottish Kirk were adept at sniffing out heresies and assiduous in exacting a price for such thinking. Smith could have rightly calculated that the cost of candor and transparency was too high.[13]

Finally, I offer a highly visible example of Smith's attempt to rouse at least some readers to think for themselves. This concerns his use of the words of Jean Baptiste Massillon, Bishop of Clermont, an early eighteenth-century preacher renowned for his exceptional achievements in a land and age where preaching had risen to a very high level. Massillon appears twice in the pages of *The Theory of Moral Sentiments*. In each case, Smith included a substantial excerpt from one of the bishop's sermons, and in each appearance he introduced him as "the eloquent and philosophical Massillon" (*TMS*, 3.2.34, 133; 3.5.11, 169). Smith's decision to include the first excerpt seems, quite frankly, bizarre. This sermon, addressed to officers of a French army regiment, carried the depressing message that all their labors and sufferings and even their readiness to lay down their lives for king and country were nothing for which they could claim recompense from the Lord. Unlike "the solitary monk in his cell, obliged to mortify the flesh and to subject it to the spirit," these military officers sacrificed in vain. The monk is buoyed up by "the hope of an assured recompence" in the hereafter. The military men, having sacrificed merely *ad gloria mundi*, deserve nothing and will receive nothing for their pains. Smith immediately followed this text with a withering outburst of rage and derision, making it clear that this "eloquent and philosophical" divine has been set up as a dupe and an easy target.

> To compare, in this manner, the futile mortifications of a monastery, to the ennobling hardships and hazards of war; to suppose that one day, or one hour,

employed in the former should, in the eye of the great Judge of the world, have more merit than a whole life spent honourably in the latter, is surely contrary to all our moral sentiments; to all the principles by which nature has taught us to regulate our contempt or admiration. It is this spirit, however, which, while it has reserved the celestial regions for monks and friars, or for those whose conduct and conversation resembled those of monks and friars, has condemned to the infernal all the heroes, all the statesmen and lawgivers, all the poets and philosophers of former ages; all those who have invented, improved, or excelled in the arts which contribute to the subsistence, to the conveniency, or to the ornament of human life; all the great protectors, instructors, and benefactors of mankind; all those to whom our natural sense of praise-worthiness forces us to ascribe the highest merit and most exalted virtue. Can we wonder that so strange an application of this most respectable doctrine should sometimes have exposed it to contempt and derision; with those at least who had themselves, perhaps, no great taste or turn for the devout and contemplative virtues? (*TMS*, 3.2.35, 134)[14]

Smith's second excerpt from another Massillon sermon is noteworthy for both its tone and how Smith used it. He did not mischaracterize either preacher or text when singling out "that passionate and exaggerating force of imagination, which seems sometimes to exceed the bounds of decorum" (*TMS*, 3.5.11, 169). It turns out, however, that Massillon's superheated rhetoric made this passage especially apt for Smith's purposes. The bishop had launched a tirade of challenges to a god who fails to remedy wrongs and correct earthly disorder and, more generally, behaves like "an indolent and fantastical tyrant, who sacrifices mankind to his insolent vanity" (*TMS*, 3.5.11, 169). A fanatical atheist could not have put it more forcibly! And that may be what motivated Smith to insert this immoderate passage in the first place and to locate it in the very center of his work. Smith followed Massillon's sermon with a quasi-sermon of his own—a page of pious platitudes rehearsing once again why the world is right to have confidence in the rectitude of a religious man's behavior.[15] So much for first impressions. Yet, having ripped Massillon's words from their context, Smith did not help readers grasp *why* that master rhetorician chose to employ near-blasphemous language with a view to making *what* point. As for Smith's own mini-sermon, it bristles with conditional sentences, other sentences that beg the question, and those little words that render meaning uncertain ("be regarded as," "appears," "seem," "imagine," "suppose"). By the end of that vastly important chapter, the situation is this: Language suggestive of blasphemous thoughts has flitted by the reader, but in a manner that leaves the speaker unidentifiable. No one uttered those words, but somehow, the sentiment has been voiced.

It is fair to wonder what drove Smith to engage in all this weaving and bobbing. Seated where he was, he surely had no reason to fear the kind of persecution that had disgraced and bloodied Lisbon, Madrid, and Rome for the past two centuries. But what of lands where Protestantism held sway? Although the authorities there were not burning bodies, they were no less assiduous in catching the scent of heresies and tirelessly hounding deviants in the hope of making them recant. Unlike Spinoza, Smith did not need a ring with an engraved message reminding him to guard his tongue and his pen. Someone with his mindfulness and experience would be aware of the burning of Rousseau's books in Geneva, of Pierre Bayle's interrogation by the Walloon Consistory in Rotterdam, and of the wary Presbyterian clerics up the road in Glasgow. If Adam Smith wrote in a guarded fashion, it was because he had something he wanted to guard. He was ever mindful of "the coarse clay of which the bulk of mankind are formed" (*TMS*, 3.5.1, 162–163).[16]

RYAN PATRICK HANLEY

Varied are the vistas opened by Ryan Patrick Hanley's richly suggestive essay. His ingenious pairing of Adam Smith and Alexis de Tocqueville on the subject of greatness evokes far-ranging thoughts. He leads readers to glimpse the larger context in which the emancipation and promotion of the commercial way of life took place. I try to follow his lead with a view to achieving a better understanding of the character of modern greatness.

Hanley's point of departure is the fact that both Smith and Tocqueville were masters of cost-benefit analysis. In their search for probable causes and possible effects, they were wary of pronouncing predictive certainties. The complexities of the human psyche had to be given their due. Yet the texts Hanley quotes abound with hard-and-fast assertions, some quite startling, some (by current standards) deeply offensive. How to make sense of this? How to proceed?

For some time there had been an ongoing and often acrimonious debate over the value and relative standing of antiquity versus modernity. This debate encompassed more than matters of literary standards and artistic practice. The ancient world's cosmic view, adorned and made more powerful by the Greek and Roman poets (even when transmuted by Christianity), was increasingly seen as an incubus to be exorcised and overthrown. Machiavelli's forthright proclamation in chapter 15 of *The Prince* that he would direct attention to the "effectual truth" might well be regarded as the opening salvo in that battle. That declaration, disdaining the imaginings his contemporaries and predecessors had been content to repeat, was at once a declaration of independence and a declaration of war. Machiavelli's campaign was carried on by Sir Francis Bacon's call to subdue nature to serve *our* human purposes; by Thomas Hobbes's proposal (in *Leviathan*, "Review and Conclusion") to replace the useless and self-serving curricula of universities (dismissed with a sneer as "Aristotelity") with his own mechanistic teaching; and by many or most of the authors discussed in my original essay.

Viewed against this background, Smith's and Tocqueville's discussions of greatness gain special resonance. However readily one might dismiss the fantasies surrounding Hercules and Achilles, there was no denying that the ancient world was peopled with noteworthy larger-than-life individuals—among them Pericles, Alcibiades, Alexander of Macedon, and Julius Caesar. Were the likes of these outstanding men even imaginable in a new world that consciously redirected and lowered the objects of ambition? And if so, how closely would that modern greatness resemble the old?

In choosing to explore Smith's and Tocqueville's views on the same plane—that of the three races then inhabiting the territory of the United States—Hanley makes a bold move. In Smith's case, it brings into sharp relief a feature of his moral philosophy that deserves greater notice by those preoccupied with his political economy. In Tocqueville's case, it points to a deeper understanding of the method he pursued in the famous chapter that concludes the first volume of *Democracy in America* ("Some Considerations on the Present State and the Probable Future of the Three Races that Inhabit the Territory of the United States").

Hanley draws special attention to *where* Smith looked for examples of greatness—emphatically not in antiquity but in modern times, and not in Great Britain but in the woods, plantations, and revolutionary assemblies of America.[17] The language he used to celebrate the "heroic firmness" of the Indians and the magnanimity of the cruelly enslaved Negro descendants of "nations of heroes" is truly extraordinary—and in each case he ended with a disparagement of their white oppressors (*TMS*, 5.2.9, 205–207). Smith's whites rise to greatness in their spirited resistance to British colonial policy, a resistance driven by their sense of offended pride. As Lincoln put it in 1838, speaking of the men who made the revolution: "Their *all* was staked upon it:—their destiny was *inseparably* linked with it."[18]

Given the importance of the comparison of the three races to Hanley's analysis of greatness, it is worth looking more closely at the chapter in which Tocqueville made that comparison thematic. It is undeniably a tour de force, but a troubling one. It is by far the longest of the work's ninety-four chapters, and it draws on Tocqueville's special strengths as an observer. The many notebooks, memoranda, letters, and drafts he preserved bear witness to his acuity as a questioner, his attentiveness to the responses of his European and American informants, and his ability to keep the myriad observations he accumulated on his journey to America from obscuring the big picture.

As Tocqueville himself announced at the beginning of the chapter, his focus was matters "American without being democratic," unlike all the preceding chapters that cited America to better show European readers the special features of the democratic revolution that was in the process of forever transforming *their* social, political, and intellectual worlds.[19] Yet if one expected this chapter to resemble a meticulous cultural anthropologist's field notes, one would be surprised and disappointed. As a case in point, consider his treatment of the people who were present before the other two races arrived in the Western Hemisphere. Tocqueville painted Indians with such broad brush strokes and at such a level of abstraction that one would hardly suspect that he had encountered members of the Iroquois, Huron, Chippewa, Creek, Cherokee, and Choctaw nations. With his own eyes he had seen these people in their different stages of decay and distress (*DA*, 310). And yet he collapsed all those distinctions into simple generalizations—as he did for all three races—stereotypes that even some current admirers of the man and his works condemn as deplorable. Applying today's sensibilities to the past, these critics view Tocqueville's characterizations as prime examples of an imperialist's essentialist thinking, expressions of a strong desire to disparage and thereby justify Western domination of the Other.

There is no denying that Tocqueville was keen on conquering and colonizing Algeria, not to benefit its Muslim Arab population but to lift Frenchmen's spirits after losing a succession of North American empires to British forces. Whether his enthusiasm for empire in North Africa bespeaks a racist state of mind is harder to say. Of the three naturally distinct races on the American continent, he wrote, "the first who attracts the eye, the first in enlightenment, in power, in happiness, is the white man, the European, man par excellence" (*DA*, 303). But this is the same thinker who emphatically and decisively rejected the racist doctrines of his erstwhile disciple and friend Arthur de Gobineau. This is the same thinker who could respond to the disaster and tragedy being played out on American soil with these bitter words: "One cannot destroy men while being more respectful of the laws of humanity" (*DA*, 325). Tocqueville did not mince words. "Tyranny" and "tyrannical" recur repeatedly in this chapter. He may have believed in the inevitable death and disappearance of the Native Americans, but he did not confront that prospect with the cool indifference of a value-free social scientist. Here is a conundrum not easily resolved.

More to the point is that Tocqueville's shorthand characterizations of the three races are better understood as Weberian ideal types he constructed to support the major theme of *Democracy in America*: the steady, ineluctable replacement of aristocratic ways of thinking and acting with democratic ones. It may be startling that "the Indian, in the depth of his misery in his woods . . . nourishes the same ideas, the same opinions as the noble of the Middle Ages in his fortified castle" (*DA*, 314), but it is no surprise that the one is vanishing just as the other has vanished. Likewise in the case of Tocqueville's white Americans. In this instance, however, he departed from his practice of lumping all Indians and all Blacks into single generalizations. Here, he drew a sharp distinction between the slaveholding American of the South and the American of the North. "The one has the tastes, prejudices, weaknesses, and greatness of all aristocracies. The other, the qualities and defects that characterize the middle class" (*DA*, 361). Predictably, and in line with Tocqueville's general thesis, the southerner's way of life is truly a lost cause. In the end, the new-model man is an Anglo-American, but only the man of the North. I conclude that Tocqueville's sweeping generalizations here are better understood as metaphors differentiating the psychic worlds of predemocratic and democratic men. His portrayal of the white northerner as a virtuoso of energy and acquisitiveness is telling, letting readers infer where Tocqueville stood in the battle between antiquity and modernity. Far from feeling revulsion at the singlemindedness of the new man of commerce, he termed it heroic greed. By not rejecting this as an *inferior* form of greatness, treating it instead as an *alternative* form of greatness, this proud scion of an old French aristocratic family showed his apparent acceptance of the new order of the ages. "We ought not to strain to make ourselves like our fathers, but strive to attain the kind of greatness and happiness that is proper to us" (*DA*, 675).

Hanley's Tocqueville leaves us pondering whether these words were uttered in a spirit of resignation by an individual who was *in* that new world but not *of* it. Or were they another instance of Tocqueville's matter-of-factness, analogous to his brilliant analysis of aristocratic and democratic notions of honor? (*DA*, 589–599). A new world is emerging; accept it. There is no place for wistful regret.

CLIFFORD ORWIN

Clifford Orwin's subtle essay brings one of Jean-Jacques Rousseau's early political writings out of the shadows. The work in question is a preface Rousseau added to *Narcisse*, a comedy he had composed some years earlier. That preface, in turn, highlights Rousseau's complicated relation to the Enlightenment. He was both a participant in that movement and one of its fiercest critics. Here, I focus on Orwin's explication of Rousseau's powerful exposure of the contradiction that lies at the heart of the Enlightenment project.

Enlightenment thinkers promised to liberate the desires of both the high and low strata of society from the constraints imposed by custom, law, and religion. All would be equally free, leaving all to pursue their own private dreams of happiness as they saw fit. At the same time, commerce and the markets through which it disciplines buyers and sellers created what Orwin calls a reciprocal, albeit impersonal, dependency among men. Orwin's Rousseau not only exposed this tension but also deepened and radicalized it through his unsparing analysis of what it takes to be a truly free man.

"All our writers," Rousseau said (presumably referring to contemporary philosophes and other deep thinkers), pride themselves on enlisting individual self-interest to tighten social ties. The sciences, the arts, luxury, commerce, the laws—all leverage self-interest to draw men closer together, the better to foster a shared common interest. So the theory goes. But the truth of the matter, "the cruelest truth," is that this fine spectacle is a sham; it has driven all individuals to adopt a false front,to live a lie, to pretend to care about others' well-being while assiduously promoting their own at the others' expense.[20]

Rousseau contrasted this depiction of the inner life of a typical citizen of a commercial republic with that of an *uncivilized* man who lives in the wilds untainted by the corruptions of city life. Whatever else he may be, Rousseau's *sauvage* is *not* a noble savage but a moral one.

> Among Savages self-interest speaks as insistently as it does among us, but it does not say the same things: love of society and care for their common defense are the only bonds that unite them: the word *property*, which causes so many crimes among our honest folk, is, for them almost devoid of meaning; discussions about interests that divide them simply do not arise among them; nothing leads them to deceive one another; public esteem is the only good to which everyone aspires and which they all deserve. It is perfectly possible that a Savage might do a bad deed, but it is not possible that he will acquire the habit of doing evil, because it would profit him nothing.[21]

Orwin clarifies what Rousseau meant by "the most astonishing and the cruelest truth." When the philosophes promoted commercial republicanism, they did so with the expectation that a wholesale liberation of humankind would follow: a reduced dependence on others, an escape from permanent grinding poverty, an exhilarating political equality. But in fact, Rousseau saw none of that occurring; rather, he saw the opposite. Worse yet—and here we have "the cruelest truth"—the philosophes were unaware that in their genuine desire to liberate humankind they were unwittingly deepening its servitude. They were victims of their own illusions.

This gap between appearance and reality has an analogue in the case being made for the promotion of commerce. Montesquieu and those who followed his lead saw the commercial way of life as a substitute for the pure mores that had largely disappeared in the modern world. In place of barbaric insularity and ferocity, a commercial people's greater engagement with the world would lead them to compare and adopt gentler mores; they would be inclined toward peace (*SL*, 4.20.1–2, 338). Military conflict would sublimate into peaceful commercial rivalry. (In this respect, as in so many others, Alexander Hamilton remained an outlier.)

But in fact, commerce among nations turned out to be neither gentle nor soft. As contributor Peter Onuf points out, the astonishingly rapid industrialization unleashed by the freeing of economic activity endowed nations in the nineteenth century with unparalleled productive capacity. The American Civil War was a preview of what was to come. This joining of science and technology made possible the overwhelming carnage of the twentieth century's two world wars. There was a second "cruelest truth" to rival the first.

Nor was this the only shattered prediction. It was expected that over time, commerce (parading as modernization) would soften despotic regimes into something more civil. One might doubt that Montesquieu or Rousseau would have put all their bets on consumerism to effect that miraculous transformation.

PETER S. ONUF

Drawing on his deep knowledge of the eighteenth-century North Atlantic world, Peter S. Onuf expands the context of the rise of the new man of commerce. The hypothetical figure I contrived out of the writings of philosophers gains three-dimensionality when viewed through the prism of national policy and emergent nation building.

My focus here is on the underlying issue raised by Onuf: before addressing the challenging question of whether we can be a nation, we must first ascertain whether we can be a *people*, and if so, what kind of a people.[22] To explore that primordial issue of identity, Onuf turns to Thomas Jefferson, an undisputed central figure in the creation of an American peoplehood.

Onuf is surely well positioned to pursue this line of inquiry. He is without rival in his grasp of Jefferson's vast literary legacy. Yet it is worth recalling the pitfalls attending any interpreter of a Jeffersonian text before addressing the substance of what Jefferson had to say and what Onuf makes of it all.

Jefferson was an accomplished writer, having developed an easy, liquid style of his own. Words came readily to him, and he was pleased to adopt the written letter as his preferred mode of communication.[23] His prescribed epitaph—"& not a word more"—memorializes him first and foremost as an "author," and a very proud one at that.[24] At the end of his life, he was still vexed by the Continental Congress's editing of his draft of the Declaration of Independence. In sum, when it came to matters of state, Jefferson was intensely and personally engaged. Behind the formal language was an individual whose head and heart were in a never-ending tug-of-war.[25] This is the public figure Onuf captures in a moment of profound self-definition and redefinition.

It is evident that Jefferson was psychically straddling two worlds long before the events leading up to the break with Britain. His youthful exposure to the languages and culture of classical antiquity, his college education in the texts of Enlightenment luminaries, and his subsequent training as a lawyer in the English common-law tradition all conspired to make him see himself as a full member in good standing of a transnational Western civilization. At the same time, he was a member of the tidewater Virginia elite (by virtue of his mother's family), though some of his tastes and preoccupations were at odds with theirs.

Even before his marriage, Jefferson had a mountaintop on the Virginia frontier decapitated and started building a home there. This project, with its never-ending revisions and improvements, would occupy his thoughts and consume a large part of his funds for the remaining fifty-seven years of his life. Monticello's symmetrical simplicity made it truly worthy of a place in Andrea Palladio's Vicenza. But Monticello is more than a beautiful object and an expression of its architect-owner's taste and skill. Rising suddenly out of the wilderness, it made a powerful statement: even here, civilization can find a home. Its portico faced west. Peering through the mists covering the Blue Ridge and turning his back on the old empire that had turned its back on him and his fellow colonials, Jefferson envisioned a new empire. It would be an empire of liberty extending over the entire continent, connected commercially to the Old World but insulated from its corruptions and oppressive social structures.

All this, Onuf shows, took place while Jefferson was reconfiguring himself from a transplanted Briton to a proud native-born American. Onuf characterizes this moment as "a revolution of political consciousness and collective identity that set the stage for regime change, nation making, and state formation." He also makes it clear that as Jefferson was "fashioning a new sense of his own person and political identity," he was laboring to awaken those around him to their true status as a free and independent people fully capable of forming and maintaining a republic of their own.

Through his detailed critique of the Virginia Constitution of 1776, Jefferson showed that he was confident about the kind of constitutional forms needed to keep government accountable and in check (*TJW*, 243–252). His anxieties about the future of America had rather to do with the capacity of the people at large to be guardians of their own liberty (*TJW*, 274).

> From the conclusion of this war we shall be going down hill. It will not then be necessary to resort every moment to the people for support. They will be forgotten, therefore, and their rights disregarded. They will forget themselves, but

in the sole faculty of making money, and will never think of uniting to effect a due respect for their rights. The shackles, therefore, which shall not be knocked off at the conclusion of this war, will remain on us long, will be made heavier and heavier, till our rights shall revive or expire in a convulsion. (*TJW*, 287)

Much of Jefferson's domestic political agenda can be understood as a response to, and an expression of, those anxieties. An inert and ignorant populace, such as he later observed in ancien régime France, would be fit for manipulation by others but for little else. Early and late, he pressed the case for bringing local government closer to the people by dividing existing counties into hundreds or into "wards of such size as that every citizen can attend, when called on, and act in person" (*TJW*, 1399). By assuming responsibility for the mundane needs of their small communities, their attachment to the larger community would follow. "These little republics would be the main strength of the great one" (*TJW*, 1227).

Onuf insists that this program of enlisting ordinary folk in the management of their own affairs was not the seedbed of a social revolution. The Virginia plantocracy, of which Jefferson was a prominent member, would remain firmly in place. The educational system Jefferson projected for Virginia would grow out of the wards and provide an appropriate education for both the laboring class and the learned class (*TJW*, 1348). Doubtless, preparing "a people fostered & fixed in principles of freedom" to defeat "the competition of wealth and birth for public trusts" was a formidable task (*TJW*, 22, 1308). Moreover, that task would have to be performed through the generations. Yet Jefferson was not relying solely on his imagined hierarchy of primary schools, secondary schools, and a university to accomplish the job. The people's participation in self-government at the ward level would constitute an education in itself. Learning to look with their own eyes and listen with attention to their neighbors' concerns, a nation of self-seekers might gradually become citizens of an enduring republic.

COLLEEN A. SHEEHAN

Colleen A. Sheehan has issued a spirited call to the better angels of our nature by bringing James Madison out from the wings and putting him up front and center stage. Her essay is a meticulous attempt to trace how Madison finally settled on his characterization of a model republican citizen. But beyond that, it calls (in a quasi-prophetic mode) for today's Americans to recognize how far our immersion in commerce and finance and their attendant consumerism has compromised our ability to be a proud, self-governing people. Sheehan's bottom line, so to speak, is that for the republic to survive and flourish, the spirit of republicanism must be embodied in the character of its citizens. The question is, how can one bring that about?

Madison was not the first to rise to this challenge. Adam Smith, the spiritual godfather of all commercial republicans, spoke clearly and sharply to that problem when he assessed the costs and benefits of the new world aborning. His *Wealth of Nations* begins with a celebrated chapter on the economic advantages of the division of labor. Almost eight hundred pages later, he finally gets around to assessing the *costs* of that great increase in productivity.

> The man whose whole life is spent in performing a few simple operations, of which the effects too are, perhaps, always the same, or very nearly the same, has no occasion to exert his understanding, or to exercise his invention in finding out expedients for removing difficulties which never occur. He naturally loses, therefore, the habit of such exertion, and generally becomes as stupid and ignorant as it is possible for a human creature to become.... Of the great and extensive interests of his country, he is altogether incapable of judging; and unless very particular pains have been taken to render him otherwise, he is equally incapable of defending his country in war.[26]

This is sterile soil indeed from which to expect to raise a citizen. Untended to, this mass of "gross ignorance and stupidity" prevailing among the inferior—that is, the laboring—ranks jeopardizes civilized society itself. "Mutilated and deformed" minds (Smith's own words) prone to "the delusions of enthusiasm and superstition" present a challenge that no free country can ignore. If commercial society cannot produce the kind of human being it requires yet normally works against, then the very safety of the government demands that *it* bear the expense of providing some rudimentary education for people of all ages.[27]

James Madison was hardly the only American who looked at the emerging commercial republic and pondered how best to mitigate its harmful effects. My 1979 essay referenced John Adams and Benjamin Rush in this regard. One could add George Washington's unheeded request that Congress establish a national university (the military academy at West Point being insufficient as a nursery of continental-minded thinkers and leaders) and, of course, Thomas Jefferson's lifelong exertions to provide his "country" of Virginia with an educational establishment starting at the local elementary level and culminating in a politically orthodox university. Sheehan's Madison was undoubtedly part of this cohort, but he introduced some considerations and grace notes expressive of his distinctive notion of *republican* citizenship.

Madison's America had a popular government, one in which the people at large were both the authors of their constitutional liberty and its vigilant guardian. In such a polity, popular opinion is sovereign. As Lincoln put it tersely in 1858: "In this age, and this country, public sentiment is every thing. *With* it, nothing can fail; *against* it, nothing can succeed."[28] This makes it all the more vital that this public opinion have a certain measure of enlightenment. Sheehan states the nub of the matter: "in popular government the majority is both a party to the case and the ultimate judge in the case." Sheehan is not seduced by the opinion widely shared by political scientists that the author of *Federalist* 10 and *Federalist* 51 was content to rely on the separation of powers, federalism, and the workings of opposite and rival interests to keep popular government safe—if not for the world, at least for the governed. To be sure, such contrivances are important in giving lawmakers and ordinary citizens the space to reconsider, to let reason engage with passion and interest. *Most* fundamental, however, is the *character* of the individuals who make up that body politic. Their collective public opinion is the real sovereign in a free government.

This brings us to Sheehan's vivid summary of Madison's model republican citizen. Standing in sharp contrast to the model commercial individual depicted by Montesquieu, Franklin, Smith, Hume, and Tocqueville, it deserves to be quoted in full:

> This person is not primarily a seller or a buyer; he is not preoccupied with material comforts and luxuries, nor is he neglectful of the spiritual life. He is not acquisitive or envious of others because he possesses what he needs to live a healthy, moderately comfortable, and, for the most part, self-sufficient life. Above all, Madison's republican citizen is an independent human being with a sense of self-assurance, dignity, and pride—a straightforward, unpretentious pride, if that is not a contradiction in terms. He is nobody's slave or servant or fool, and he does not make slaves or dependents or dupes of others.

If one could imagine an American populace in which such fine fellows constituted a critical mass, one might hope to see a society very different from the one presumed in *The Federalist Papers*. And in fact, Madison offered a sketch of that happy world in a strikingly utopian vision. As part of a campaign he and Jefferson mounted against the centralizing policies of Alexander Hamilton and his followers, Madison wrote and published a series of highly partisan essays. In the 1791 essay "Consolidation," he offered some unsolicited advice to those against whom he and Jefferson had already drawn battle lines. He urged "those who may be inclined to contemplate the people of America in the light of one nation"—namely, the Federalist Party—"to employ their utmost zeal, by eradicating local prejudices and mistaken rivalships, to consolidate the affairs of the states into one harmonious interest" with a view to erecting "one paramount Empire of reason, benevolence and brotherly affection."[29] I need hardly dwell on how far the underlying political psychology of this passage lies from the sober, unblinking expectations voiced by Madison in his contributions to *The Federalist Papers*.

I am struck by how closely Sheehan's fine summation of Madison's model republican citizen tracks the youthful Franklin's portrayal of a country Cato in "The Busy-Body No. 3." This rough-shod rustic, living in the most obscure part of the country, is depicted as being free of false humility and any tinge of cunning. "The Consciousness of his own innate Worth and unshaken Integrity renders him calm and undaunted in the Presence of the most Great and Powerful, and upon the most extraordinary Occasions."[30] This man, Franklin asserted, embodies true glory. Nonetheless, Sheehan insists on drawing a sharp contrast between the kind of character Madison sought to foster and nourish and the cramped, diminished souls of the self-seeking new men of commerce whose way of life Smith and Franklin were promoting.

In the case of Smith, Sheehan's strictures are demonstrably overstated. In his view, small-bore prudence, "when directed merely to the care of the health, of the fortune, and of the rank and reputation of the individual"—in other words, the preoccupations of the run-of-the-mill new man of commerce as Sheehan imagines him—was not much to crow about. Taking care of oneself with a view to securing one's comfort and happiness in this life may pass for prudence in common language, but Smith is barely willing to concede even this much. "It commands a certain cold esteem, but seems not entitled to any very ardent love or admiration" (*TMS*, 6.1.5, 14; 213, 216).

As for Franklin, as someone who has spent the better half of his life keeping company with that engaging, feisty, and ultimately enigmatic man, I am obliged to say that Sheehan's arrows have fallen wide of the mark. She readily grants that Franklin the man should not be conflated with what she takes to be his model of an ideal man: "From the classical perspective"—and, I would add, from her perspective as well—"Franklin's ideal man looks bourgeois and banal, someone who has a great deal in common with the Walmart shopper of today." Here, Sheehan joins a large cohort of interpreters, most notably Ernest Renan, Max Weber, and D. H. Lawrence, who simply failed to recognize that they had encountered a virtuoso of irony and indirection. Thus, when reading his preface to 1758's *Poor Richard Improved* and enduring the tedious litany of Father Abraham's truisms, platitudes, and moralisms, they concluded that the author was the quintessential killjoy. Failing to recognize a masterpiece of American comic writing, somber readers mistook not only the whole drift of his work but also the man himself. To conclude that Franklin was somehow endorsing the character of doorbusters on Black Friday is possible only by ignoring the framing story in which Franklin placed Father Abraham's sermon.[31]

Franklin's preface to his 1758 almanac was his hail and farewell to the fictional almanac maker Richard Saunders, to his henpecking wife Bridget, and to *Poor Richard's Almanac* altogether. He was off to pursue a diplomatic career that would consume most of the next quarter century, further evidence (if one needed it) that indifference to the needs of his country was not part of his makeup. Notwithstanding the astonishing variety and richness of his private life, Franklin was not a cool citizen. Much earlier, when proposing the founding of an academy in Pennsylvania, he published a lengthy and detailed description of his recommended curriculum. "The first Principles of sound Politicks," he urged, ought to be "fix'd in the Minds of Youth." And to this end, quoting John Milton, "that they may not, in a dangerous Fit of the Commonwealth, be such poor, shaken, uncertain Reeds, of such a tottering Conscience, as many of our great Councellors have lately shewn themselves, but stedfast Pillars of the State."[32]

This was a maxim by which Franklin lived. An education directed toward character formation was a prerequisite to meaningful citizenship. As Madison later put it: "a people who mean to be their own Governors, must arm themselves with the power which knowledge gives." And, he asked, "What spectacle can be more edifying or more seasonable, than that of Liberty & Learning, each leaning on the other for their mutual & surest support?"[33] These were maxims and hopes to which Benjamin Franklin, Adam Smith, Thomas Jefferson, James Madison, and Colleen Sheehan could all heartily subscribe.

PETER MCNAMARA

Peter McNamara's essay takes a deep dive into Alexander Hamilton's thoughts about the advantages and disadvantages a people dedicated to commerce might expect. Both the intended and unintended consequences are truly far-reaching, shaping the behavior and thinking of the individual and extending to the conduct of foreign and military policy. Let this striking passage from *Federalist* 12 be our point of departure:

> The prosperity of commerce is now perceived and acknowledged, by all enlightened statesmen, to be the most useful as well as the most productive source of national wealth; and has accordingly become a primary object of their political cares. By multiplying the means of gratification, by promoting the introduction and circulation of the precious metals, those darling objects of human avarice and enterprise, it serves to vivify and invigorate the channels of industry, and to make them flow with greater activity and copiousness. The assiduous merchant, the laborious husbandman, the active mechanic, and the industrious manufacturer, all orders of men look forward with eager expectation and growing alacrity to this pleasing reward of their toils.[34]

This paean to commerce was neither Hamilton's first nor last word on the subject. It does, however, shed light on the framework within which he thought about commerce. This new world was a place of change and boundless expectations, a world constantly in motion and in flux. Even the farmer, who is ordinarily thought of as being rooted to a particular place, partakes of the unbridled spirit of enterprise.[35]

Hamilton, too, was very much a man *of* this world as well as its promoter. Thanks to his vaulting ambition and good luck in finding sponsors, he was able to extricate himself from his island birthplace and make a new life on the North American mainland. I am tempted to think of him as having no parochial attachments at all and that when he arrived as a seventeen-year-old in New York City, he was mentally prepared to view men, policies, and events with the eyes and understanding of a *continental* thinker. If Virginia was Jefferson's "country," America was Hamilton's. This predisposition is evident in his emphatic use of the word "empire" in his contributions to *The Federalist Papers*. America is *already* "an empire, in many respects, the most interesting in the world." He spoke of the perverted ambition of some men who hoped to benefit from "the subdivision of the empire" and its "dismemberment."[36]

Hamilton's *Federalist* essays were directed at persuading his audience in New York State and beyond that America was not only an empire—which is to say, a whole—but also a specific kind of whole. To write of "commercial republics like ours" was perhaps to assume what he hoped to promote and establish more fully.[37] So, when he wrote more than once, "if we mean to be a commercial people," he was preparing his audience to hear some possibly unwelcome news about what it would take to sustain and protect their commercial way of life.[38] It would be a mistake to think of Hamilton as an uncritical admirer of commerce. Commercial society, like so many other features of life, would prove to be a mixed blessing.[39] For all that, a dedication to commerce was Americans' present and future fate. What would that entail?

Montesquieu thought he saw modern men in the process of curing themselves of Machiavellianism (*SL*, 4.21.20, 389). Quite a few commercial republicans welcomed that hopeful prognosis and publicized it. Especially for those writing in America, such as Benjamin Rush and Thomas Paine, the preoccupation with conquest and glory in ancient Sparta and Athens was bizarre and, even worse, irrelevant. Here in the United States, there was a wilderness to tame, a virgin land filled with riches to unearth and exploit. Setting the old world at defiance was not our business; commerce and free trade with the whole world were.

In contrast to Montesquieu and Hume (both of whom he refrained from naming in this context), Hamilton rejected the notion that the spirit of commerce would soften men's manners to the point that their passionate urgings to lord it over others would wither away. There would be no golden age. America was no exception to what history and experience have shown to be the sad truth about human nature and the behavior of all states, be they monarchies or republics.[40] Hamilton unleashed all his rhetorical prowess against the purveyors of such dangerous expectations.

McNamara asserts that Hamilton was no Machiavellian, and he may well be right.[41] Yet even while heaping disdain on those who expected commerce to lead to a more tranquil world, Hamilton displayed more than a little of the thinking of Machiavelli and Hobbes.[42] Those who fancied the American states living in a *disunited* condition, as well as those who imagined that the European powers would watch quietly while a *united* nation grew in strength and prosperity, were guilty of an inexcusable forgetfulness. The accumulated experience of the ages tells us that "men are ambitious, vindictive and rapacious."[43] They will never lack reasons for conducting hostile operations against one another. These are constants. Furthermore, commerce itself provides new incentives for aggrandizement by others. European commercial competitors would take note of the "unequalled spirit of enterprise, which signalises the genius of the American Merchants and Navigators." Foreseeing what the United States might yet become, they would strive to "[clip] the wings, by which we might rise to a dangerous greatness."[44]

When Hamilton thought about commerce, he framed it in geopolitical terms. "Our situation invites, and our interests prompt us, to aim at an ascendant in the system of American affairs."[45] That meant bringing an end to the domestic disunion and weakness that only encouraged European colonial powers to extend their dominion. America needed not a standing army (politically impossible, given the fresh memories of British occupation forces) but a small army whose cadre could quickly train a large number of recruits should the occasion require it. Most especially, the nation needed a navy. The comparative advantage shown by American seamen and navigators in the fisheries and in the carrying trade to China and Japan guaranteed a rivalry with the European maritime powers monopolizing that commerce. In the final analysis, the United States had to rely on its own arms to protect its own interests and defend its own commerce. And that, in turn, required a government with the political strength and financial resources to support all those military ventures. Given the inherent uncertainty of how foreign rivals might challenge the United States in the future, Americans must prepare to wage both defensive war and, if it comes to that, "offensive war, founded upon reasons of state." Hamilton noted, "To judge from the history of mankind, we shall be compelled to conclude, that the fiery and destructive passions of war, reign in the human heart, with much more powerful sway, than the mild and beneficent sentiments of peace; and, that to model our political systems upon speculations of lasting tranquility, is to calculate on the weaker springs of the human character."[46]

Thanks to his insatiable ambition, his lust for glory, his profoundly analytical mind, and even his Machiavellianism, Alexander Hamilton was able to envision and work toward an American polity vastly different from the one that existed in his time.[47] As he was devising his geopolitical plans for American hegemony, western settlement barely extended past Pittsburgh and what would become Syracuse, New York. It is unlikely that any white person living on America's Atlantic seaboard was aware of the existence of the Rockies, that massive geological barrier blocking easy passage to the Pacific Ocean. Overleaping these rude beginnings, Hamilton planned for a nation that would supplant European states as the dominant power in the Western Hemisphere and, more generally, would be capable of setting the terms for its political and commercial relations with the rest of the world.

In 1802, disheartened by the decisive electoral victory of Jefferson and Madison's Democratic-Republican Party, which opposed his vision of an energetic, strong, well-mounted national government, Hamilton wrote to his political soulmate Gouverneur Morris: "Every day proves to me more and more that this American world was not made for me."[48] And yet, before the century was out—though only after passing through a horrendous ordeal of fire—the America he had envisioned and labored to bring about would become a reality. *His* American world had arrived.

JOHN C. KORITANSKY

John C. Koritansky has produced a lucid and impressive meditation on Tocqueville's consideration of the place of religion in a democratic and commercial society. His Tocqueville is at once subtle, ironical, and reserved in examining the subject. This beautiful essay stimulates further wonderment.

Early on, Koritansky asks why the passion for gain that is so pronounced in the commercial republic Tocqueville observed in America does not "dissolve into the mud of selfish venality." Might not Tocqueville's famous analytical tool in *Democracy in America*—the doctrine of self-interest rightly understood—be taken as "a mantra for a shrewd and selfish knave"? Yet there is this striking fact: Americans insist that their behavior is governed by a hardboiled calculation befitting practical men of the world—nothing more, nothing grander. In Tocqueville's memorable words: "they would rather do honor to their philosophy than to themselves" (*DA*, 502).

Rather than take the Americans at their word, Koritansky applies a large discount to their insistent assertion—for two reasons. The first is prompted by a suspicion: Americans *enjoy* explaining their behavior in such unsentimental terms. The truth may be more complex. The second derives from his close reading of Tocqueville's presentation of religion in a democratic age.

Provocatively, Koritansky treats the doctrine of self-interest rightly understood as a *moral* doctrine. Yet unlike other dogmas that claim to derive from some higher power's incontestable fiat, this one is ultimately sustained in America by mere popular sentiment, albeit a nearly unanimous sentiment. How sturdy is this support for public-spirited behavior? Tocqueville's answer is that it suffices because behind that sentiment and propping it up is a religion that tempers or moderates behavior that otherwise would be all-absorbing and corrosive of society itself. Koritansky asks, Where does this religion come from? Why do the democrats think they need God? His answer is that Tocqueville looked into himself and found a yearning, a hope, for something more meaningful than an ordinary life span, and he proceeded to project his yearning and hope onto humankind at large—now calling it religion.[49] "In considering religions from a purely human point of view, one can therefore say that all religions draw from man himself an element of strength that can never fail them, because it depends on one of the constituent principles of human nature" (*DA*, 284).

It is hard to know how to evaluate this claim by Tocqueville and, accordingly, the validity of Koritansky's explanation. Tocqueville was notably cautious and reserved in exposing his own spiritual journey. Add to this his highly rhetorical style, and we are left to ponder two additional questions. The first concerns the adequacy of his description of Americans' religion. The second asks to what audience Tocqueville was addressing his great work and how that decision might have shaped the way he presented his thoughts on religion.

Although Tocqueville noted the multiplicity of associations formed by Americans to promote their favorite social causes, he did not relate that activity to the Second Great Awakening, which was then fueling enthusiasm for reform movements of every kind. Rather than take note of the *intemperance* of those moral crusaders and the frenzy of evangelical camp meetings, he surveyed the entire American religious landscape with a seemingly calm confidence.[50] I strongly suspect that Tocqueville arrived at his confidence about religion's continuing role in buttressing and tempering democracy by focusing on a generic New World religion that had already been tempered and rendered mild by the psychic effects of commercial thinking. In this case, Americans, like other peoples before them, had succeeded in modeling their heaven after their earth.

Finally, I believe that the peculiar shape and tone of Tocqueville's discussion of religion had less to do with the Americans (who would gladly hear his praises and blithely ignore his criticisms and warnings) than with his audience back home. There was a lesson for the French to learn from America. They were still struggling with the ghosts of their violent and troubled past. The reactionaries among them would extirpate every vestige of the thinking that had fired the revolutionaries of 1789. They would restore the alliance of throne and altar that Tocqueville regarded as fatal to religion and freedom alike. Their opponents, for whom Voltaire's "*Ecrasez l'infâme*" was still a rallying cry to finish the job of purging superstition, looked to replace despotic rule with a meddlesome centralized state based on the latest science. Tocqueville rejected both camps. Neither understood how a mild Christianity that knows its place and avoids the imprudent excesses that disfigured religion in the Old World could support religious feeling *and* freedom. Let them go to America and see for themselves, he advised. "I therefore await them on their return" (*DA*, 281).

ENVOI

Clifford Orwin's essay includes a vivid recollection of the first time we met, an occasion I can recall with almost the same clarity close to six decades later. His recollection is marked by such a generosity of spirit that I feel obliged to respond to it, if only by adding some relevant details. I already had some experience engaging with students of high intelligence and high motivation, but it was obvious to me that the young men and women registered for this particular course presented a vastly different challenge. Never before—nor ever since—had I encountered such a density of high intellect and great intensity. Having already been instructed by a charismatic virtuoso teacher, they were fired up (this phrase is well chosen) for learning. I soon found myself entering marginalia in the text before me to record the insights emerging from our give-and-take across the table. I tried my best to rise to the challenge and to the occasion. But just as it takes two to tango, I must add this to Orwin's account: I labored to respond to the occasion, but it was those memorable young men and women who constituted the occasion.

Chaucer heaped high praise on his Oxford Cleric when he wrote of him, "Gladly wolde he lerne and gladly teche." I would add this gloss to that line: what so great a reward as to learn from those one has taught!

NOTES

1. John Locke, *Two Treatises of Government*, ed. Peter Laslett (Cambridge: Cambridge University Press, 1988), I:42.

2. A perfect example of this modus operandi is Locke's constant reevaluation of how much human cultivation adds to the productivity of nature's uncultivated waste (II:37).

3. Locke, II:5. See Leviticus 19:9–10, Deuteronomy 15:7–11, 2 Corinthians 9:6–8.

4. Locke, II:41.

5. Montesquieu, *The Spirit of the Laws*, trans. Anne M. Cohler, Basia Carolyn Miller, and Harold Samuel Stone (Cambridge: Cambridge University Press, 1989), xlv; hereafter cited as *SL*, followed by part, book, chapter, and page numbers in this edition.

6. The ever-ironic Lord Melbourne is a case in point. "'No, my Lord,' he replied to the disconcerted Archbishop of York, who had invited him to attend the evening service, 'once is orthodox, twice is puritanical.'" Lord David Cecil, *Melbourne* (Indianapolis: Bobbs-Merrill, 1962), 181.

7. Or, as happened more than a few times, clerics turned instead to investigating local history or local natural history and composing very fine works in the manner of Gilbert White's *Selborne*.

8. See Montesquieu's litany of reasons justifying "the right we had of making Negroes slaves" (*SL*, 3.15.5, 250) and the "very humble remonstrance to the inquisitors of Spain and Portugal" occasioned by the burning at the stake of an eighteen-year-old Jewess—a fictitious document that Montesquieu pronounced "the most useless that has ever been written" (*SL*, 5.25.13, 490–492).

9. Translation courtesy of Stuart D. Warner.

10. I list here (in no particular order and with no claim to being exhaustive) the locutions Smith used in *The Theory of Moral Sentiments* to refer to the divine or to some higher power: God; gods; that Great Superior; the great Superintendant of the universe; the great Dictator of the universe; divine Being; Deity; Author of nature; the great Judge of hearts; Nature, when she formed man for society; Fortune, which governs the world; superintending Power; the great Director of nature; infinite Creator; the great judge of the world; the all-seeing Judge of the world; that great, benevolent, and all-wise Being; the great Director of the world; the great Genius of human nature and the world; Infinite Wisdom and Infinite Power; mysterious beings, whatever they are; our Saviour's precept. Confronted with such wordiness, a reader might well cry, "Enough!" and treat it as an extreme case of what H. W. Fowler dismissed as "elegant variation." That hasty judgment, I believe, would be a mistake. Smith was a deliberate writer, even taking pains to change capitalization from one edition to another (unlike his older friend Benjamin Franklin, he had abandoned the custom of starting all nouns with uppercase). The Glasgow edition of *The Theory of Moral Sentiments* lists forty pages of minor variants occurring in the six editions. The implications of the more significant changes related to religious orthodoxy and justice are discussed by the editors in a nineteen-page appendix. Adam Smith, *The Theory of Moral Sentiments*, in *The Works and Correspondence of Adam Smith*, Glasgow ed., ed. D. D. Raphael and A. L. Macfie (Oxford: Clarendon Press, 1976; reprint, Indianapolis: Liberty Fund, 1982), 343–381, 383–401; hereafter cited as *TMS*.

11. Ryan Patrick Hanley, "Adam Smith on the 'Natural Principles of Religion,'" *Journal of Scottish Philosophy* 13, 1 (2015): 47. The promise of Sabbath Psalm 97:7 remains unfulfilled.

12. See Gavin Kennedy, "The Hidden Adam Smith in His Alleged Theology," *Journal of the History of Economic Thought* 33, 3 (September 2011): 385–402.

13. See Kennedy, 390, 394.

14. If one consults *An Inquiry into the Nature and Causes of the Wealth of Nations*, Glasgow ed., ed. R. H. Campbell, A. S. Skinner, and W. B. Todd (Oxford: Clarendon Press, 1979; reprint, Indianapolis: Liberty Fund, 1981), 5.1.f.30, 2:771, where Smith contrasts the "austerities and abasement of a monk" with the "liberal, generous, and spirited conduct of a man," one sees that there is no "Adam Smith problem" on this important issue.

15. The effectual truth about that "confidence" is laid out in Smith, *Wealth of Nations*, 5.1.g.22, 2:802.

16. D. D. Raphael, "Adam Smith and 'The Infection of David Hume's Society,'" *Journal of the History of Ideas* 30, 2 (April–June 1969): 245–248; Peter Minowitz, *Profits, Priests, and Princes: Adam Smith's Emancipation of Economics from Politics and Religion* (Stanford, CA: Stanford University Press, 1993), 5–9, 188–234; Arthur M. Melzer, *Philosophy between the Lines: The Lost History of Esoteric Writing* (Chicago: University of Chicago Press, 2014), 28–29, 372–373nn44–45.

17. Although Smith spoke more than once of "a Grecian patriot or hero" and of the fortitude of the ancient philosophers (*TMS*, 7.2.1.28–30, 282–283), that is not where he would have his readers look for examples of greatness. Similarly, his singular paean to John Churchill, the Duke of Marlborough, is the exception that proves the rule.

18. Abraham Lincoln, *Abraham Lincoln: Speeches and Writings*, ed. Don E. Fehrenbacher (New York: Library of America, 1989), 1:34.

19. Alexis de Tocqueville, *Democracy in America*, trans. Harvey C. Mansfield and Delba Winthrop (Chicago: University of Chicago Press, 2000), 303; hereafter cited as *DA*.

20. Jean-Jacques Rousseau, "Preface to *Narcissus*," in *Rousseau: The Discourses and Other Early Political Writings*, 2nd ed., ed. and trans. Victor Gourevitch (Cambridge: Cambridge University Press, 2019), 102–103.

21. Rousseau, 103n–104.

22. On the first question, see Richard B. Bernstein, *Are We to Be a Nation? The Making of the Constitution* (Cambridge, MA: Harvard University Press, 1987).

23. Perhaps words came too readily, as Jefferson was given to overstatement, leaving it to others to tamp down the troubling implications. Examples include Madison responding to Jefferson's enthusiastic endorsement of the proposition that "the earth belongs always to the living generation" or, decades later, Madison fighting a rearguard action against Calhounians citing, on Jefferson's authority, a state's natural right to nullify what it considers the federal government's encroachment. James Madison, *James Madison: Writings*, ed. Jack N. Rakove (New York: Library of America, 1999), 863, 453.

24. Thomas Jefferson, *Thomas Jefferson Writings*, ed. Merrill Peterson (New York: Library of America, 1984), 706; hereafter cited as *TJW*.

25. In his infinitely patient dissection of Jefferson's tangled feelings and thoughts about

race, Winthrop D. Jordan draws this conclusion from the "Dialogue between my head & my heart" inserted in Jefferson's famous love letter to Mrs. Maria Cosway: "beneath its stiltedness one senses a man not naturally cool but thoroughly air-conditioned." Winthrop D. Jordan, *White over Black: American Attitudes toward the Negro, 1550–1812* (Chapel Hill: University of North Carolina Press, 1968), 462.

26. Smith, *Wealth of Nations*, 782.
27. Smith, 788.
28. Lincoln, *Speeches and Writings*, 1:493.
29. James Madison, "Consolidation," in *Writings*, 499–500.
30. Benjamin Franklin, "The Busy-Body No. 3," in *Benjamin Franklin: Writings*, ed. J. A. Leo Lemay (New York: Library of America, 1987), 96–97.
31. For a detailed account of Franklin's rhetorical strategy in this piece, see Ralph Lerner, "The Gospel According to the Apostle Ben," in *Naïve Readings: Reveilles Political and Philosophic* (Chicago: University of Chicago Press, 2016), 33–38.
32. Franklin, *Writings*, 337.
33. Madison, *Writings*, 790, 793.
34. Alexander Hamilton, *Federalist* 12, in *Alexander Hamilton: Writings*, ed. Joanne B. Freeman (New York: Library of America, 2001), 209; subsequent references to Hamilton's *Federalist* essays are to this work, cited as *AHW*.
35. Hamilton, *Federalist* 7, *AHW*, 186.
36. Hamilton, *Federalist* 1 and 13, *AHW*, 171, 172, 215. See also *Federalist* 22, 23, and 28, *AHW*, 252, 257, 283.
37. Hamilton, *Federalist* 6, *AHW*, 178.
38. Hamilton, *Federalist* 24 and 34, *AHW*, 262, 312.
39. See the discussion of this feature of Hamilton's 1795 "Defense of the Funding System" in Karl-Friedrich Walling, *Republican Empire: Alexander Hamilton on War and Free Government* (Lawrence: University Press of Kansas, 1999), 193–194.
40. See the classic discussion of Hamilton's insistence on the primacy of foreign policy and what follows from that in Gerald Stourzh, *Alexander Hamilton and the Idea of Republican Government* (Stanford, CA: Stanford University Press, 1970), 148–153.
41. But see Karl Walling, "Was Alexander Hamilton a Machiavellian Statesman?" *Review of Politics* 57, 3 (Summer 1995): 419–447, especially 442–447.
42. Hamilton's barrage of derision in *Federalist* 6 includes "Utopian speculation," "visionary or designing men," "projectors in politics," "reveries," and "idle theories" (*AHW*, 176, 178, 181).
43. Hamilton, *Federalist* 6, *AHW*, 176.
44. Hamilton, *Federalist* 11, *AHW*, 207.
45. Hamilton, *Federalist* 11, *AHW*, 207.
46. Hamilton, *Federalist* 34, *AHW*, 312.
47. For this phenomenon of an opposition to Machiavellianism that rests on Machiavellian premises, see Paul A. Rahe, "Montesquieu's Anti-Machiavellian Machiavellianism," *History of European Ideas* 37, 2 (June 2011): 128–136; Randal R. Hendrickson, "Montesquieu's

(Anti-)Machiavellianism: Ordinary Acquisitiveness in *The Spirit of Laws*," *Journal of Politics* 75, 2 (April 2013): 285–296.

48. Alexander Hamilton to Gouverneur Morris, February 29, 1802, in *AHW*, 986.

49. It is tempting to think of Jefferson as a case in point. He amassed a large written record of his lifelong struggle with the hope religion offers. But his point of departure—a fervent deism—differed from Tocqueville's, as did the terminus where he came to rest.

50. Jefferson's calmness, in contrast, bespeaks a total indifference to doctrine. Thus, on neighboring Pennsylvania's refusal to have an established church, he wrote, "Religion [nevertheless] is well supported; of various kinds, indeed, but *all good enough*; all sufficient to preserve peace and order." "Notes on Virginia," query xvii, in *TJW*, 287; emphasis added. The italicized words speak volumes. As for his confidence that his ferocious hatred of kingcraft and priestcraft would end in victory for his cause, that confidence was based on *faith in reason*. He believed that the "counter-religion made up of the *deliria* of crazy imaginations" being taught by usurpers of the Christian name would be driven out by refocusing on the pure moral teaching of Jesus of Nazareth. That being accomplished, "I trust that there is not a *young man* now living in the United States who will not die a Unitarian." Thomas Jefferson to Dr. Benjamin Waterhouse, June 26, 1822, in *TJW*, 1459.

Selected Bibliography

Adair, Douglass. *Fame and the Founding Fathers*, ed. Trevor Colbourn. New York: Norton, for the Institute of Early American History and Culture, 1974.
Adams, John. *Diary and Autobiography of John Adams*, ed. L. H. Butterfield, Leonard C. Faber, and Wendell D. Garrett. Cambridge, MA: Harvard University Press, 1961.
———. *The Works of John Adams, Second President of the United States, with a Life of the Author, Notes and Illustrations*, ed. Charles Francis Adams. Boston, 1850–56.
Adams, John, Samuel Adams, and James Warren. *Warren-Adams Letters: Being Chiefly a Correspondence among John Adams, Samuel Adams, and James Warren*, ed. Worthington C. Ford. Boston: Massachusetts Historical Society, 1925.
Adams, John, and Benjamin Rush. *The Spur of Fame: Dialogues of John Adams and Benjamin Rush, 1805–1813*, ed. John A. Schutz and Douglass Adair. San Marino, CA: Huntington Library, 1966.
[Alembert, Jean Le Rond d']. "Éloge de M. le President de Montesquieu." In *Encyclopédie, ou Dictionnaire raisonné des sciences, des arts, et des métiers*, ed. Denis Diderot and Jean Le Rond d'Alembert. Paris: Briasson, 1751–72; Neuchâtel: S. Faulche, 1765; Amsterdam: M. M. Rey, 1776–77; Paris: Panckoucke, 1777–80.
Anderson, Benedict. *Imagined Communities: Reflections on the Origin and Spread of Nationalism*. Rev. ed. London: Verso, 2006.
Appleby, Joyce. *Capitalism and a New Social Order*. New York: New York University Press, 1984.
———. *Liberalism and Republicanism in the Historical Imagination*. Cambridge, MA: Harvard University Press, 1992.
Aristotle. *Politics*, trans. Carnes Lord. Chicago: University of Chicago Press, 1986.
Atanassow, Ewa. "Colonization and Democracy: Tocqueville Reconsidered." *American Political Science Review* 111 (2017): 83–96.
Bailyn, Bernard. *The Ideological Origins of the American Revolution*. Cambridge, MA: Harvard University Press, 1967.
Barbon, Nicholas. *A Discourse of Trade*. 1690. Reprinted in *Commerce, Culture and Liberty: Readings on Capitalism before Adam Smith*, ed. Henry C. Clark, 66–99. Indianapolis: Liberty Fund, 2003.
Bernstein, Richard B. *Are We to Be a Nation? The Making of the Constitution*. Cambridge, MA: Harvard University Press, 1987.
Boyd, Richard. "Tocqueville and the Napoleonic Legend." In *Tocqueville and the Frontiers of Democracy*, ed. Ewa Atanassow and Richard Boyd, 264–288. Cambridge: Cambridge University Press, 2013.
Brubaker, Lauren. "Adam Smith on Natural Liberty and Moral Corruption: The Wisdom of Nature and Folly of Legislators?" In *Enlightening Revolutions: Essays in Honor of Ralph Lerner*, ed. Svetozar Minkov, 191–217. Lanham, MD: Lexington Books, 2006.

Bumsted, J. M. "'Things in the Womb of Time': Ideas of American Independence, 1633 to 1763." *William and Mary Quarterly* 31 (1974): 534–564.

Cecil, David. *Melbourne*. Charter ed. Indianapolis: Bobbs-Merrill, 1962.

Cogliano, Francis D. *Emperor of Liberty: Thomas Jefferson's Foreign Policy*. New Haven, CT: Yale University Press, 2014.

———. *Thomas Jefferson: Reputation and Legacy*. Charlottesville: University of Virginia Press, 2006.

Cooke, Jacob E., ed. *The Federalist*. Middleton, CT: Wesleyan University Press, 1961.

Corsa, Andrew. "Modern Greatness of Soul in Hume and Smith." *Ergo* 2 (2015): 27–58.

Countryman, Edward. *A People in Revolution: The American Revolution and Political Society in New York, 1760–1790*. Baltimore: Johns Hopkins University Press, 1981.

Courtney, Cecil Patrick. "Montesquieu et les imprimeurs de *L'Esprit des lois* (1748–1758)." In *L'Écrivain et l'imprimeur*, ed. Alain Riffaud, 193–216. Rennes, France: Presses Universitaires de Rennes, 2010.

Cropsey, Joseph. *Political Philosophy and the Issues of Politics*. Chicago: University of Chicago Press, 1977.

———. *Polity and Economy*. South Bend, IN: St. Augustine's Press, 2001.

Crowley, John C. *The Privileges of Independence: Neomercantilism and the American Revolution*. Baltimore: Johns Hopkins University Press, 1993.

Crowley, J. E. *This Sheba, Self: The Conceptualization of Economic Life in Eighteenth-Century America*. Johns Hopkins University Studies in Historical and Political Science, 92nd ser., no. 2. Baltimore: Johns Hopkins University Press, 1974.

Desgraves, Louis, and Catherine Volpilhac-Auger. *Catalogue de la bibliothèque de Montesquieu à La Brède*. Naples: Liguori Editore, 1999.

Diamond, Martin. "Ethics and Politics: The American Way." In *The Moral Foundation of the American Republic*, ed. Robert H. Horwitz, 39–72. Charlottesville: University of Virginia Press, 1977.

Dumont, Louis. *From Mandeville to Marx: The Genesis and Triumph of Economic Ideology*. Chicago: University of Chicago, 1977.

Dwyer, John. *The Age of the Passions: An Interpretation of Adam Smith and Scottish Enlightenment Culture*. Edinburgh: Tuckwell Press, 1998.

Edling, Max. *Perfecting the Union: National and State Authority in the US Constitution*. New York: Oxford University Press, 2019.

———. *A Revolution in Favor of Government: Origins of the U.S. Constitution and the Making of the American State*. New York: Oxford University Press, 2003.

Englert, Gianna. "Tocqueville's Politics of Grandeur." *Political Theory* 50 (2022): 477–503.

Faulkner, Robert. *The Case for Greatness: Honorable Ambition and Its Critics*. New Haven, CT: Yale University Press, 2007.

Filmer, Robert. *Patriarcha*. In *Patriarcha and Other Writings*, ed. Johann Sommerville. Cambridge: Cambridge University Press, 1991.

Fliegelman, Jay. *Declaring Independence: Jefferson, Natural Language & the Culture of Performance*. Stanford, CA: Stanford University Press, 1993.

Franco, Paul. "Tocqueville and Nietzsche on the Problem of Greatness in Democracy." *Review of Politics* 76, 3 (2014): 439–467.

Franklin, Benjamin. *The Autobiography of Benjamin Franklin*, ed. Leonard W. Labaree, Ralph L. Ketcham, and Helen C. Boatfield. New Haven, CT: Yale University Press, 1964.

———. *The Papers of Benjamin Franklin*, ed. Leonard W. Labaree. New Haven, CT: Yale University Press, 1963.

Frost, Robert. "A Talk for Students." Commencement address, Sarah Lawrence College, 1956. https://scholarworks.uni.edu/cgi/viewcontent.cgi?article=1055&context=hearst_documents.

Gordon-Reed, Annette, and Peter S. Onuf. *Most Blessed of the Patriarchs: Thomas Jefferson and the Empire of the Imagination*. New York: Liveright, 2016.

Greene, Jack P. *The Constitutional Origins of the American Revolution*. New York: Cambridge University Press, 2011.

———. *Imperatives, Behaviors, and Identities: Essays in Early American Cultural History*. Charlottesville: University of Virginia Press, 1992.

———. *Peripheries and Center: Constitutional Development in the Extended Polities of the British Empire and the United States, 1607–1788*. Athens: University of Georgia Press, 1986.

Griswold, Charles L., Jr. *Adam Smith and the Virtues of Enlightenment*. Cambridge: Cambridge University Press, 1999.

———. *Jean-Jacques Rousseau and Adam Smith: A Philosophical Encounter*. London: Taylor & Francis, 2017.

Grotius, Hugo. *The Rights of War and Peace*, ed. Richard Tuck. Indianapolis: Liberty Fund, 2005.

Hamilton, Alexander. *The Papers of Alexander Hamilton*, ed. Harold C. Syrett and Jacob E. Cooke. New York: Columbia University Press, 1961.

Hamilton, Alexander, John Jay, and James Madison. *The Federalist*, ed. George W. Carey and James McClellan. Indianapolis: Liberty Fund, 2001.

Hamowy, Ronald. *The Scottish Enlightenment and the Theory of Spontaneous Order*. Carbondale: Southern Illinois University Press, 1987.

Hanley, Ryan Patrick. *Adam Smith and the Character of Virtue*. Cambridge: Cambridge University Press, 2009.

———. "Adam Smith on the 'Natural Principles of Religion.'" *Journal of Scottish Philosophy* 13, 1 (2015): 37–53.

———. "Commerce and Corruption: Rousseau's Diagnosis and Adam Smith's Cure." *European Journal of Political Theory* 7 (2008): 137–158.

———. "Magnanimity and Modernity: Greatness of Soul and Greatness of Mind in the Enlightenment." In *The Measure of Greatness: Philosophers on Magnanimity*, ed. Sophia Vasalou, 176–196. Oxford: Oxford University Press, 2019.

———. *Our Great Purpose: Adam Smith on Living a Better Life*. Princeton, NJ: Princeton University Press, 2019.

———. "Political Economy and Individual Liberty." In *The Challenge of Rousseau*, ed. Eve Grace and Christopher Kelly, 34–57. Cambridge: Cambridge University Press, 2012.

———. "Rousseau, Smith, and Kant on Becoming Just." In *Justice*, ed. Mark Le Bar, 39–66. Oxford: Oxford University Press, 2018.

———. "Tocqueville and the Philosophy of the Enlightenment." In *The Cambridge Companion to Democracy in America*, ed. Richard Boyd, 47–68. Cambridge: Cambridge University Press, 2022.

Hattem, Michael D. *Past and Prologue: Politics and Memory in the American Revolution*. New Haven, CT: Yale University Press, 2020.

Hendrickson, David. *Peace Pact: The Lost World of the American Founding*. Lawrence: University Press of Kansas, 2003.

Hendrickson, Randal R. "Montesquieu's (Anti-)Machiavellianism: Ordinary Acquisitiveness in *The Spirit of Laws*." *Journal of Politics* 75, 2 (April 2013): 285–296.

Hirschman, Albert O. *The Passions and the Interests: Political Arguments for Capitalism before Its Triumph*. Princeton, NJ: Princeton University Press, 1977.

Hobbes, Thomas. *Leviathan*. New York: Collier Books, 1962.

———. *Leviathan; or the Matter, Forms and Power of a Commonwealth, Ecclesiastical and Civil*, ed. Michael Oakeshott. Oxford: Oxford University Press, 1946.

Hobsbawm, Eric. *Nations and Nationalism since 1780: Programme, Myth, Reality*. 2nd ed. Cambridge: Cambridge University Press, 1992.

Howard Campbell, Sally, and John T. Scott. "Rousseau's Politic Argument in the *Discourse on the Sciences and Arts*." *American Journal of Political Science* 49, 4 (2005): 818–828.

Hulliung, Mark. *The Autocritique of Enlightenment. Rousseau and the Philosophes*. Cambridge, MA: Harvard University Press, 1994.

Hume, David. *Essays Moral, Political and Literary*. Oxford: Oxford University Press, 1963.

Hurtado, Jimena. "Adam Smith and Alexis de Tocqueville on the Division of Labour." *European Journal of the History of Economic Thought* 26 (2019): 1187–1211.

Hutson, James. *John Adams and the Diplomacy of the American Revolution*. Lexington: University Press of Kentucky, 1980.

Jaffa, Harry V. *Crisis of the House Divided: An Interpretation of the Issues in the Lincoln Douglas Debates*. Garden City, NY: Doubleday, 1959.

Jefferson, Thomas. *Notes on the State of Virginia*, ed. William Peden. Chapel Hill: University of North Carolina Press, 1954.

———. *The Papers of Thomas Jefferson*, ed. Julian P. Boyd. Princeton, NJ: Princeton University Press, 1950–.

———. *The Papers of Thomas Jefferson Digital Edition*, ed. James P. McClure and J. Jefferson Looney. Charlottesville: University of Virginia Press, Rotunda, 2008–22. https://rotunda.upress.virginia.edu/founders/TSJN.html.

———. *Thomas Jefferson Writings*, ed. Merrill Peterson. New York: Library of America, 1984.

Jordan, Winthrop D. *White over Black: American Attitudes toward the Negro, 1550–1812*. Chapel Hill: University of North Carolina Press, 1968.

Kennedy, Gavin. "The Hidden Adam Smith in His Alleged Theology." *Journal of the History of Economic Thought* 33, 3 (September 2011): 385–402.
Keohane, Nannerl O. "The Masterpiece of Policy in Our Century: Rousseau on the Morality of the Enlightenment." *Political Theory* 6, 4 (1978): 457–484.
Lawler, Peter. "Tocqueville on Greatness and Justice." In *Magnanimity and Statesmanship*, ed. Carson Holloway, 83–108. Lanham, MD: Lexington Books, 2008.
Lerner, Ralph. "Commerce and Character: The Anglo-American as New-Model Man." *William and Mary Quarterly* 36, 1 (January 1979): 3–26.
———. "The Constitution of the Thinking Revolutionary." In *Beyond Confederation: Origins of the Constitution and American National Identity*, ed. Richard Beeman, Stephen Botein, and Edward C. Carter II, 38–68. Chapel Hill: University of North Carolina Press, 1987.
———. *Maimonides' Empire of Light: Popular Enlightenment in an Age of Belief*. Chicago: University of Chicago Press, 2000.
———. *Naïve Readings: Reveilles Political and Philosophic*. Chicago: University of Chicago Press, 2016.
———. "The Supreme Court as Republican Schoolmaster." *Supreme Court Review* 1967 (1967): 127–180.
———. *The Thinking Revolutionary: Principle and Practice in the New Republic*. Ithaca, NY: Cornell University Press, 1987.
Lincoln, Abraham. *The Collected Works of Abraham Lincoln*, ed. Roy P. Basler, Marion Dolores Pratt, and Lloyd A. Dunlap. New Brunswick, NJ: Rutgers University Press, 1953.
Locke, John. *Two Treatises of Government*, ed. Peter Laslett. Cambridge: Cambridge University Press, 1960.
Lovejoy, Arthur O. *Reflections on Human Nature*. Baltimore: Johns Hopkins University Press, 1961.
Machiavelli, Niccolò. *Tutte le opera*, ed. Mario Martelli. Florence: G. C. Sansoni, 1971.
Madison, James. *The Papers of James Madison*, ed. William T. Hutchinson et al. 17 vols. Vols. 1–10, Chicago: University of Chicago Press, 1962–77; vols. 11–17, Charlottesville: University Press of Virginia, 1977–91.
Mandeville, Bernard. *The Fable of the Bees: or, Private Vices, Publick Benefits*, ed. F. B. Kaye. Oxford: Clarendon Press, 1924.
Manent, Pierre. "Tocqueville, Political Philosopher." In *The Cambridge Companion to Tocqueville*, ed. Cheryl Welch, 108–120. Cambridge: Cambridge University Press, 2006.
Mansfield, Harvey. "Party Government and the Settlement of 1688." *American Political Science Review* 58, 4 (1964): 933–946.
———. *Tocqueville: A Very Short Introduction*. Oxford: Oxford University Press, 2010.
Marshall, Terence. "Rousseau and Enlightenment." *Political Theory* 6, 4 (1978): 421–455.
McDonald, Robert M. S. *Confounding Father: Thomas Jefferson's Image in His Own Time*. Charlottesville: University of Virginia Press, 2016.
Meek, Ronald L. *Social Science and the Ignoble Savage*. New York: Cambridge University Press, 1976.

Melzer, Arthur M. "The Origin of the Counter-Enlightenment: Rousseau and the New Religion of Sincerity." *American Political Science Review* 90, 2 (1996): 344–360.
———. *Philosophy between the Lines: The Lost History of Esoteric Writing*. Chicago: University of Chicago Press, 2014.
Meyers, Marvin. *The Jacksonian Persuasion: Politics & Belief*. Stanford, CA: Stanford University Press, 1957.
Minowitz, Peter. *Profits, Priests, and Princes: Adam Smith's Emancipation of Economics from Politics and Religion*. Stanford, CA: Stanford University Press, 1993.
Montesquieu, Charles-Louis de Secondat, baron de La Brède et de. *Discourses, Dissertations, and Dialogues on Politics, Science, and Religion*, ed. and trans. David W. Carrithers and Philip Stewart. Cambridge: Cambridge University Press, 2020.
———. *Œuvres complètes de Montesquieu*, ed. Roger Caillois. Paris: Bibliothèque de la Pléiade, 1949–51.
———. *Œuvres complètes de Montesquieu*, ed. André Masson. Paris: Les Éditions Nagel, 1950–55.
———. *Œuvres complètes de Montesquieu*, ed. Jean Ehrard and Catherine Volpilhac Auger. Oxford: Voltaire Foundation, 1998–2008; Paris: Éditions Classiques Garnier, 2010–.
———. *Pensées, Le Spicilège*, ed. Louis Desgraves. Paris: Robert Laffont, 1991.
———. *The Spirit of the Laws*, trans. Anne M. Cohler, Basia Carolyn Miller, and Harold Samuel Stone. Cambridge: Cambridge University Press, 1989.
Morgan, Edmund S. *Inventing the People: The Rise of Popular Sovereignty in England and America*. New York: W. W. Norton, 1988.
Ockham, William of. *A Letter to the Friars Minor and Other Writings*, ed. Arthur McGrade and John Kilcullen. Cambridge: Cambridge University Press, 1995.
Onuf, Nicholas, and Peter S. Onuf. *Federal Union, Modern World: The Law of Nations in an Age of Revolutions, 1776–1814*. Madison, WI: Madison House, 1993.
———. *Nations, Markets, and War: Modern History and the American Civil War*. Charlottesville: University of Virginia Press, 2006.
Onuf, Peter S. *Jefferson and the Virginians: Democracy, Constitutions, and Empire*. Baton Rouge: Louisiana State University Press, 2018.
———. *Jefferson's Empire: The Language of American Nationhood*. Charlottesville: University of Virginia Press, 2000.
Paine, Thomas. *The Life and Major Writings of Thomas Paine*, ed. Philip S. Foner. New York: Citadel Press, 1961.
Palmer, Robert R. *The Age of the Democratic Revolution*. 2 vols. Princeton, NJ: Princeton University Press, 1959–64.
Pangle, Lorraine Smith, and Thomas L. Pangle. *The Learning of Liberty: The Educational Ideas of the American Founders*. Lawrence: University Press of Kansas, 1993.
Pangle, Thomas. *Montesquieu's Philosophy of Liberalism: A Commentary on "The Spirit of the Laws"* Chicago: University of Chicago Press, 1973.
———. *The Spirit of Modern Republicanism: The Moral Vision of the American Founders and the Philosophy of Locke*. Chicago: University of Chicago Press, 1990.
Peled, Yoav. "Rousseau's Inhibited Radicalism: An Analysis of His Political Thought

in Light of His Economic Ideas." *American Political Science Review* 74, 4 (1980): 1034–1045.

Pincus, Steve. *The Heart of the Declaration: The Founders' Case for an Activist Government.* New Haven, CT: Yale University Press, 2016.

Pitts, Jennifer. "Empire and Democracy: Tocqueville and the Algeria Question." *Journal of Political Philosophy* 8 (2000): 295–318.

Pocock, J. G. A. *The Machiavellian Moment: Florentine Political Thought and the Atlantic Republican Tradition.* Princeton, NJ: Princeton University Press, 1975.

Postigliola, Albert. "Editer L'Esprit des lois." In *Editer Montesquieu, Publicare Montesquieu*, ed. Alberto Postigliola, 65–77. Naples: Liguori Editore, 1998.

Price, Richard. *A Discourse on the Love of Our Country, Delivered on November 4, 1789.* Boston, 1790.

Rahe, Paul A. "Beyond Confessional Paradigms: Re-Grounding Virtue on Secular Calculation Alone." In *Recht, Konfession und Verfassung im 17. Jahrhundert*, ed. Mathias Schmoeckel and Robert von Friedeburg, 269–283. Berlin: Duncker & Humbolt, 2015.

———. "Blaise Pascal, Pierre Nicole, and the Origins of Liberal Sociology." In *Enlightenment and Secularism: Essays on the Mobilization of Reason*, ed. Christopher Nadon, 129–140. Lanham, MD: Lexington Books, 2013.

———. "The Book that Never Was: Montesquieu's *Considerations on the Romans* in Historical Context." *History of Political Thought* 26, 1 (Spring 2005): 43–89.

———. "Carthage Can Now Defeat Rome: Political Order, Seaborne Commerce, and the Projection of Power in Barbon and Montesquieu." In *Applied History and Contemporary Policymaking: School of Statecraft*, ed. Robert Crowcroft, 53–66. London: Bloomsbury, 2022.

———. *Montesquieu and the Logic of Liberty: War, Religion, Commerce, Climate, Terrain, Technology, Uneasiness of Mind, the Spirit of Political Vigilance, and the Foundations of the Modern Republic.* New Haven, CT: Yale University Press, 2009.

———. "Montesquieu's Anti-Machiavellian Machiavellianism." *History of European Ideas* 37, 2 (June 2011): 128–136.

———. "Montesquieu's Critique of Monarchy: A Self-Destructive Anachronism." *Montesquieu et la civilité*, Annuaire de l'Institut Michel Villey 2010, 2 (2011): 209–228.

———. *Soft Despotism, Democracy's Drift: Montesquieu, Rousseau, Tocqueville and the Modern Prospect.* New Haven, CT: Yale University Press, 2009.

———. "Was Montesquieu a Philosopher of History?" In *Montesquieu et les philosophies de l'histoire au XVIIIe siècle*, ed. Lorenzo Bianchi and Rolando Minuti, 71–86. Naples: Liguori Editore, 2013.

Raphael, D. D. "Adam Smith and 'The Infection of David Hume's Society.'" *Journal of the History of Ideas* 30, 2 (April–June 1969): 225–248.

Reid, John Phillip. *Constitutional History of the American Revolution: The Authority of Rights.* Madison: University of Wisconsin Press, 1986.

Richter, Melvin, ed. *Essays in Theory and History: An Approach to the Social Sciences.* Cambridge, MA: Harvard University Press, 1970.

Rodgers, Daniel. "Republicanism: The Career of a Concept." *Journal of American History* 79 (1992): 11–38.

Rousseau, Jean-Jacques. *The Collected Works of Rousseau*, ed. Roger D. Masters and Christopher Kelly. Hanover, NH: Dartmouth College/University Press of New England, 1992.

———. *The Discourses and Other Early Political Writings*, ed. Victor Gourevitch. 2nd ed. Cambridge Texts in the History of Political Thought. Cambridge: Cambridge University Press, 2018.

———. *Emile, or On Education*, trans. Allan Bloom. New York: Basic Books, 1979.

———. *The First and Second Discourses*, trans. Roger D. and Judith R. Masters. New York: St. Martin's Press, 1964.

———. *The Social Contract*, trans. Maurice Cranston. London: Penguin Group, 1968.

Rush, Benjamin. *Essays, Literary, Moral and Philosophical*. 2nd ed. Philadelphia: Kessinger, 1806.

———. *Letters of Benjamin Rush*, ed. L. H. Butterfield. Princeton, NJ: Princeton University Press, 1951.

———. *A Plan for the Establishment of Public Schools and the Diffusion of Knowledge in Pennsylvania*. Philadelphia, 1786.

———. *The Selected Writings of Benjamin Rush*, ed. Dagobert D. Runes. New York: Philosophical Library, 1947.

Ryerson, Richard A. *The Revolution Is Now Begun: The Radical Committees of Philadelphia, 1765–1776*. Philadelphia: University of Pennsylvania Press, 1977.

Schliesser, Eric. *Adam Smith: Systematic Philosopher and Public Thinker*. Oxford: Oxford University Press, 2017.

———. "The Obituary of a Vain Philosopher: Adam Smith's Reflections on Hume's *Life*," *Hume Studies* 29 (2003): 327–362.

Shalhope, Robert E. "Republicanism and Early American Historiography." *William and Mary Quarterly* 39 (1982): 334–356.

———. "Toward a Republican Synthesis: The Emergence of an Understanding of Republicanism in American Historiography." *William and Mary Quarterly* 29 (1972): 49–80.

Shaw, Peter. *The Character of John Adams*. Chapel Hill: University of North Carolina Press, 1976.

Sheehan, Colleen A. *The Mind of James Madison: The Legacy of Classical Republicanism*. Cambridge: Cambridge University Press, 2015.

Shell, Susan Meld. "Rousseau, Kant, and the Beginning of History." In *The Legacy of Rousseau*, ed. Clifford Orwin and Nathan Tarcov, 45–64. Chicago: University of Chicago Press, 1997.

Shy, John. *A People Numerous and Armed: Reflections on the Military Struggle for American Independence*. New York: Oxford University Press, 1976.

Skinner, Andrew S., and Thomas Wilson, eds. *Essays on Adam Smith*. Oxford: Oxford University Press, 1975.

Smith, Adam. *An Inquiry into the Nature and Causes of the Wealth of Nations*, ed. R. H. Campbell and A. S. Skinner. 2 vols. Indianapolis: Liberty Fund, 1981.

———. *An Inquiry into the Nature and Causes of the Wealth of Nations*, ed. Edwin Cannan. Chicago: University of Chicago Press, 1976.

———. *Lectures on Justice, Police, Revenue and Arms, Delivered at the University of Glasgow by Adam Smith, Reported by a Student in 1763*, ed. Edwin Cannan. Oxford: Clarendon Press, 1896.

———. *The Theory of Moral Sentiments*, ed. D. D. Raphael and A. L. Macfie. Indianapolis: Liberty Fund, 1982.

Stewart, Reginald C. *The Half-Way Pacifist: Thomas Jefferson's View of War*. Toronto: University of Toronto Press, 1978.

Stourzh, Gerald. *Alexander Hamilton and the Idea of Republican Government*. Stanford, CA: Stanford University Press, 1970.

———. "Alexander Hamilton: The Theory of Empire Building." Presented at the American Historical Association meeting, New York, December 30, 1957.

———. "Die tugendhafte Republik: Montesquieus Begriff der 'vertu' und die Anfänge der Vereinjgten Staaten von Amerika." In *Österreich und Europa*, ed. Heinrich Fichtenau and Hermann Peichl, 247–267. Graz, Austria: Verlag Styria, 1965.

Strauss, Leo. *Natural Right and History*. Chicago: University of Chicago Press, 1953.

Tocqueville, Alexis de. *Democracy in America*, ed. and trans. Harvey C. Mansfield and Delba Winthrop. Chicago: University of Chicago Press, 2000.

———. *Democracy in America*, ed. J. P. Mayer and Max Lerner. New York: Harper & Row, 1966.

———. *The Old Regime and the Revolution*, ed. François Furet and Françoise Mélonio, trans. Alan S. Kahan. Chicago: University of Chicago Press, 1998.

———. *Recollections*, ed. J. P. Mayer and A. P. Kerr. New Brunswick, NJ: Transaction, 2009.

———. *Writings on Empire and Slavery*, ed. and trans. Jennifer Pitts. Baltimore: Johns Hopkins University Press, 2006.

Tomlins, Christopher L. *Freedom Bound: Law, Labor, and Civic Identity in Colonizing English America, 1580–1865*. New York: Cambridge University Press, 2010.

Velkley, Richard L. *Freedom and the End of Reason: On the Moral Foundations of Kant's Critical Philosophy*. Chicago: University of Chicago Press, 1989.

Vickers, Daniel. "Competency and Competition: Economic Culture in Early America." *William and Mary Quarterly* 47, 1 (January 1990): 3–29.

Walling, Karl. *Republican Empire: Alexander Hamilton on War and Free Government*. Lawrence: University Press of Kansas, 1999.

———. "Was Alexander Hamilton a Machiavellian Statesman?" *Review of Politics* 57, 3 (Summer 1995): 419–447.

Warren, Mercy. *History of the Rise, Progress and Termination of the American Revolution, Interspersed with Biographical, Political and Moral Observations*. London: British Library, 1804.

Washington, George. *The Papers of George Washington Digital Edition*. Charlottesville: University of Virginia Press, Rotunda, 2008. https://rotunda.upress.virginia.edu/founders/GEWN.html.

Williams, David Lay. *Rousseau's Platonic Enlightenment*. University Park, PA: Penn State University Press, 2007.
Winch, Donald. *Riches and Poverty: An Intellectual History of Political Economy in Britain, 1750–1834*. Cambridge: Cambridge University Press, 1996.
Winthrop, Delba. Review of *Writings on Empire and Slavery*, Society 40 (2002): 110–113.
Wood, Gordon S. *The Creation of the American Republic, 1776–1787*. Chapel Hill: University of North Carolina Press, 1969.
Yarbrough, Jean. *American Virtues: Thomas Jefferson on the Character of a Free People*. Lawrence: University Press of Kansas, 1998.
———. "Tocqueville on the Needs of the Soul." *Perspectives on Political Science* 47, 3 (2018): 123–141.
Zaretsky, Robert, and John T. Scott. *The Philosophers' Quarrel: Rousseau, Hume, and the Limits of Human Understanding*. New Haven, CT: Yale University Press, 2009.

Contributors

Ann Charney Colmo is professor emeritus of political philosophy at Dominican University in River Forest, Illinois. Her publications include "What Sophie Knew: Rousseau's Émile et Sophie, ou Les Solitaires," in *Finding a New Feminism* (edited by Pamela K. Jensen); "Spiritedness and Piety in Aristotle," in *Understanding the Political Spirit: Philosophical Investigations from Socrates to Nietzsche* (edited by Catherine H. Zuckert); "The Virtues in Aristotle's Rhetoric," in *Interpretation*; and "Splendid Equality in the Nicomachean Ethics: Munificence," in *Equality and Excellence in Ancient and Modern Political Philosophy* (edited by Steven Frankel and John Ray).

Steven Frankel is the Stephen S. Smith Professor of Political Economy at Xavier University, where he teaches in the Department of Philosophy and directs the Smith Scholars Honors Program. After earning his PhD from the Committee on Social Thought at the University of Chicago in 1997, he joined the faculty at the American University of Paris, where he received the Board of Trustees Award for Distinguished Teaching in 2001. Frankel's scholarly work focuses on the relationship between philosophy and religion. In 2014 he published a collection of essays with John Ray on intellectual and cultural life in France titled *French Studies: Literature, Culture, and Politics*. He published *Civil Religion and Early Modern Philosophy*, with coauthor Martin Yaffe, in 2020 and, more recently, an edited collection titled *Equality and Excellence in Ancient and Modern Political Philosophy*, with John Ray. He is currently writing a book on the philosophy of Spinoza.

Ryan Patrick Hanley is professor of political science at Boston College. Prior to joining the faculty there he was the Mellon Distinguished Professor of Political Science at Marquette University and held visiting appointments or fellowships at Yale, Harvard, and the University of Chicago. A specialist on the political philosophy of the Enlightenment period, he is the author of *Adam Smith and the Character of Virtue* (2009), *Love's Enlightenment: Rethinking Charity in Modernity* (2017), and *Our Great Purpose: Adam Smith on Living a Better Life* (2019). His most recent book is *The Political Philosophy of Fénelon* (2020) and its companion translation volume, *Fénelon: Moral and Political Writings* (2020).

John C. Koritansky is emeritus professor of political science at Hiram College, where he has taught since 1970. He is also a founding member and was the initial chair of Hiram's Garfield Institute for Public Leadership. He has published several articles and book chapters on American politics, public law, and political philosophy, including interpretive comments on Aristotle, Thomas Hobbes, Thomas Paine, and Leo Strauss, in addition to his work on Tocqueville. His book *Alexis de Tocqueville and the New Science of Politics* is in its second edition. He is currently engaged in analyzing how Strauss's reading of Lucretius informs or illuminates his understanding of classical political rationalism.

Ralph Lerner is the Benjamin Franklin Professor Emeritus of Social Thought at the University of Chicago. His books include *The Founders' Constitution* (coedited with Philip B. Kurland), *The Thinking Revolutionary: Principle and Practice in the New Republic, Revolutions Revisited: Two Faces of the Politics of the Enlightenment, Maimonides' Empire of Light: Popular Enlightenment in an Age of Belief*, and, most recently, *Naïve Readings: Reveilles Political and Philosophic*.

Peter McNamara has taught at Utah State University, Boston College, and Clemson University, where he was a Hayek Visiting Scholar. His research and teaching focus on American political thought, early modern political thought, and political economy. He is the author of *Political Economy and Statesmanship: Smith, Hamilton and the Foundation of the Commercial Republic* and the editor of *The Noblest Minds: Fame, Honor and the American Founding* and (with coeditor Louis Hunt) *Liberalism, Conservatism and Hayek's Idea of Spontaneous Order*. He has written on a wide variety of other topics, including Hayek's moral theory, political opportunism, Jefferson's federalism, and the intellectual origins of business schools.

Peter S. Onuf is the Thomas Jefferson Foundation Professor Emeritus in the Corcoran Department of History at the University of Virginia and senior research fellow at the Robert H. Smith International Center for Jefferson Studies (Monticello). A specialist in the history of the early American republic, Onuf earned his PhD in 1973 at Johns Hopkins University and has taught at Columbia University, Worcester Polytechnic Institute, and Southern Methodist University before arriving in Virginia in 1990. From 2008 to 2009 Onuf was the Harmsworth Professor of American History at the University of Oxford; in

2014, he was elected to the American Academy of Arts and Sciences. Onuf's early scholarship includes *The Origins of the Federal Republic: Jurisdictional Conflicts in the United States* (1983) and *Statehood and Union: A History of the Northwest Ordinance* (1987). He collaborated with his brother, international relations theorist Nicholas G. Onuf, on *Federal Union, Modern World: The Law of Nations in an Age of Revolutions, 1776–1814* (1993) and *Nations, Markets, and War: Modern History and the American Civil War* (2006). Onuf's work on Thomas Jefferson's political thought, culminating in *Jefferson's Empire: The Language of American Nationhood* (2000) and *The Mind of Thomas Jefferson* (2007), grows out of earlier studies on the history of American federalism, foreign policy, and political economy. His most recent books are *Most Blessed of Patriarchs: Thomas Jefferson and the Empire of the Imagination* (2016), with coauthor Annette Gordon-Reed, and *Jefferson and the Virginians: Democracy, Constitutions, and Empire* (2018).

Clifford Orwin is professor of political science, classics, and Jewish studies and a fellow at St. Michael's College. He is also a senior fellow of Massey College at the University of Toronto and a senior fellow of the Berlin/Bochum Thucydides Center. He is the author of *The Humanity of Thucydides* (1994; 5th edition, 2021) and has written dozens of chapters and articles on classical, modern, contemporary, and Jewish political thought. He is currently working on a book about the thought of Flavius Josephus. He has won three major teaching awards at the University of Toronto, including the inaugural J. J. Berry Smith Prize for Excellence in Doctoral Supervision (2013).

Paul A. Rahe is the Charles O. Lee and Louise K. Lee Chair in the Western Heritage at Hillsdale College, where he is professor of history. He is the author of *Republics Ancient and Modern: Classical Republicanism and the American Revolution* (1992), *Against Throne and Altar: Machiavelli and Political Theory under the English Republic* (2008), *Montesquieu and the Logic of Liberty: War, Religion, Commerce, Climate, Terrain, Technology, Uneasiness of Mind, the Spirit of Political Vigilance, and the Foundations of the Modern Republic* (2009), and *Soft Despotism, Democracy's Drift: Montesquieu, Rousseau, Tocqueville, and the Modern Prospect* (2009). More recently, he has published a series of books on the grand strategy of classical Sparta.

John Ray is associate professor of political science at Xavier University, where he teaches political philosophy and constitutional law. With Steven Frankel, he coedited *French Studies: Literature, Culture and Politics* (2014) and *Equality and Excellence in Ancient and Modern Political Philosophy* (2023). He has published on political leadership in Xenophon's *Education of Cyrus* and in George Washington's writings and on Rousseau's understanding of civil religion.

Colleen A. Sheehan is professor of politics in the School of Civic and Economic Thought and Leadership at Arizona State University. She previously served in the Pennsylvania House of Representatives and on the Pennsylvania State Board of Education. She has been an Earhart Fellow, Bradley Fellow, Mary and Kennedy Smith Fellow, and Garwood Fellow at the James Madison Program of Princeton University. Sheehan is the author of *The Mind of James Madison: The Legacy of Classical Republicanism* (2015), *James Madison and the Spirit of Republican Self-Government* (2009), *Friends of the Constitution: Writings of the "Other" Federalists, 1787–88* (with Gary L. McDowell, 1998), and *The Cambridge Companion to The Federalist* (with Jack Rakove, 2020). Her articles have appeared in *American Political Science Review*, *William and Mary Quarterly*, *Review of Politics*, and *Persuasions: The Jane Austen Journal*. Her current projects include an interpretation of Jane Austen's *Emma* and "The Madisonian Moment."

Michael Zuckert is the Nancy R. Dreux Professor of Political Science Emeritus and the Thomas Smith Distinguished Visiting Professor at Arizona State University. He has published extensively in the fields of political theory and constitutional studies. His books include *Natural Rights and the New Republicanism*, *Natural Rights Republic*, *Launching Liberalism*, and (with Catherine Zuckert) *The Truth about Leo Strauss* and *Leo Strauss and the Problem of Political Philosophy*. He coedited (with Derek Webb) *The Antifederal Writings of the Melancton Smith Circle*. His most recent work is *A Nation so Conceived: Abraham Lincoln and the Paradox of Democratic Sovereignty*.

Index

Adams, John: analyses of the world of commerce, 1, 123, 142, 164; on division of labor, 228; on government, 25, 26; on human ambitions, 25, 26–27, 30, 155; Model Treaty of 1776, 149; on new man of commerce, 12, 25, 191; on passion for wealth, 6; on pride, 30; on Spartan regime, 20; vision of America, 25, 30
African Americans: greatness of, 105–6, 112
agriculture, 36n46, 44, 59, 141, 171
Alembert, Jean le Rond d', 214
Alexander, the Great, 105, 220
Algeria: French colonization of, 221–222
ambitions: of commercial republicans, 5–6, 27–28, 68–69; danger of, 15, 26–27, 99, 155; democratic, 7, 18; of old aristocratic order, 13, 14
America: break with Britain, 136, 147; as commercial republic, 107, 150, 179n8, 234; constitutional structures, 195–196; egalitarianism and social mobility of, 31–32, 165; as empire, 152–153, 154, 232–233; freedom of association in, 198; geopolitical expansion of, 234–235; love of equality and greatness, 103; mobilization of citizens in, 152, 156; as model for a new world order, 149; popular government, 150, 229; vs. Russia, 32; self-preservation of, 155; slavery in, 150, 153; state building, 153–154; three races of, 105, 112, 220, 221–222
American Civil War, 224
American Pilgrims, 39–40
American Revolution, 106, 144, 147, 148–149, 155, 156
Americans: claim to sovereignty, 147; cooperation between, 199; greatness of, 31–32, 106, 113–114, 220–221, 222–223; individualism of, 32, 116, 192; national character of, 24–25, 137, 138, 148–149, 151; as new-model men, 9, 222; patriotism, 143–144; political and military mobilization, 141–142, 143–144, 149; religious beliefs of, 192, 201–2, 203, 204, 241n50; sense of self-importance, 106; understanding of self-interest, 206; virtues of, 24, 151, 178–179
Ancien Régime (Tocqueville), 114
ancient-modern dichotomy, 176
appropriation, 43–44
aristocratic order: critique of, 14, 16, 17
Aristotle: on commerce, 57; democratic model of farmer-citizen, 181n27; on friendships of utility, of pleasure, and of the good, 95; on good legislator, 180–181n27; influence of, 166; moral discourse of, 85, 97, 99, 100; *Politics*, 10, 55, 181n27; on private property, 39, 40; on three types of goods, 180n27; on virtue, 95, 100
Art of War (Machiavelli), 62
Athens: as commercial nation, 72–73, 170; imperial ambitions of, 73; wars of, 186

Bacon, Francis, 11n3, 13, 220
Barbon, Nicholas, 62; *A Discourse of Trade*, 60, 61
Barthélemy, Jean Jacques: *Voyage of the Young Anacharsis in Greece*, 166
Bayle, Pierre, 70, 71, 219
beneficence, 86, 94, 95, 96–97
Blenheim, Battle of, 60
Bloom, Allan, 133
Bradford, William, 40
Burke, Edmund, 206, 209

Caesar, Julius, 105, 220
capitalism, 8, 39, 40, 46, 83, 93

258 Index

Carr, Peter, 144
Carthage, 61, 64, 66, 67, 72, 177, 186
Catholicism, 202
centralized authority: tyranny of, 193–194
Christianity, 16, 69, 72, 176, 201, 237
citizens. *See* republican citizens
citizenship, 108
civic virtue, 12, 57, 123, 163, 191
civil religion, 205, 207n4
civil society, 124, 139, 193, 196, 228
Colmo, Ann Charney, 8, 214, 215
colonialism, 59, 221–222
Columbus, Christopher, 59
commerce: ambitions and, 24–25, 28–29; ancient Greeks on, 57, 58; benefits of, 109; civil society and, 124, 171, 188, 225; corruption and, 70; critique of, 131; democracy and, 69, 70, 71; domestic security and, 6, 10, 234; driving force of, 115; effect on civic and social lives, 162–163; Enlightenment view of, 124, 125–126; generation of wealth and, 126, 130; geopolitics and, 234; harmful effects of, 6–7, 29–31, 32–33, 78, 172–173, 224, 228–229; human nature and, 19, 185, 189; as idea of free trade, 167; international relations and, 23; liberty and, 3, 59–60, 124, 126; moral effects of, 107–108, 109; national interest and, 19; pacifying tendencies of, 122; political interests and, 2, 58, 188–189; pride and, 28, 29; as relation between demanders and suppliers, 19, 145, 167; technology and, 61; unity of nation and, 60, 146, 172
"Commerce and Character" (Lerner), 1, 138, 162, 191, 208–209
commerce of economy, 22, 64, 72
commercial republic: in antiquity, 72; civic virtue of, 12–13, 29–31; definition of, 124; ethos of, 157, 162; fanaticism in, 16; focus on market, 125, 153–154, 157; freedom from tradition and hierarchy, 147; idea of equality in, 156; institutional infrastructure, 151–152; mitigation of harmful effect of, 228–229; morality of, 8; new form of citizenship, 147, 167; *vs.* old regimes, 3, 13–15, 16, 20, 24; organization of state in, 33n1; passion and interest in, 4, 5, 164; spirit of enterprise, 18–19, 70–73; warfare and, 22–23, 61, 62, 150, 186–187, 188
commercial republican. *See* new-model commercial man
commercial revolution, 8, 58, 59, 60
commercial society, 39, 40, 49, 104, 108, 125, 162
common good, 39, 46, 49, 173, 180n27, 181, 203
conscience, 90, 102n16, 169
Considerations on the Causes of the Greatness of the Romans and Their Decline (Montesquieu), 62, 63
Constitution of 1787, 2
Continental Congress, 107, 140
Cosway, Maria, 154, 155, 240n25
Creoles: displacement of, 139; identity of, 139–140; nationalism of, 152

Declaration of Independence: Jefferson's draft of, 9, 136–137, 138, 139, 140, 142, 154, 225
democracy: commerce and, 69, 70, 71, 72, 78; degeneration into tyranny, 115; problem of, 194–195; religion and, 202–203
Democracy in America (Tocqueville): on Americans, 220, 222; on centralized authority, 193; on commercial republican ethos, 157; on constitutional structures, 195–196; on degeneration of democracy into tyranny, 115; on doctrine of self-interest, 192, 199–200, 235; on Enlightenment, 11; on equality, 32; on greatness, 114, 121n21, 220–221, 222–223; on individualism, 192; on provincial governmental freedoms,

196–197; on religion, 192; on voluntary associations, 196–197
democratic republicanism, 68
Democratic-Republican Party, 235
Descartes, René, 11n3, 13
despotism, 63, 193, 195–196
Diamond, Martin, 179n8
Diderot, Denis, 132
Discourse of Trade, A (Barbon), 60, 61
Discourse on Political Economy (Rousseau), 130
Discourse on the Origins of Inequality (Rousseau), 127–128, 131
Discourse on the Sciences and the Arts (Rousseau), 9, 127, 131
divine right of kings, 40–41
division of labor, 108, 109, 131, 228, 229
doux commerce: concept of, 10–11, 167–168, 183, 190
Dutch Republic, 61, 64, 186, 208

economics, 2
egalitarianism, 32, 111, 165
egoism, 33, 192
Emile (Rousseau), 129
Enlightenment: conception of national character, 140; conception of universal human nature, 145; critique of, 122–124, 127, 131–133; impact on American revolutionaries, 2; notion of equality, 126–127, 129; on progress in history, 138–139; on property, 7–8; on removal restraints on human freedom, 124–125; "universal histories" of, 147; view of commerce, 124, 126, 129
Epicureans, 85
equality, 103–104, 126, 148
Eugene, Prince of Savoy, 60
extended republic, 154, 174

Fable of the Bees, The (Mandeville), 70
fanaticism, 5, 16
Federalist Papers, The: on causes of war, 186–187; on commerce, 10, 188, 232; debate on republican government, 166–167, 169, 183, 184, 229–230; on extended republic, 174; ideas of *Federalist* 6, 183, 186, 188–189; on limitations on the national government's power, 187; on people's republican virtue, 165–166; on problem of domestic faction, 187
federal republic, 140, 154, 187
Ferguson, Adam, 8
Filmer, Robert, 40–41; *Patriarcha*, 40
Franklin, Benjamin: autobiography, 37n47; on commercial republicanism, 12, 123, 191; comparison to Washington, 165; ideal man of, 164–165, 230, 231
freedom: as threat to despotism, 193
French Revolution, 119, 237

George III, King of Great Britain, 136, 137, 139, 149, 154
Gibbon, Edward, 166
Gobineau, Arthur de, 222
good legislator, 180–181n27
goodwill, 89, 96, 178
Great Britain: America's break with, 136, 147; as collective security organization, 149–150; colonialism, 65–66; as commercial republic, 3, 33n1, 64, 65–67, 72–77, 212; geographic location, 66; politeness of, 75–76; political and commercial interests, 73; public opinion in, 75; relations with colonies, 170–171; religion in, 74–75; rivalry with France, 61–62; rule of law in, 74, 75, 76, 77; sense of self-importance, 106; supremacy at sea, 67; wars, 186
great mercantile republic, 3, 19, 141, 145, 167
greatness: American, 103, 105–106, 112; of ancient and aristocratic societies, 4, 8, 14, 20–21, 105, 111, 239n17; aspiration to, 111–112; in democratic age, 8–9, 103–104, 114, 115–116, 117–119; equality and, 103; improper ways to,

greatness (*continued*): 110–111; military, 14, 114–115, 117; national, 114, 116, 117; of Native Americans, 105, 112; of new commercial men, 104–105, 113–114; of politicians, 106–107, 117; vs. prudence, 104–105; truth and, 119
great-souled man, 165, 179n9, 214
Grotius, Hugo, 41

Hamilton, Alexander: on American exceptionalism, 186; on benefits of a federal republic, 187; on causes of war, 186–187; on centralizing policies, 230; on commerce, 29, 122, 185, 189, 232, 233–234; on commercial republic, 22–23, 191; criticism of, 169; on *doux commerce* thesis, 10–11, 167, 183, 190; *Federalist* essays, 183, 232–233; on French Revolution, 189; on golden age, 188; on likelihood of conflict among states, 184; on love of wealth, 6; on men of "irregular ambition," 26; on modern armies, 187; Montesquieu's influence on, 184–185; on private motives that lead to war, 185, 186; on problem of domestic factions, 184; rejection of notion of spirit of commerce, 233; on religion, 192; on war, 234
Hanley, Ryan Patrick, 8, 215, 219, 220, 221, 223
happiness, 94, 102n23
health of the soul, 171
heroism, 113, 114
Hobbes, Thomas: on anarchic state of nature, 143; on curricula of universities, 220; influence of, 11n3, 13, 163, 164, 167, 176, 233; on intentions and actions, 102n16; moral discourse, 82, 85, 99; on reason, 5; Smith's critique of, 84–85, 98, 143, 146
Homo economicus (Smith), 141
Hooker, Richard, 210
Huart (printer in Paris), 54, 56, 57, 79n6

human beings: faculties of, 169; origin of association of, 71; temporal structure of, 43
human labor, 44–45. *See also* division of labor
human nature, 15, 20, 83, 99, 109, 111, 236; commerce and, 19, 185, 189
Hume, David: on ambitions, 15, 27; on commercial republic, 7, 12, 39, 123, 178, 190; comparison between Locke and, 209–211; critique of older order, 15–16; on *doux commerce* thesis, 183; on expansion of empire, 154; on inequalities, 210–211; influence of, 1, 10, 166, 208; on modern republican citizen, 163, 164, 175, 191; on passions, 21, 23; on reliance on charity, 210–211; on right of self-preservation, 48–49; on rules of justice, 47–48; on sovereign's "best policy," 152; on Spartan nation, 14, 20–21; theory of property, 8, 46–49, 50–51, 52; *A Treatise of Human Nature*, 47; on virtue, 4

impartial spectator, 8, 15, 86, 88–89, 91, 92, 101
individualism, 11, 116, 151, 192, 194, 199
industrialization, 129
intentions, 84, 85, 89, 99, 102n12, 102n16
internal tribunal, 90–91
"invisible hand," 8, 82, 83, 93, 101
irregularity in moral sentiments, 89, 96

Jackson, Andrew, 114–115, 120n20
Jay, John, 19, 183, 184
Jefferson, Thomas: on agriculture, 36n46, 141; background of, 136, 226; career of, 157; on causes of war, 187; on commerce-based peace, 188; criticism of centralizing policies, 230; domestic political agenda, 227, 229; draft of the Declaration of Independence, 9, 136–137, 138, 139, 140, 142, 154, 225;

identity of, 137–138, 140, 143; literary legacy of, 225, 241n49; on new man of commerce, 145; plantation of, 226; on popular political participation, 143, 144, 156; on race, 239n25; on religion, 241n50; on republican citizen, 231; on self-preservation, 156; on "spirit of 1776," 140; on trade, 141; on virtues of his countrymen, 151; vision of America, 150, 152–153, 154–155, 226–227
Jenkins, Robert, 186
justice, 47–49, 84, 95

Kant, Immanuel, 122, 123
Kent, James, 190
Koritansky, John C., 11, 235–236

Lawler, Peter, 121n21
Lawrence, D. H., 231
Lee, Henry, 137
Lerner, Ralph: analysis of Tocqueville, 191–192; on commerce, 167; "Commerce and Character" essay, 1, 133, 138, 162, 191, 208; on commercial republic, 2, 4–5, 123, 124, 126, 140, 142–144, 147, 151, 153, 154, 156, 157, 191; on Enlightenment, 2, 122, 125; on Jefferson, 141, 145; on liberty, 3; on Madison, 165–167, 170; on new-model commercial man, 9, 143, 162, 163, 164, 175; on passion and interest, 164; on Rousseau, 9, 122, 123, 124, 129, 130; scholarship of, 1, 7, 142; on separation of rhetoric from argument, 11n3; on Smith, 4; *The Thinking Revolutionary*, 1–2, 5–7; on Washington, 165–167
liberty, 3, 125–126
limited government: doctrine of, 169, 176, 178
Lincoln, Abraham, 221, 229
Livy, 61
Locke, John: on America, 31; on capitalism, 50; comparison between Hume and,
209–211; on division of labor, 44–45; on inequalities, 210–211; influence of, 7, 13, 208; on natural right to property, 8, 39, 40, 41–42, 46–52, 210; on prices, 44; on rationale for political action, 51; on reliance on charity, 210–211; on self-ownership, 42, 43–45, 49; theory of capitalism, 40; *Two Treatises on Civil Government*, 210
lógos, 55
Louis XIV, King of France, 61, 62, 65
Louis XV, King of France, 63
Lovejoy, Arthur O., 34n9
Lycurgus, 68

Machiavelli, Niccoló: *Art of War*, 62; break with the classical world, 176; influence of, 11n3, 13, 141, 189, 233, 234; *The Prince*, 220; on revolution and commerce, 61
Madison, James: advocacy of free enterprise, 168–169; on agriculture, 171; on ancient political practice, 170; on causes of war, 187; on commerce-based peace, 187; "Consolidation" essay, 230; criticism of Hamilton, 169; critique of Montesquieu, 172; on division of labor, 229; on *doux commerce*, 167–168; *Federalist* essays, 166–167, 179n8, 182n42; on government, 169, 174, 229, 230; on "health of the soul," 171; on individual liberty, 178; on laws against perpetuating the national debt, 168; on limited government, 176, 178; on model republican citizen, 10, 154, 170, 175, 178, 179, 191, 228, 229, 230, 231; "Notes on Government," 181n27; "Notes on Vices of the Political System of the United States," 174; on occupations of republican citizens, 171–172; on passion and interest, 168; on political ambitions, 26; on property, 169; on protection of freedom of the mind

Madison, James (*continued*): and conscience, 169–170; on public good, 168; on public opinion, 174–175; references to Aristotle, 181n27; on religion, 192; "Republican Distribution of Citizens," 170, 177; on republican virtues, 165–166; on self-government, 178; "Spirit of Governments," 172; study of Greek authors, 166; on true republic, 173–174; on virtue and intelligence of American people, 181n27; vision of American republic, 173–174, 175–176, 177

Mandeville, Bernard, 71, 85; *The Fable of the Bees*, 70

Manent, Pierre, 124, 128

market: discipline of, 125, 126; impersonality of, 124; inequality and, 126; leftist critique of, 129; moderation power of, 17–18, 22; as natural system of liberty and justice, 5, 17, 18–19, 125–126; paradoxical logic of, 145; universal laws of, 146–147

Marlborough, John Churchill, Duke of, 60, 105

martial virtues, 108–109

Marx, Karl, 129

Massillon, Jean Baptiste, Bishop of Clermont: sermons of, 217–218

McGiffert, Michael, 208

McNamara, Peter, 10, 232, 233

merits, 75, 87–88, 90

Meyers, Marvin, 119n1

Milton, John, 231

Model Treaty of 1776, 149, 156

moderation: virtue of, 5, 164

monarchy, 64, 65, 78

money, 58–59, 60, 62–63, 65

Montesquieu, Charles de Secondat, baron de: on ambitions, 168; on ancien régime, 14, 78; on battle of Blenheim, 60; on benefits of a federal republic, 187; on character of a people, 138; on commerce, 8, 22, 146, 149, 164, 188–189, 224, 225; conception of modern commercial republic, 2, 12, 29, 123, 125, 167, 172–173, 178, 184, 190; *Considerations on the Causes of the Greatness of the Romans and Their Decline*, 62, 63; on democracy based on commerce, 68, 69, 70, 71, 72, 78; depiction of France, 213; on *doux commerce* thesis, 183; on England and English people, 3, 33n1, 74–77, 177, 212; on excessive self-esteem, 34n9; imitation of Rousseau, 78; influence of, 7, 9, 10, 166; on laws, 212; on moderate government, 59–60; on money, 58–59; on new man of commerce, 162, 163, 175, 212–213, 233; new regime classification, 172; personality of, 214; on pursuit of comfort, 6; *Reflections on Universal Monarchy in Europe*, 61, 62, 63, 64; reliance of Greek thinkers, 20; on size of republic, 153–154; on slavery, 238n8; travels of, 213–214; on universal monarchy, 62, 63–65; on virtue, 20; on war, 60, 62–63, 65. *See also Spirit of the Laws, The* (Montesquieu)

Monticello plantation, 226

moral dogma, 192

morality: as act of sympathizing with others, 85, 86–87, 88; human sentiments and, 8; justice and, 84, 95; merit as aspect of, 87–88; passion and, 84–85; propriety as aspect of, 87, 97; rules of, 91, 92, 214, 216, 217; self-interest and, 8, 82–83, 85–86; Smith's vs. ancient, 97–98

"moral sense," 144

Nantucket whalemen, 35n19, 141

Narcisse (Rousseau), 127, 130, 133, 223

National Gazette, 166, 169

national identity, 138

Native Americans, 105, 221, 222; greatness of, 105, 112–113

new-model commercial man: ambitions of,

25; *vs.* ancient aristocrat, 170; character of, 24–25, 126, 143–144, 148–149, 163, 175; egalitarianism and individualism of, 32; emergence of, 12, 31, 141, 145–146, 212–213; Franklin's ideal of, 164–165; practical reasoning of, 143, 164; predisposition to liberty, 32; prudence of, 17; republican citizen as, 9–10, 12; self-interest and, 104
Nicole, Pierre, 70, 71
Nozick, Robert, 50

Onuf, Peter, 9, 224, 225, 226, 227
Orwin, Clifford, 9, 223, 224, 237

Paine, Thomas, 22, 151, 188, 233
Pascal, Blaise, 200, 201
passions: actions and, 87, 98; as causes of labour, 21; as causes of war, 186; morality and, 84–85, 86; propriety of, 87, 97; sympathy and, 98; *vs.* virtues, 4–5; for wealth, 4–5, 6, 25, 30
Patriarcha (Filmer), 40
patriotism, 21, 22, 96
Pericles, 185, 220
personhood, 42–43
philosophic reasoning, 142
Plato: on commerce, 57, 70; on communism of property holdings, 39, 40; influence of, 85, 97, 99, 100, 115, 117, 118, 166; *Laws*, 55; on political regimes, 56; *Republic*, 55, 99, 180n27
political associations, 197–198
political equality, 129
politics: ambitions in, 15, 26; economics and, 7, 156; goal of, 5, 6, 169; motives in, 106; virtue and, 6
Politics (Aristotle), 10, 55, 181n27
Poor Richard's Almanac, 231
popular sovereignty, 144
Price, Richard, 139
prices, 44–45
pride: aristocratic, 16; civility and, 14, 71; of commercial republicans, 28, 148, 155; forms of, 28; of nobility, 30; of politicians, 106; Smith's doctrine of, 34n9
private ownership, 39, 45–46
private vices, 70
property: communal, 39–40; Enlightenment's view of, 7; government regulation of, 169; "greater good" and protection of, 51; irregularities in matters of, 87, 93, 100; justice and, 48; natural right to, 40, 41–42, 46, 47, 48, 49–50, 52; philosophical views of, 39; political control of, 49, 50, 51; as prerequisites of capitalism, 46; as social utility, 47–48, 49, 50; theory of the divine source of, 40–41; utility and, 100; virtue and, 99–100. *See also* self-ownership
Protestantism, 202
prudent man, 104–105
public good: notion of, 4, 13, 14, 21, 23, 168; private ownership and, 39, 45–46; private vices and, 70
public opinion, 174–175
Publius. *See* Madison, James
pursuit of rank, 93–94

Rahe, Paul, 8, 211, 212
Reflections on Universal Monarchy in Europe (Montesquieu), 61, 62, 63, 64
religion: in democratic age, 192, 202–203, 205, 206–207, 235; as form of hope, 204–205; moral utility of, 203, 204; political freedom and, 203; psychological core of, 205
Renan, Ernest, 231
Republic (Plato), 55, 99, 180n27
republican citizens: ambitions of, 6, 10, 23–24, 25, 27–28, 68–69; character of, 10, 178–179, 191, 229; *vs.* conventional aristocrats, 24; obligations of, 175; occupations fit for, 171–172, 180–181n27; virtues of, 24

reward of action, 86, 87, 88, 89, 91
right to charity, 210–211
Robertson, William, 166
Rousseau, Jean-Jacques: on arts, 127; on citizen of a commercial republic, 223–224; on civil religion, 207n4; on commerce, 7, 9, 129, 130–131, 225; critique of Enlightenment, 122–123, 127, 130, 131–133, 223; critique of Hobbes, 193; *Discourse on Political Economy*, 130; *Discourse on the Origins of Inequality*, 127–128, 131; *Discourse on the Sciences and the Arts*, 9, 127, 131; *Emile*, 129; on finance, 3, 28–29, 130; on human society, 127–128, 129; on leadership and civic education, 130; on legitimate authority, 193; *Narcisse*, 127, 130, 133, 223; on philosophes, 131, 132; on savages, 224; on self-interest, 128–129; *The Social Contract*, 207n4; on will of sovereign, 129
rule of the majority, 194, 198
rules of morality, 91, 92, 214, 216, 217
Rush, Benjamin: Adams and, 27; on citizens of a commercial republic, 191; on commerce, 23, 30, 164, 228; on commercial republicanism, 123, 148, 233; on influence of commerce on character, 6, 12, 148

Saint-Simon, Louis de Rouvroy, duc de, 213–214
Saunders, Richard, 231
self-conscious individual, 146
self-fortification, 98–99
self-importance, 106, 107
self-interest: doctrine of, 33, 192, 199–200, 201; morality and, 8, 82–83, 85–86, 235, 236; religion and, 200–201; social context of, 128–129
"self-interest properly understood," 8, 11, 21–22, 98, 185, 200, 206
self-judgment, 90

self-ownership, 42–43, 49, 52
self-preservation, 8, 48–49, 82, 95, 98–99, 100, 155
self-sacrifice, 4, 192, 199, 200, 201
Shays's Rebellion, 185
Sheehan, Colleen A., 10, 227–228, 229, 230–231
slavery, 150, 153, 238n8
Smith, Adam: on African Americans, 105–106; on American War of Independence, 155; on aristocratic order, 14–15, 16–17; on capitalism, 8, 83, 93; on character of merchants, 141; on commerce, 7, 8, 164; on commercial republicanism, 14, 123, 178, 190; critique of Hobbes, 84–85, 102n16; critique of mercantilism, 141; on death, 98; on demagogues, 118; on democratic future, 118; on division of labor, 108; on Enlightenment, 122; as future-oriented man, 117; on greatness, 9, 104, 105, 106, 107, 110–111, 118, 219, 220–221, 239n17; on happiness, 94, 102n23; on history, 101; *Homo economicus*, 141; on human nature, 83; idea of great mercantile republic, 3, 19, 141, 145, 167; on ignorance, 110; influence of political thought of, 101, 208; on intentions, 85, 89, 99; on irregularities of sentiments, 89, 91–92, 100; on market economy, 5, 17–18, 139, 140–141, 143; moral discourse of, 6, 8, 84–85, 95, 97–100, 216; on new man of commerce, 8–9, 12, 24, 146; on New World colonies, 4, 16; notion of "invisible hand," 8, 82, 83, 93; on pacific effects of commerce, 188; on patriotism, 96; on politician's motives, 106; on primary care, 98; on propriety, 99–100; on prudent man, 85, 104; on religion, 215–219, 238n10; on republican citizen, 191, 231; on self-preservation, 98–99, 100; on system of liberty and justice, 143; on "the great mob of mankind," 14; on

utility, 92–93, 100; on vanity and pride, 16, 34n9; on virtues, 87, 88, 94, 95–96, 99–100, 108–109
social compact, 176
social utility, 47, 48, 49
Socrates, 105
Spartan regime, 14, 20, 68, 233
specialized labor. *See* division of labor
Spinoza, Baruch, 11n3, 13, 203, 219
"spirit of commerce": notion of, 22, 59–60, 71, 77, 146, 185, 213, 233
Spirit of the Laws, The (Montesquieu): on agriculture, 59; on commerce, 57–59; editions of, 56–57, 67, 79n6, 80n14; on England, 3, 65–67, 73–78, 212; influence of, 8, 56, 188; on laws, 55–56, 212; map of the world in, 57, 59; on monarchy, 64–65; on new man of commerce, 162, 170; on political liberty, 55; publishers of, 54; on real estate, 59; structure of, 54–55; on technological inventions, 59; on universal monarchy, 61, 63; on war, 55
Stoics, 85
Strabo, 166
Strauss, Leo, 176
Sumner, William Graham, 210
Swift, Jonathan, 167, 176; *The Battle of the Books*, 162
sympathizing: act of, 86–87

Theory of Moral Sentiments, The (Smith): on beneficence, 95, 96–97; connection between *The Wealth of Nations* and, 83, 101n8; discussion of religion, 238n10; editions of, 214–215, 238n10; excerpt from sermons of Massillon, 217–219; on greatness, 105, 106; on human nature, 109; on human sentiments, 8, 85; on intention, 84; on internal tribunal, 90–91; on justice, 95; on morality, 8, 82, 83, 84, 95; significance of, 215–216; time of writing, 101n5; on virtues, 84, 89–90, 94

Thinking Revolutionary, The (Lerner), 1–2, 5–7
Thomas Aquinas, Saint, 41
Thucydides, 166
Tocqueville, Alexis de: on Americans, 24–25, 31–32, 113, 191–192, 195–196; *Ancien Régime*, 114; on commerce, 6–7, 115; on commercial republic, 18–19, 28, 32, 33, 82, 164; comparison of America and Russia, 32; on democracy, 25, 116, 117–119, 119n1, 129–130, 141, 194–195; description of America, 165, 179; doctrine of "self-interest properly understood," 8, 11, 21–22, 185, 200; on freedom, 193; on future of democratic societies, 117–119, 129–130; on greatness, 9, 103–104, 111–117, 219, 220–223; on individualism, 192, 194, 199; on Jackson, 114–115, 120n20; on morality, 8, 82–83, 192; on Native Americans, 112–113, 221, 222; on new heroism, 115; on new-model men, 7, 8–9, 12, 141, 162; new science of politics of, 198, 206; on political consequences of centralization, 194; on religion, 192, 201, 202–204, 205, 206–207, 236–237; on Revolution of 1789, 119; on self-interest, 33, 206; on self-sacrifice, 201; on "standards of mediocrity," 18; support for colonialism, 121n22, 221–222; on tyranny of the majority, 198; on voluntary associations, 197–198, 199. *See also Democracy in America* (Tocqueville)
trade, 2, 59, 145
Treatise of Human Nature, A (Hume), 47
Two Treatises on Civil Government (Locke), 210
tyranny of the majority, 198

universal benevolence, 96, 97
universal human nature, 138, 145
universal monarchy, 62, 63–64

vanity, 15, 16, 34n9, 64, 70
Venice, 61, 64, 186
Vernet, Jacob, 54, 56
Virginia Constitution of 1776, 226
Virginia plantocracy, 151, 227
virtue(s): of ancient republic, 4; corruption of, 109; friendships and, 95; happiness and, 94; "impartial spectator" as judge of, 8, 86, 88–89; of others, judgment of, 89–90; *vs.* passions, 4–5, 100; philosophical contemplation as, 95; politics and, 6; propriety and, 99–100; root of, 99; sympathy as, 95
Voltaire: "*Ecrasez l'infâme*," 237
voluntary associations, 196–197, 199
Voyage of the Young Anacharsis in Greece (Barthélemy), 166

war: causes of, 185–187; change of nature of, 186–187; financial consequences of, 62–63, 187; money as sinews of, 60, 62; poverty and, 63; as spirit of monarchy, 64; technology and, 61
War of Jenkins' Ear (1739–1748), 186
Washington, George, 149, 165, 179n9, 228

wealth: accumulation of, 18; corruption and, 69; generated by commerce, 126, 130; pursuit of, 6, 93; redistribution of, 71, 126
Wealth of Nations, The (Smith): on ambitious men, 26; on British politics, 106–107; on capitalism, 8; connection between *The Theory of Moral Sentiments* and, 83, 101n8; on division of labor, 108, 228; on human nature, 109; on increase in productivity, 108; influence of, 82; moral discourse in, 214; notions of "invisible hand," 82, 83; time of writing, 101n5; on universal laws of market, 146–147
Weber, Max, 231
William of Ockham, 41
Winthrop, D. Jordan, 239n25
Winthrop, James, 184
Wood, Gordon, 21

Xenophon: *The Constitution of the Athenians*, 72

Zeno, 85, 97
Zuckert, Michael, 7, 8, 209, 210

www.ingramcontent.com/pod-product-compliance
Lightning Source LLC
Chambersburg PA
CBHW031803220426
43662CB00007B/507